Campaigning in the Aftermath of the 2020 Elections

Campaigning in the Aftermath of the 2020 Elections

A Communications Perspective

Edited by
Robert E. Denton Jr.

ROWMAN & LITTLEFIELD
Lanham • Boulder • New York • London

Published by Rowman & Littlefield
An imprint of The Rowman & Littlefield Publishing Group, Inc.
4501 Forbes Boulevard, Suite 200, Lanham, Maryland 20706
www.rowman.com

86-90 Paul Street, London EC2A 4NE

British Library Cataloguing in Publication Information Available

Library of Congress Cataloging-in-Publication Data

ISBN: 978-1-5381-6125-8 (cloth)
ISBN: 978-1-5381-6126-5 (paperback)
ISBN: 978-1-5381-6127-2 (electronic)

This book is dedicated to my dear friend Andrew Vos. He is one of the kindest, most charming, and most generous persons I have ever known. He is loving, caring, and courageous. He adores his family and loves this nation. He is a fellow veteran and historian of World War II. I was honored when Andrew and his wife, Laurie, would visit my political communication classes. Our discussions afterward affirmed my commitment to reach out beyond campus. He is a New Jersey native who became a genuine Appalachian mountain man. Over time, he came to understand my North Carolina mountain accent and appreciated my grandpa's sayings. The sharing of food, fires, and laughter has enriched my life. With my love and utmost admiration.

Contents

Acknowledgments

I have had the privilege of editing more than twenty volumes over the years. I had no intention of editing so many volumes, but they have provided opportunities to share many perspectives and ideas from outstanding scholars within the discipline. Chapters provide snapshots of investigations and studies of communication. Early on I discovered there were sometimes challenges working with very smart, busy, and diverse groups of scholars. However, over the years, I have come to enjoy the process. I am pleased to share that this project was no exception. This project brought together "new" colleagues and "old" friends. Once again, the contributors have made this a most rewarding and enjoyable endeavor. I genuinely appreciate their participation in this volume. I also value their friendship.

I want to thank my colleagues in the School of Communication at Virginia Polytechnic Institute and State University (Virginia Tech). As now a long-term administrator of various sorts over the years, I am grateful to my colleagues for their continued collegiality and encouragement, as well as for their recognizing the importance of maintaining an active research agenda. Thanks also to Robert Sumirchrast, dean of the Pamplin College of Business, whose support allows my continued association with the Department of Marketing and the college. I am also most grateful to Lura Belmonte, dean of the College of Liberal Arts and Human Sciences, who understands the importance of the "right mix" that makes the job of school director a privilege and pleasure. I am fortunate, indeed. They both are outstanding mentors and administrators.

Finally, as always, countless thanks to my wonderful wife, Rachel, a true blessing, friend, colleague, and partner in my life. She made the pandemic bearable. And I also must pay homage to my now-grown sons, Bobby and Chris, who have their own wonderful spouses, Christen and Sarah. The boys and Rachel have always been tolerant of the countless hours in the study (and now upon reflection, perhaps too tolerant and too many hours). Together the five, plus our dog, little Abby girl, enrich and fulfill every moment of my life.

Preface

Since 1992, I have edited a volume on the presidential campaigns from a communication perspective. Each chapter focuses on a specific area of political campaign communication. While in the final stages of preparing the manuscript on the 2020 presidential campaign for submission to Rowman & Littlefield, several authors expressed concern about the lack of attention to or acknowledgment of the unprecedented postelection challenges and capitol riots. The postelection period of the 2020 presidential campaign is historic for numerous reasons, culminating in the mob attacks on the Capitol on January 6, 2021, and the dramatic inauguration of Joe Biden as the forty-sixth president of the United States. The situation presented a dilemma. Should the project be delayed to include additional analyses of topics in the postelection period? A consensus emerged that the events, activities, and actions postelection were very much an essential part of the 2020 presidential campaign and warranted their own dedicated analyses of the historic period. Thus, in the preface it would be noted that the volume focused on the general election phases of the campaign and largely completed well before the events of January 6, 2021. In addition, a brief epilogue was included in the volume.[1]

Historically, the literature identifies four phases of a modern political campaign: preprimary, primary, convention, and general election. Each phase of a campaign has relatively discrete functions. Of course, the functions of each stage affect the entire campaign. Traditionally, there really is not a postelection phase, per se. Within a day or so, the outcome becomes clear. The loser concedes and a form of transition begins. There are two forms of transition phases depending upon whether an incumbent is reelected or a new president is selected. The former is certainly less dramatic. However, the latter is viewed as the beginning of a new presidency and era in American history.

However, in 2020, there was a distinct and active postelection campaign, culminating in the riots and attempted siege of the Capitol on January 6, 2021. President Donald Trump vigorously challenged the election, calling for recounts and court challenges amid charges of voter fraud and irregularities. Speeches, rallies, fundraising, and advertising continued weeks past the election. In effect, for the first time in modern electoral history, there was an active, dramatic, and decisive postelection phase of the 2020 presidential campaign.

This volume explores the postelection phase of the campaign from election day until the inauguration of Joe Biden. Collectively the chapters focus on communication aspects and dynamics during this phase. Virtually all the contributors provide analysis of the same communication variables and issues as in the general election volume noted above. Topics examined during this phase include political branding, the nature of argumentation in the era of partisanship, the themes and issues of media coverage, examination of Trump's January 6 address in terms of inciting an insurrection or free speech, Trump's discursive strategy, political advertising, and political cartoons during this period, concluding with an examination of the postelection lawsuits.

In chapter 1, Lisa Burns and Courtney Marchese continue their analysis of the political branding and messaging strategies of Trump and Biden during the postelection period. They examine the speeches and social media messaging of Trump and Biden during four distinct phases of the period: the immediate aftermath of the election, the challenge period, the Capitol insurrection, and the inauguration. Although the brands of Trump and Biden were polar opposites, both candidates stayed true to their brands during this phase. Biden's brand was a calm, casual, and cool image. Biden stressed his experience, competence, sincerity, and desire to be president of all Americans. Trump's brand was big, bold, and defiant. Trump relied on his cult brand, celebrity status, and his antipolitician "superhero" persona. Biden's messaging was low-key and reassuring, and it stressed unity. In contrast, Trump's messaging was divisive, utilizing a "paranoid" rhetorical style. Biden's political branding was more traditional; Trump's was novel, aggressive, and antipolitician.

Benjamin Voth in chapter 2 provides an argumentation analysis of the postelection by comparing the political rhetoric of the summer of 2020 and the Trump rally of January 6. The comparison contextualizes how political arguments are understood through partisan lens. The contrast, presentations, and explanations contribute to the ongoing cycle of political cynicism. Voth suggests that the partisan framing of the events of violence and frustrations of the summer of 2020 and of January 6 forbodes that violence as an extreme response may well continue to be a part of American politics.

Chapter 3 provides an overview of some of the issues and characterizations of how primarily the news media covered the postelection through the inauguration. I surveyed news articles and opinion pieces focusing on how the media covered the events, activities, and "drama" of this period. Interestingly, many of the concerns were raised by the media themselves, but their perspectives varied a great deal. The themes that emerged include the general lack of trust in media broadly defined, general right/left bias, press and corporate censorship, rush to judgment, and the question of systemic election fraud. In terms of January 6, there was a wide-range debate in characterizing the events and participants of the day, comparisons of coverage of the events of the day to those of the summer riots of 2020, the role Trump played in the day's events, and the anticipation leading up to the inauguration of Joe Biden. Within each theme and issue of coverage there was a clear divergence of bias, arguments, and presentations. Thus, what also becomes clear are the troubling implications resulting from the transformation of the practice of journalism across platforms and media. Today's tribal and partisan practice of journalism has contributed to the formation of our political, partisan, and ideological divides and echo chambers. The current media environment does threaten our democracy.

Wat Hopkins, in chapter 4, analyzes Trump's speech of January 6 from a legal and historical perspective to determine whether the speech indeed incited the riot or was simply protected speech. Hopkins argues that based on the legal elements of intent, imminence, likelihood, and context, Trump's speech certainly met the legal standards for inciting a riot that resulted in death, injury, and property destruction. For Hopkins, the time, place, and context of the speech were clearly outside the protection of the First Amendment.

In chapter 5, Theodore Sheckels examines the events of January 6 from a Bakhtinian perspective utilizing a refinement of the concept "carnivalesque." His exploration of the work of Bakhtin and the application of carnivalesque contributes to rhetorical inquiry. In addition, the analysis of the events of January 6 leads to a richer and broader understanding of that day. The spectacle of the participants—the joy, and, yes, the violence, irreverence, and rallying cries to confront those in power—was evident. Indeed, it was a "carnivalesque" crowd with mixed motives and intentions of participation. In short, there were multiple ideologies, multiple views, and multiple emotions on display that day. For the critic, the events were multivoiced and multifaceted.

During the postelection period with claims of fraudulent ballots, Trump was fundraising through social media to support the expenses of court challenges of voter fraud. Some of those funds were used in paid advertising on both sides of the debate. The Trump campaign spent over $4 million; and the anti-Trump PAC, the Lincoln Project, spent over $7 million. John

Tedesco and Scott Dunn in chapter 6 examine the political advertising during the postelection. The Lincoln Project's ads went well beyond attempting to expose the lies of fraudulent voting but also addressed larger issues such as Republican leadership failing to support true conservative values. Some ads targeted potential GOP 2024 presidential candidates. The group was most successful in shaping the political environment of the general election campaign and postelection.

Natalia Mielczarek identifies and interprets the major themes and recurring visual signifiers that emerged in political cartoons published during the postelection period. Chapter 7 begins with an overview of the role editorial cartoons have played in American press and impact as visual rhetoric. In analyzing over nine hundred political cartoons, Mielczarek describes four major textual areas: the presidential election of 2020, Trump's legacy, the Capitol siege, and the transition of power. Across the four dominant themes, most of the cartoons expressed anti-Trump sentiment. The textual hooks emerged around Trump, Biden, the Statue of Liberty, and Uncle Sam. In relation to Trump, the likeness of Trump appeared in the majority of the cartoons across the themes. Trump supporters were also frequently featured in textual hooks. Finally, the GOP and Republicans were also among the most popular visual hooks displayed throughout the four themes. Biden's likeness began to appear as Inauguration Day drew closer. The various themes and visual hooks are described in detail and illustrated as examples in four cartoons.

Finally, in chapter 8, Cayce Myers provides an analysis of the 2020 postelection lawsuits. Actually, litigation was discussed during the campaign by both candidates and used the prospects of fundraising opportunities. The chapter examines federal and state lawsuits filed before and after the election. While claims of election fraud did not meet the legal threshold for overturning the election, various concerns that emerged are prompting legislation at the federal and state levels. After a brief overview of constitutional issues and enfranchisement, the chapter concludes with an analysis of both the legal and political impact of the lawsuits in 2020 and speculation about the role such suits may play in future elections.

Without question, the postelection period of the 2020 presidential campaign and January 6 will be an important part of the history of the election. I am sure there will be numerous studies and accounts of the postelection. Even now, months past January 6, there continues to be new information and revelations of that time. And the nation is as polarized as ever, and viewpoints are firm. We are indeed in a time of political realignment, generational transition, and rapid communication technology advancements.

I often refer to former mentor and early scholar of political communication Bruce Gronbeck, who argued that campaigns "get leaders elected, yes, but ultimately, they also tell us who we as a people are, where we have been and where we are going; in their size and duration they separate our culture from all others, teach us about political life, set our individual and collective priorities, entertain us, and provide bases for social interaction."[2]

There are many lessons to learn from the election of 2020. I wish to reiterate my thirty-thousand-foot view from the epilogue to the initial edited volume on the election written in the shadows of January 6. My thinking has not changed.

A democratic government is a reflection of its citizens. And the values of the citizens will be reflected in the behaviors of elected officials and government. Our body politic is fractured in many ways. There are important and systemic issues we must address. I think we are at a critical point in our republic. I am encouraging a broader view and perspective. The last four to five years are just a reflection and culmination of decades of political, cultural and social fragmentation. In many ways, Trump is not "the" or "an issue," either good or bad. He is merely a symptom of the state of our polity. I am certainly not suggesting the demise of our nation. I am suggesting we need a national recommitment to the core principles of the American experiment. Although we remain divided, appeals and messages must be grounded in the principles that created and defined America. They are there in the Declaration of Independence and in the Constitution. We need an understanding and some agreement on the fundamental values essential to our nation. And civic responsibility and initiative should once again become a keystone of social life. Whether we like it or not, as Americans, we do have a "social contract" with one another. We can negotiate the terms of the contract, perhaps, but we are bound together based upon national values.[3]

NOTES

1. Robert E. Denton Jr., ed., *The 2020 Presidential Campaign: A Communication Perspective* (Lanham, MD: Rowman & Littlefield, 2021).

2. Bruce Gronbeck, "Functions of Presidential Campaigning," in *Political Persuasion in Presidential Campaigns,* ed. Lawrence Devlin (New Brunswick, NJ: Transaction Books, 1987), 496.

3. Robert E. Denton Jr., "Epilogue," in *The 2020 Presidential Campaign: A Communication Perspective,* Robert E. Denton Jr., ed. (Lanham, MD: Rowman & Littlefield, 2021), 193.

Chapter 1

Political Branding and Messaging Strategies in the 2020 Postelection Presidential Campaign

Lisa M. Burns and Courtney L. Marchese

INTRODUCTION

The 2020 U.S. presidential campaign was like no other, in part because it lasted well after Election Day. Donald Trump refused to concede and challenged the election results in court, waging a campaign of disinformation about voter fraud via speeches and social media. Joe Biden continued his campaign message of unity by saying he would be a president for all Americans, including the over seventy-four million people who voted for Trump. This chaotic postelection period came down to two days in early 2021: January 6 and January 20. The images from those dates are a study in contrasts that sum up the 2020 election cycle. On January 6, a swarm of Trump supporters— many wearing the iconic red MAGA hats and waving Trump flags—stormed the U.S. Capitol, scaling the walls, smashing windows, and desecrating the symbolic and literal seat of U.S. democracy. On January 20, Democratic and Republican members of Congress, former U.S. presidents and their spouses, and celebrities gathered on the same Capitol steps to witness the peaceful transition of power as Joe Biden and Kamala Harris took their oaths of office at a subdued and socially distanced inauguration ceremony.

As remarkable as the events of the postelection period were, both candidates stayed true to their campaign brands. From the beginning of his political career, Trump positioned himself as the antipolitician. His bombastic, brash, and bullying style are trademarks of the Trump brand. His public image is based on winning and success, so his refusal to accept a loss or the fairness of the election was not surprising. Everything about his brand foreshadowed his challenge of the election results and his willingness to question the integrity of the voting process, even if such claims were potentially damaging to democracy. In stark contrast, Biden's brand is the experienced elder statesman

1

who is reliable, kind, a tad old-fashioned, and even a bit boring. If Trump is the antipolitician, Biden is the anti-Trump. Where Trump is divisive, Biden seeks to unite. His efforts to bring the country together were not only in response to a contested election and false claims of voter fraud, but also an attempt to manage the continuing COVID-19 pandemic and begin to address social inequities.

This chapter examines how the candidates' brands influenced their 2020 postelection campaign strategies by analyzing the speeches and social media messaging of Trump and Biden. After a brief overview of each candidate's brand, we'll look at four distinct periods in the postelection campaign: the immediate aftermath of the election (November 3–7), the challenge period (November 7–January 6), the Capitol insurrection (January 6), and the Biden-Harris inauguration (January 20).

CANDIDATE BRANDS IN CAMPAIGN 2020

Branding has always been a central part of presidential campaigns. An effective logo, slogan, and imagery help campaigns deliver consistent messaging and sum up their candidate's political ideology.[1] However, the study of political candidates as brands didn't start receiving serious scholarly attention until the 1990s[2] even though campaigns had been "selling candidates exactly the way Madison Avenue sells corn flakes and soap" for many years.[3] While much of the research on candidate branding has been done from a political marketing standpoint, we approach the topic from a communication perspective that takes into account the rhetorical dimensions of the campaigns' brand messaging strategies.

Political branding uses symbols and concepts to shape how a candidate is perceived by the public.[4] A strong political brand sums up the personality and reputation of the candidate through a combination of a clear purpose, concise and consistent messaging, compelling storytelling, emotional appeal, and memorable visual imagery that is designed to target key voting demographics.[5] A campaign creates their candidate's brand personality by using value-laden words and images to construct a public persona possessing traits valued by voters.[6] These identities are designed to "appeal to their target publics and the general public, and as such to encourage identification of citizens with their personas."[7] The "Big Five" dimensions of brand personality are sincerity (down-to-earth, honest, kind, empathetic), competence (reliable, successful, knowledgeable), excitement (daring, spirited, carefree), sophistication (upper-class, prestigious, wealthy), and ruggedness (rough, tough, outdoorsy).[8]

Trump and Biden have very different brand personalities. Trump's brand, which he's spent years cultivating, is BIG, BOLD, and DEFIANT. His brand personality is a mix of excitement, sophistication, and ruggedness. Andrea Schneiker describes Trump's distinctive brand as a "superhero anti-politician celebrity" who used his wealth and fame to propel himself to the presidency by positioning himself as the ultimate political outsider.[9] He is a rugged individualist and "outlaw who doesn't have time for politeness or political correctness."[10] He embraces what Richard Hofstadter calls a "paranoid style" rhetoric that promotes conspiracy theories about "vast and sinister plots"[11] involving political corruption as reflected in slogans like "Drain the Swamp" and "Stop the Steal." He's an antagonist, bully, Twitter troll, and "American strongman" who listens to his gut instead of relying on facts or expert opinions.[12] These characteristics, often construed as negative, are seen as positive by Trump's intensely loyal base. Trump has successfully built a "cult brand," which is a brand with "a relatively small but loyal customer base that verges on fanaticism" where followers "feel a sense of self-ownership or vested interest in the brand's popularity and success."[13] Cult brands become part of their followers' identity, creating a strong sense of community by embracing "a certain way of being, aligned to a specific set of beliefs,"[14] such as those embodied by Trump's "Make America Great Again" mantra. Cult brands are powerful because they "don't just foster casual relationships with consumers, they find ways to play an integral part in their lives."[15] These followers believe in the brand no matter what, just as Trump's base believe his claims about a stolen election regardless of the lack of evidence.

Most importantly, Trump's brand is defined by winning. According to *ABC News* White House correspondent Jonathan Karl, "His brand is everything. And his brand is being the winner."[16] Jonathan Allen of *NBC News* similarly states, "The core of that brand is the notion that superhuman instincts and physical capabilities enable him to win at everything all the time."[17] The result, as communication scholar Mary E. Stuckey notes, is that Trump "is unwilling to admit failure or weakness, and he cannot admit lapses in judgment or mistakes."[18] For example, rather than admitting Hillary Clinton won the popular vote in the 2016 presidential election, Trump blamed voter fraud. So, it should not have been surprising when the same thing occurred in 2020. Karl claims, "Trump could not take the idea that he lost. He was worried his followers would abandon him if he lost. It's why he's so desperate to say he didn't lose. But it's a huge hit to his brand because he didn't win."[19]

On the campaign trail, Biden cultivated a calm, casual, and cool image. He also represented himself as a knowledgeable leader who could unite, rather than divide, the country. He came off as experienced, likable, and trustworthy, which stressed the brand personality traits of competence and sincerity. Biden's brand personality lacked the excitement and ruggedness of Trump's, but that ultimately worked to his advantage. In a market research study by Ipsos, Brand Biden was deemed "nondescript" because participants' descriptions of Biden were rather generic. When participants were asked what popped into their minds when they thought of Biden, the number one response was "great (potential) President/person," but "old" was a close second followed by "cares about the people/kind." Other positive attributes associated with Biden included likable, trustworthy, qualified, and stands up for people while his negatives were being irresponsible, boring, and old. In contrast, participants had very intense positive or negative reactions to Trump. "Great President/person" was also the top response for Trump, but "arrogant/rude" and "bad President/person" received the second and third most mentions. Trump supporters' reflected his "superhero anti-politician celebrity" brand, describing him as someone who's "bold, good for the economy, [and] intelligent" and who "respects law and order while fighting political correctness." But over half of the respondents had strong negative perceptions of Trump, using words like corrupt, racist, reckless, bully, liar, arrogant, and narrow-minded when discussing him. Researchers concluded that Brand Trump is well defined in both positive and negative ways, causing people to be either extremely loyal to or repelled by his brand, which is characteristic of cult brands. Meanwhile, Biden's supporters were more anti-Trump than pro-Biden.[20] The Biden team seized on this sentiment. If Trump was the antipolitician, then Biden was the anti-Trump. He also embraced the traditions and traits of the presidency, promising a return to normalcy after the disruption of the Trump era.

The differences between the candidates' brands became even more pronounced during the postelection campaign. Biden represented order, tradition/convention, calm, peaceful transition of power, faith in political institutions, trusting the system, and unity. Trump's brand represented chaos, nonconformity, disruption, refusal to relinquish power and begin transition, undermining of confidence in political institutions, distrust of the system, and divisiveness. As the president-elect, Biden sought to unite a divided country and reinforce faith in democratic processes and institutions, branding himself as a president for all Americans. Meanwhile, Trump privileged his personal brand over the institution of the presidency, which he had done from the start. In *Unmaking the Presidency*, Susan Hennessey and Benjamin Wittes argue that Trump elevated "the expressive, vanity-plate dimensions of the office . . . making it a personal vehicle for the public self-expression of the office holder." In doing so, he rejected "nearly all other traditional features of the presidency" including "its expectation of ethical conduct, truthfulness, and service."[21] This was evident in the postcampaign period as Trump spread disinformation about how he won the election "by a lot" and that it was being stolen from him through election fraud—all unsubstantiated claims that sought to undermine faith in the electoral system. Similarly, Stuckey observes, "In both his substance and in his style, Trump changed the way Americans consider national politics; he altered the personal presidency to make it a presidency that focused on the president as an individual and not the presidency as an institution, unheeding of the requirements of civic virtue and subject to the whims of the individual president."[22] Because of his disregard for the presidency and political institutions in general, Trump had no qualms about undermining them or attacking "the norms and values that have long underpinned national politics."[23]

In the postelection period, Biden's brand personality focused on being presidential, stressing his competence and sincerity, while Trump continued to be the defiant individualist disrupting democratic institutions. Stuckey explains that, in their performance of the presidency, presidents model for citizens "behavior and attitudes appropriate for the sustenance of a democratic republic." She says, "Most presidents, most of the time, understand that they continue to model the dispositions that make democracy possible, and they adhere to these norms, as do most presidential candidates, who are interested in presenting themselves as already 'presidential.'" Consequently, "a large amount of presidential public speech is essentially interchangeable" with each president offering their own take on what it means to be a "good citizen."[24] This strategy is evident in Biden's messaging with his focus on unity and faith in the electoral process. However, Trump isn't most presidents and has "performed the presidency largely in ways that undermine its place in the American political system and has weakened the entire political system."[25] Being presidential was never part of Trump's brand. Stuckey notes, "Like the other norms he violates, this is also an attack on the processes that underpin democracy."[26] His sustained attacks on the electoral system not only undermined faith in free and fair elections, but resulted in an attack on the Capitol aimed at disrupting one of the foundations of American democracy.

Campaigns, candidacies, and even presidencies have clear end points, but brands do not. Prioritizing his personal brand helps explain why Trump refused to acknowledge the end of the campaign, especially since the results did not support a brand that puts winning above all else. Thus, the campaign extended well beyond election night. While Biden recognized the traditional markers of the postelection period—waiting for the final election results, delivering an acceptance speech, carrying out the transition process, and taking the presidential oath of office at the inauguration—Trump did not. Instead, Trump declared preemptive victory before all votes were counted, refused to concede and challenged the election results, would not cooperate with the transition, and snubbed the inauguration. Yet, in spite of their very different approaches to the postelection campaign, the one thing Biden and Trump had in common was staying true to their brands. The remainder of the chapter will analyze how the candidates' brand messaging in speeches and social media posts reflected their brand personalities and the potential consequences of political branding in the postelection campaign.

IMMEDIATE AFTERMATH: NOVEMBER 3–7, 2020

The 2020 presidential election was unique for a variety of reasons, including the challenges of conducting an election during a pandemic. Many states expanded voting access, including mail-in balloting, to avoid long lines and super-spreader conditions on Election Day. This meant results would most likely not be known on November 3.[27] Election officials and the news media tried to prepare the public for the delay by detailing the vote counting process in different states.[28] Biden frequently discussed the need for patience in the final days of the campaign since Democrats were more likely to vote by mail, messaging that continued in the immediate aftermath of the election. In stark contrast, Trump spent months calling into question the validity of mail-in balloting, planting the seeds of a "rigged" election and the idea that only votes cast on Election Day, where in-person voting largely favored Republicans, were legitimate.[29] It took four days for enough votes to be tallied that state election officials and news outlets felt confident in declaring a winner. During that time, the messaging by the candidates was on-brand, but radically different.

The Trump campaign held their election night event in the East Room of the White House. About two hundred administration officials, top Republicans, and donors gathered to watch the results on monitors broadcasting Fox News.[30] At 12:49 a.m. on November 4, Trump tweeted his first claims that election officials were trying to "steal" the election: "We are up BIG, but they are trying to STEAL the Election. We will never let them do it. Votes cannot be cast after the Polls are closed!" Twitter put a warning label on this particular tweet for "making a potentially misleading claim about an election," the first of many in the coming days.[31] Around 2:30 a.m., Trump addressed the White House crowd and TV cameras. No network had called the election yet since most battleground states had too many outstanding votes, mainly mail-in ballots. Yet Trump both claimed victory and called into question the integrity of the vote. At the very start of his speech, he thanked the "millions and millions of people" who voted for him, but then said, "And a very sad group of people is trying to disenfranchise that group of people and we won't stand for it." He mentioned his wins in Florida, Ohio, and Texas. But he also claimed it was "clear that we have won Georgia," that "we're winning Pennsylvania by a tremendous amount," and that he was winning Michigan and Wisconsin even though all of those states had significant amounts of ballots yet to count and were ultimately won by Biden. Next, Trump shifted to unfounded allegations that the election was being stolen. He proclaimed: "This is a fraud on the American public. This is an embarrassment to our country. We were getting ready to win this election. Frankly, we did win this election. We did win this election. So our goal now is to ensure the integrity for the good of this nation." He then announced he'd be "going to the US Supreme Court. We want all voting to stop." Before handing the podium over to Mike Pence, Trump once again thanked his supporters and said, "To me this is a very sad moment and we will win this. And as far as I'm concerned, we already have won it."[32] In less than twelve hours, the Trump campaign filed lawsuits to stop vote counting in Michigan and Pennsylvania, challenged ballot handling in Georgia, and requested a recount in Wisconsin.[33]

Trump's speech was not surprising given he'd spent months asserting without evidence that mail-in balloting was rife with fraud as well as years of questioning the integrity of U.S. elections. *CNBC* reported that Trump "sought to undermine faith in the multiday process of vote tallying, and to lay the groundwork for insisting that the only valid election results were those tallied on election night."[34] By July of 2020, Trump had made ninety-one claims that "questioned voting or suggested that an election would be rigged, unfair, or otherwise compromised," according to Factbase, a website tracking Trump's public statements and tweets. This was a familiar mantra for Trump, who made over seven hundred such comments dating back to 2012.[35] In an August 19 *New York Times* op-ed, political scientist Richard Hasen posited that Trump was either using fraud as "an excuse for a possible loss to his Democratic opponent, Joe Biden" or "seeking to sow chaos to drive down turnout and undermine the legitimacy of the election, laying the groundwork for contesting a close election if he loses."[36] Both of Hasen's predictions played out. Trump used this same strategy in the 2016 campaign as a way to buffet against a potential election loss to Hillary Clinton and later to explain losing the popular vote to Clinton by over three million votes.[37] Since Trump's brand cannot accept a loss, he needed to justify why he didn't win. So Trump employed paranoid style rhetoric to rationalize the results, well before votes were even cast, to shift blame to mysterious outside forces, a corrupt system, and conspiracy theories.[38]

Throughout the day on November 4, Trump continued to spread falsehoods about so-called "ballot dumps" costing him the election. At 4:56 p.m.,

Trump decided to call the election himself: "We have claimed, for Electoral Vote purposes, the Commonwealth of Pennsylvania (which won't allow legal observers) the State of Georgia, and the State of North Carolina, each one of which has a BIG Trump lead. Additionally, we hereby claim the State of Michigan." Of course, Trump had no authority to claim victory with the vote count still underway. On November 5, Trump started his day by tweeting "STOP THE COUNT!," which became a rallying cry for his supporters. About an hour later he followed up with, "ANY VOTE THAT CAME IN AFTER ELECTION DAY WILL NOT BE COUNTED!" and repeated "STOP THE FRAUD" soon after. That evening during a White House press conference, Trump reasserted election fraud claims without providing evidence, telling reporters, "If you count the legal votes, I easily win. If you count the illegal votes, they can try to steal the election from us."[39] Trump contended he had already won states including Michigan, Georgia, and Pennsylvania by "a lot" even though his lead was shrinking. He once again blamed mail-in voting, calling it "a corrupt system." But, as *NBC News* pointed out, votes weren't being "found." They were legitimate mail-in ballots that couldn't be processed until after polls had closed: "This claim, casting doubt on the integrity of American elections, is false. There's no evidence of widespread voter fraud, according to numerous studies, and there are a number of safeguards in place to ensure the security of mail ballots and prevent fraud."[40] Meanwhile, throughout the week, Twitter continued to label Trump's posts as "misleading," while Facebook and Instagram also attached warnings noting that "final results may be different from the initial vote counts."[41]

Trump's paranoid rhetoric continued on November 6 with a 2:22 a.m. tweet that stated, "I easily WIN the Presidency of the United States with LEGAL VOTES CAST." He spent the rest of the day retweeting news about his legal challenges. By the morning of November 7, he was once again falsely claiming "tens of thousands of votes were illegally received" on Election Day and that "People were screaming STOP THE COUNT & WE DEMAND TRANSPARENCY." Trump's morning ended with the announcement of his lawyers' press conference at Four Seasons Landscaping in Philadelphia followed by the proclamation, "I WON THIS ELECTION, BY A LOT!" Within the hour, the election was called for Joe Biden.[42] Minutes after networks made the call, the Trump campaign released a statement that said, "The simple fact is this election is far from over. Joe Biden has not been certified as the winner of any states, let alone any of the highly contested states headed for mandatory recounts, or states where our campaign has valid and legitimate legal challenges that could determine the ultimate victor."[43] The campaign promised to fight the results in court, making it clear that Trump would not concede. Trump tweeted just two more times later that day, yet again stating,

"I WON THE ELECTION, GOT 71,000,000 LEGAL VOTES" and repeating charges of election fraud. His messaging continued to vacillate between claiming victory and complaining the election was rigged.

Unlike Trump, Biden did not immediately declare victory. Instead, he focused on counting all votes. His tone was cautiously optimistic given that the mail-in vote was projected to be heavily in his favor. Shortly after midnight on November 4, Biden and wife ,Jill, appeared in front of the drive-in rally crowd outside of the Chase Center in Wilmington, Delaware. In a brief speech, Biden said he was "feeling good" about the results but stressed the need for patience: "We're going to have to be patient until the hard work of tallying the votes is finished. And it ain't over until every vote is counted." After thanking his team, Biden told the crowd, "Keep the faith guys, we're going to win this."[44] That messaging continued on social media. On November 4, the Biden team switched its banners across platforms to the slogan "Keep the Faith!" The Biden camp also called on supporters to remain calm. One clever take on this was a deep-breathing GIF on Instagram featuring Biden's iconic aviators—a frequently used campaign image—that signaled when to inhale, hold, and exhale. The accompanying text read, "Folks—I know this is a stressful time. I want to remind you to breathe and keep the faith. We'll come out on the other side."

The campaign's other postelection slogan was "Count Every Vote"/"Contar Cada Voto." Biden stated on Instagram on November 4, "Let me be clear—every American's vote matters and deserves to be counted," while on Facebook and Twitter he vowed, "We won't rest until everyone's vote is counted." Another Instagram post noted, "It's not my place or Donald Trump's place to declare who has won this election. That's the decision of the American people." Biden delivered a similar message during a press briefing on November 5 telling reporters, "It is the will of the voters. Not one, not anyone else that chooses the President of the United States. So each ballot must be counted." He also stressed the need for patience, noting, "Democracy is sometimes messy. It sometimes requires a little patience as well. But that patience has been rewarded now for more than 240 years with a system of governance that has been the envy of the world."[45] The message on Twitter was, "Be patient, folks. Votes are being counted, and we feel good about where we are." Again he called for calm, saying, "The process is working. The count is being completed." This defense of the vote counting process was a direct response to the Trump camp's efforts to undermine the public's faith in the election. As Trump continued his attacks on the election's integrity, Biden countered by tweeting on November 6, "The people will not be silenced, be bullied, or surrender. Every vote must be counted." Across platforms, he stated, "No one is going to take our democracy away from us. Not now, not ever. America has come too far, fought too many battles, and endured too much to let that happen."

By the evening of November 6, with counts in key battlegrounds wrapping up in Biden's favor, his messaging shifted to calls for unity. In a speech at 10:45 p.m., he told the nation, "The purpose of our politics isn't to wage total and unrelenting war. It's to solve problems. . . . We may be opponents, but we're not enemies. We're Americans."[46] This message was repeated across Biden's social media accounts. He also said in his speech, "We're certainly not going to agree on a lot of issues but at least we can agree to be civil with one another. We have to put the anger and the demonization behind us. It's time for us to come together as a nation to heal."[47] Biden repeated his campaign pledge to be a president for all Americans: "My responsibility as president will be to represent the whole nation. And I want you to know that I'll work as hard for those who voted against me as those who voted for me, that's the job."[48] But his calls for unity did not ignore the divisiveness promoted by Trump's challenge of the election results. Biden proclaimed, "Democracy works. Your vote will be counted. I don't care how hard people try and stop it. I will not let it happen."[49]

At 11:24 a.m. on November 7, CNN was the first network to declare Biden the winner of the 2020 presidential election after the latest Pennsylvania results showed Biden with an insurmountable margin over Trump. The other networks quickly followed suit, with Fox News being the last to declare Biden's victory at 11:40 a.m.[50] At 11:52 a.m., Biden posted the following message across platforms, "America, I'm honored that you have chosen me to lead our great country. The work ahead of us will be hard, but I promise you this: I will be a President for all Americans—whether you voted for me or not. I will keep the faith that you have placed in me." The posts included a 1:56-minute video set to Ray Charles's rendition of "America the Beautiful" featuring a montage of average people from diverse backgrounds across the United States. The closing tag was "A COUNTRY for all Americans. A FUTURE for all Americans. A PRESIDENT for all Americans," projected over video of a sunrise. His feeds then announced his address to the nation that evening proclaiming, "A new day in America has come." The text appeared on a yellow-to-blue-gradient background reminiscent of a sunrise. The imagery and language of these posts were reminiscent of Ronald Reagan's famous "Morning in America" ad. Biden's Instagram feed also featured an artistic rendering of Biden's and Harris's profiles surrounded by the faces of a diverse group of Americans. The combined faces formed the shape of the continental United States (with Alaska and Hawaii included below) and the text "ALL OF US UNITED." This image was sold as a poster in Biden's online campaign store.

Biden's acceptance speech the evening of November 7 was a culmination of his campaign's messaging. At a drive-in rally outside the Chase Center in Wilmington, attendees were socially distanced and wearing masks along with their Biden campaign merch. According to *BuzzFeed News*, it was likely the largest crowd of Biden's entire campaign: "All day, people had been gathering in Wilmington's surrounding Riverfront district eager to see history. Hundreds of cars made it into the lot. Supporters stood outside them, wearing their masks, waving their American flags."[51] Biden focused much of his speech on unity. After pointing out his victory had been "clear" and "convincing," he immediately turned his attention to the more than seventy million Americans who voted for Trump. He pledged "to be a president who seeks not to divide but unify, who doesn't see red states and blue states, only sees the United States. I'll work with all my heart, with the confidence of the whole people, to win the confidence of all of you." A bit later, he said, "For all those of you who voted for President Trump, I understand the disappointment tonight. I've lost a couple of times myself. But now, let's give each other a chance. It's time to put away the harsh rhetoric, lower the temperature, see each other again. Listen to each other again. And to make progress, we have to stop treating our opponents as our enemies. They are not our enemies. They are Americans." And toward the end, he declared, "I'm a proud Democrat, but I will govern as an American president. I'll work as hard for those who didn't vote for me as those who did. Let this grim era of demonization in America begin to end here and now."[52] His speech mirrored predecessors Barack Obama and George W. Bush, who also called for unity following bitterly fought elections.[53] Biden's call for calm and empathy reflected his brand as a sincere leader who could be trusted. He positioned himself yet again as the anti-Trump with statements alluding to Trump's polarizing appeals solely to his supporters without ever referencing his opponent by name. The closest Biden came was when he noted, "Our nation is shaped by the constant battle between our better angels and our darkest impulses. What presidents say in this battle matters. It's time for our better angels to prevail."[54]

As with most acceptance speeches, Biden also touted his win as a mandate for his agenda. He thanked his supporters, celebrating what he called "the broadest and most diverse coalition in history. Democrats, Republicans, independents, progressives, moderates, conservatives, young, old, urban, suburban, rural, gay, straight, transgender, white, Latino, Asian, Native American" and including a special thanks to the African American community. Biden promised to continue supporting diversity and inclusion in his presidency: "I said at the outset, I wanted this campaign to represent and look like America. We've done that. Now that's what I want the administration to look like and act like."[55] When his speech concluded and the extended Biden and Harris families came to the stage to watch a massive fireworks display, the image represented and looked like America, reinforcing Biden's unifying rhetoric and his inclusive brand.

The themes of Biden's victory speech were shared across his social media platforms, with the majority of posts focusing on unity and celebrating the end of a hard fought campaign. Traditionally, acceptance and concession speeches mark the official end of the campaign and the start of the transition period. Following his November 7 acceptance speech, Biden embraced his new title of president-elect and his team shifted their focus to the transition of power. But their efforts were hindered by a Trump administration that refused to cooperate and a lame duck president unwilling to admit defeat. Trump never conceded. Instead, he continued to make unfounded claims of election fraud. For nearly nine weeks, the country was confronted with competing performances of the presidency: one that focused on the individual over the institution and another that showed reverence for the traditions of the office.

CHALLENGE AND TRANSITION PERIOD: NOVEMBER 7, 2020–JANUARY 6, 2021

Trump spent the final two months of his presidency declaring the election had been stolen and he was the true winner. A search of Trump's tweets on Factbase shows that he made 426 references to "election fraud," used "steal/ stole" 154 times, made 100 mentions of "rigged election," and referenced "voter fraud" 91 times between November 7, 2020, and January 6, 2021. During that same period he used the word "win" 2,238 times and "won" on 403 occasions. Most of the comments were the same claims Trump made immediately following the election. Trump appeared on camera on just a handful of occasions during this period. He spent much of his time sequestered in the White House or golfing at one of his properties while his legal team led by Rudy Giuliani handled the court battles. But in his few public appearances and prerecorded messages, he repeated the unfounded accusations of election fraud, never wavering from his conviction that he was not a loser.

One of Trump's only interactions with reporters was following a Thanksgiving phone call with troops on November 26. He spent twenty-five minutes taking questions and once again mentioned the rigged election, telling them, "The numbers are corrupt. It was a rigged election, 100%, and people know it."[56] For the first time since the election, he said he would "leave the White House" if the Electoral College voted for Biden, but he still refused to concede. "It's going to be a very hard thing to concede because we know there was massive fraud," Trump said, comparing the election to one in "a

Third World country." Meanwhile, he scoffed repeatedly at the election results, saying, "There's no way that Biden got 80 million votes" and claimed
there would "be a lot of things happening" before the inauguration, holding
out hope that he'd prevail in overturning the election.[57]

On December 2, Trump uploaded a forty-six-minute prerecorded speech to
his social media platforms that repeated his unsubstantiated claims of election
fraud and served as a "call to arms to his supporters."[58] He opened by saying,
"This may be the most important speech I've ever made," before launching
into an update on his team's "efforts to expose the tremendous voter fraud
and irregularities."[59] The *New York Times* described the speech as "the
in-person embodiment of Mr. Trump's staccato tweets over the past three
weeks: one falsehood after another about voting irregularities in swing states,
attacks on state officials and signature verifications, and false accusations
against Democrats."[60] Without evidence, Trump asserted, "This election
was rigged. Everybody knows it," and declared, "If we don't root out the
fraud, the tremendous and horrible fraud that's taken place in our 2020 election, we don't have a country anymore." Throughout the speech he claimed
he was challenging the election results to defend the Constitution and
"protect our election system, which is now under coordinated assault and
siege," which was possibly an attempt to answer those who said his efforts
to overturn the election were having the opposite effect. Trump positioned
himself as the antipolitician superhero who was fighting a rigged system
on behalf of his supporters. But this fight was also personal because, for
his brand, losing wasn't an option. So, instead he talked about how he was
being robbed, declaring, "You can't let another person steal that election
from you,"[61] employing the paranoid-style rhetoric that defined most of
his postcampaign messaging.

In fact-checking the speech, news media outlets noted that Trump continued to repeat the same disinformation he'd been spreading on social media
since election night. But they also questioned the potential consequences of
Trump's messaging. The *Washington Post* described Trump as "escalating his
attack on democracy from within the White House" and attempting "to lever-
age the power of the presidency to subvert the vote and overturn the election
results." The story continued, "Although his words actually worked to undermine democracy, he cast himself as the protector of democracy, saying his
single greatest achievement as president would be to restore 'voter integrity
for our nation.'"[62] The *Associated Press* called Trump "increasingly detached
from reality" and argued his "baseless claims" were "undermining public faith
in the integrity of U.S. elections."[63] *U.S. News & World Report* observed that
the speech "shows a man who seems not just willing to repeat discredited
information from the powerful perch of the White House but who appears

genuinely incapable of comprehending the reality of the election results. The president is known for his bombastic speeches and insult-laden tweets, but the rant against his perceived enemies was a new level even for Trump."[64] *The Hill* said Trump was "increasingly isolated in his refusal to accept the outcome of the election" and remarked there were "no signs that the president will ever accept the outcome of the election or seek to unify a divided country on his way out."[65] These statements echo the concerns of scholars who questioned whether "Trump's presidency further weakened a political system that was already being increasingly seen as unworthy of trust."[66]

Trump appeared at his first rally since Election Day on December 5, traveling to Valdosta, Georgia, to campaign for David Perdue and Kelly Loeffler in their Senate runoff elections. But instead of promoting the candidates, Trump spent most of his one-hundred-minute speech rehashing his conspiracy theories of voting fraud and claiming he won the election. He opened by stating, "We've never lost an election. We're winning this election," and later shouted, "They cheated and rigged our presidential election, but we'll still win." He continued that theme, telling the crowd, "If I lost, I'd be a very gracious loser. If I lost, I would say I lost and I'd go to Florida and I'd take it easy and I'd go around and I'd say I did a good job. But you can't ever accept when they steal and rig and lie."[67] Trump even claimed to have won Georgia's electoral votes despite the state certifying Biden's win. Trump had called Republican governor Brian Kemp earlier that same day asking him to convene a special session of the legislature to overturn the results, which Kemp refused to do.[68] Throughout the speech, in response to Trump's unproven claims, the crowd repeatedly chanted "Stop the Steal."

A similar scene played out on January 4 at a Dalton, Georgia, rally the night before Perdue and Loeffler's election. For over eighty minutes, Trump once again railed about the "rigged election" and "how badly screwed we got" while still declaring a "landslide" victory. He bragged: "I've had two elections. I've won both of them. It's amazing."[69] He also ratcheted up his rhetoric. With the Electoral College certification just two days away, he still refused to accept the loss: "They're not going to take this White House. We're going to fight like hell, I'll tell you right now." He used the speech to put pressure on members of Congress to challenge the certification. Trump berated Republicans who refused to support his attempt to overturn Biden's win, telling the crowd, "People will remember the people who don't support us." Trump also called out Vice President Mike Pence, hoping that Pence "comes through for us" when presiding over the joint session of Congress and "if he doesn't come through, I won't like him so much."[70] While Trump quickly played it off as a joke, such comments had consequences, making Pence a primary target during the storming of the Capitol.

While Trump and his team continued to promote baseless claims of election fraud, president-elect Biden focused on COVID-19, Cabinet picks, and uniting a divided country. The Trump administration initially refused to cooperate with the transition process, forcing the Biden team to do what they could without government funding or support. They used a series of press events to highlight their work, starting with a briefing by Biden's newly formed COVID-19 Advisory Council on November 10. During these briefings, Biden and Harris were seated on stage in the campaign's Delaware headquarters in front of a giant screen where their guests appeared via video conferencing while reporters sat socially distanced in the audience. They met with national security experts, bipartisan groups of governors and mayors, frontline workers, and small business owners. The goal was to show Biden and Harris engaging with both experts and average Americans. The same venue was used to introduce Biden's Cabinet picks, starting with his national security and foreign policy team on November 24. The nominees were announced via press release and on social media followed by the official press briefings, which were usually aired live by the TV news networks. Staying true to his campaign pledge, the Biden administration was on course to become one of the most diverse and representative in history with several nominees poised to be the first to hold their intended post.[71] The history-making nature of Biden's appointments generated positive press coverage. With an average of two briefings a week through early January, Biden was able to keep himself and his agenda in the news. He even hit the campaign trail again, visiting Georgia to support Reverend Raphael Warnock and Jon Ossoff's Senate bids in their January runoff elections. But unlike previous presidential transitions, he had to compete with stories of the Trump campaign's latest legal challenges or court decisions, which dominated the news cycle.

Biden's social media posts focused on moving forward and uniting the nation by promoting the inclusivity of his Cabinet picks and highlighting his agenda for his first one hundred days, particularly his planned response to the pandemic. His posts conveyed competence, sincerity, and a sense of hope for the future. As part of their transition strategy, Biden's social media platforms also showcased him performing the typical ceremonial duties of the presidency. He took congratulatory calls from world leaders telling them America was "going to be back in the game." On Veteran's Day, he and wife, Jill, laid wreaths at a Korean War Memorial in Philadelphia and spoke with veterans and their families. He sent prayers to families in the path of Tropical Storms Eta and Iota and congratulated NASA and SpaceX on a successful launch. On Thanksgiving, he and Jill made video calls to frontline workers to thank them for their service during the pandemic. In a recorded message, he encouraged families to sacrifice their typical Thanksgiving gatherings for the larger public good: "And while I know this isn't the way many of us hoped to spend the holiday, the small act of staying home is a gift to our fellow Americans." The Bidens offered a similar message on Christmas while also acknowledging the loss and hardships brought on by the pandemic and the hope for brighter days ahead. On a lighter note, they posted a video of dogs Champ and Major enjoying their Christmas presents. His social media team also recognized holidays including Diwali, Hanukkah, and Kwanzaa with greeting card–style posts and acknowledged events like Transgender Remembrance Day, National Indigenous Heritage Day, World AIDS Day, the International Day for Elimination of Violence Against Women, International Day of People with Disabilities, Pearl Harbor Day, and the anniversaries of the Sandy Hook school shooting and the ISIS terrorist attacks in France. By performing these typical duties of the presidency, Biden was consciously shifting his branding from personal to presidential.

The theme of unity continued to permeate Biden's messaging. Many of his Twitter posts referred back to his November 7 acceptance speech call "to put aside the partisanship and the rhetoric designed to demonize one another" and "stop treating our opponents as our enemy. We are not enemies. We are Americans." He also reiterated his pledge "to be a president who seeks not to divide, but to unify. Who doesn't see red and blue states, but a United States" and to "be a president for all Americans." While Biden generally ignored the Trump campaign's efforts to overturn the election results (Trump was rarely mentioned by Biden during this period), there were a few occasions when his team used social media to reaffirm the democratic process. A tweet from November 24 noted, "Despite overt political pressure from the president, over the last 24 hours, MI, PA, and NV certified their results and the GSA began the transition. Still, President Trump has not conceded." On December 14, the day of the Electoral College vote, Biden said on Twitter, "In America, politicians don't take power—the people grant it to them. The flame of democracy was lit in this nation a long time ago. And we now know that nothing—not even a pandemic or an abuse of power—can extinguish that flame." These messages promoted faith in the democratic process and the voting results. On January 4, Biden posted what now seems like a prophetic warning, "In America, politicians can't assert, take, or seize power. It has to be given by the American people. We can't ever give that up. The will of the people must always prevail." But two days later following a "Save America/Stop the Steal" rally where Trump repeated claims of election fraud, attendees marched on the U.S. Capitol and stormed the building as a joint session of Congress was conducting the Electoral College vote certification, attempting to seize power and undermine the will of the people.

INSURRECTION: JANUARY 6, 2021

The Electoral College vote certification is typically a ceremonial affair symbolic of the peaceful transition of power, a foundation of American democracy. But in this unique postelection campaign, the date took on new significance and became a "last stand" for Trump and his supporters in their efforts to overturn Biden's victory.[72] The *New York Times* described it as "a day of reckoning. A day to gather in Washington to 'save America' and 'stop the steal' of the election [Trump] had decisively lost, but which he still maintained—often through a toxic brew of conspiracy theories—that he had won by a landslide."[73] It appears Trump himself was the first to call on supporters to gather in D.C. on January 6. On December 19, Trump tweeted, "Big protest in D.C. on January 6. Be there, will be wild!"[74] By early January, the event organized by "Women for America First" effectively became a White House production with Trump himself planning to speak and discussing things like the lineup and music.[75]

On the morning of January 6, thousands of Trump supporters gathered in downtown D.C. "forming rivers of Trump red that commingled the Trump and American flags."[76] The sea of red MAGA hats and "Trump 2020" flags were dotted with camouflage, the other popular attire color that day. Trump took the stage at noon, riling up the crowd during his seventy-minute speech that was consistent with his postcampaign messaging. He began by praising the crowd size and questioning the election results: "Hundreds of thousands of American patriots are committed to the honesty of our elections and the integrity of our glorious Republic. All of us here today do not want to see our election victory stolen." He then vowed, "We will never concede. It doesn't happen. You don't concede when there's theft involved." He used the word "we" 379 times in the speech, making emotional appeals to his loyal cult brand followers and calling them to action. Much of the speech was a rehash of his previous public comments, like telling supporters "We must stop the steal" and claiming he won the election "by a landslide." The most-used words in the speech were "fraud" (twenty-two references) and "win/won" (twenty-one mentions). But he also said the word "fight" twenty times. He told the crowd, "If you don't fight like hell you're not going to have a country anymore," adding, "You will never take back our country with weakness." Trump also called on Republican lawmakers to "fight much harder," including Pence.[77] His new speech material focused mainly on Pence and his false claims that the vice president could stop the Electoral College certification, even though Pence himself released a statement earlier that day noting it was not within his constitutional power to do so.[78] Trump referenced Pence by name a half-dozen times. "I hope Mike is going to do the right thing . . .

because if Mike Pence does the right thing, we win the election," Trump said. "All Vice President Pence has to do is recertify, and we become president, and you are the happiest people."[79] He then warned if Pence didn't "come through" it would "be a sad day for our country."[80] Trump also called Republican lawmakers refusing to object to the certification "weak" and "pathetic," promising to "primary the hell out of the ones that don't fight."[81] With such messaging, it's not surprising that Pence and members of Congress were primary targets of the mob that Trump all but led to the Capitol steps. At two different points in the speech, Trump encouraged the crowd to march on the Capitol, claiming he'd be among them: "After this, we're going to walk down and I'll be there with you." He ended the speech with the following call for action: "We are going to walk down Pennsylvania Avenue . . . to give our Republicans—the weak ones because the strong ones don't need any of our help . . . the kind of pride and boldness that they need to take back our country."[82] With those words, Trump "unleashed a mob."[83] The *New York Times* called the speech "incendiary,"[84] while the *Washington Post* asserted that "Trump's angry rant amounted to a call to arms."[85]

Before Trump's speech even ended, upwards of fifteen thousand rallygoers streamed toward the Capitol where hundreds of protestors were already gathered.[86] The first breach of Capitol security came at 12:53 p.m. when protestors brandishing Trump flags and clad in MAGA hats and "Trump 45" winter beanies overwhelmed three Capitol Police officers, breaking through four temporary barricades to reach the west Capitol steps. At 1:10 p.m., when Trump concluded his speech, many in the crowd "did as they were told. By the thousands, they walked 16 blocks down Pennsylvania Avenue NW and surrounded the U.S. Capitol."[87] By then, the vastly outnumbered Capitol Police in riot gear were trying to hold back an angry mob chanting, "Whose house? Our house."[88] Rioters forced their way up the stairs while others scaled the Capitol walls and scaffolding set up for Biden's inauguration. Just one hour after Trump's speech, the first rioters breached the Capitol using flagpoles and riot shields to break windows and crawl into the building while Congress continued to meet just steps away.[89] Within a few minutes, rioters were roaming freely throughout the building while members of Congress and staffers were evacuated or sheltered in place, barricading doors and fearing for their lives.[90] Some rioters posed for selfies, wandering around like tourists, while others ransacked the historic site. Packs of protestors roamed the halls searching for Pence and members of Congress. The mob halted the constitutional process of completing Biden's election, "raising the specter of a coup."[91]

Most of the footage from inside the Capitol was captured on participants' cell phones and shared on social media where rioters bragged about their involvement. This very modern need to document the event via social media led to over four hundred arrests as of April 2021.[92] These posts dominated media coverage of the insurrection. Meanwhile, news cameras on the Capitol grounds recorded Trump supporters attacking police and celebrating their takeover of the Capitol by hanging Trump banners from the building.[93] From a branding perspective, the most striking image of the insurrection was the amount of Trump merch on display. Media reports noted that many members of the mob "smashing their way into the Capitol were wearing Trump regalia"[94] and "carrying flags and wearing clothes that bore his name."[95] They waved Trump 2020 flags alongside American and Confederate flags in the Capitol rotunda and chanted "Fight for Trump." It is nearly impossible to find a photo or video of the rioters that does not feature some item of Trump paraphernalia, with the iconic red MAGA hats and blue "Trump 2020" flags being the most visible products. Thus, the Trump brand will forever be associated with the Capitol insurrection.

Meanwhile, Trump's response to the riot stayed true to his brand messaging. Trump reportedly watched the day's events unfold on TV in the Oval Office.[96] At 2:24 p.m., just minutes after rioters broke into the Capitol, Trump tweeted, "Mike Pence didn't have the courage to do what should have been done to protect our Country and our Constitution, giving States a chance to certify a corrected set of facts, not the fraudulent or inaccurate ones which they were asked to previously certify. USA demands the truth!" That was mere moments before Pence and his family were moved from an office to a more secure location. Trump's closest advisors convinced him to call for calm. At 2:38 p.m., Trump tweeted, "Please support our Capitol Police and Law Enforcement. They are truly on the side of our Country. Stay peaceful!" But he did not encourage the rioters to stop. About thirty-five minutes later, he posted a slightly stronger tweet: "I am asking for everyone at the U.S. Capitol to remain peaceful. No violence! Remember, WE are the Party of Law & Order." At 4:17 p.m., minutes after Biden addressed the nation, Trump uploaded a one-minute video to Twitter denouncing the riots but maintaining the false claims that the election was stolen.[97] In the video, Trump sympathized with his violent followers, "I know your pain, I know you're hurt. We had an election that was stolen from us. It was a landslide election and everyone knows it, especially the other side. But you have to go home now. We have to have peace. We have to have law and order." He continued, "There's never been a time like this where such a thing happened where they could take it away from all of us—from me, from you, from our country. This was a fraudulent election, but we can't play into the hands of these people. We have to have peace. So go home. We love you. You're very special."[98] Not once did Trump blame or disavow his supporters.[99]

That evening, Trump continued to insist the election was stolen tweeting at 6:01 p.m., "These are the things and events that happen when a sacred landslide election victory is so unceremoniously & viciously stripped away from great patriots who have been badly & unfairly treated for so long. Go home with love & in peace. Remember this day forever!" This tweet, which "edged close to celebrating the day's events,"[100] finally caused the social media companies to act. At 7 p.m., Facebook and Instagram removed Trump's video addressing the protests and his subsequent posts noting that they "contribute to, rather than diminish, the risk of ongoing violence," and at 8:36 p.m. they blocked his page for twenty-four hours. Twitter followed suit at 7:02 p.m., shutting down Trump's account for twelve hours for "severe and repeated" violations of the company's Civic Integrity policy. YouTube also removed the video.[101]

Trump was back on Twitter the evening of January 7. He released a video statement declaring he was now focused on a "smooth, orderly, seamless transition of power." Many thought his calls for healing and reconciliation were too little, too late. Yet according to a senior White House official, Trump said he wished he hadn't released the message because "he feared that the calming words made him look weak."[102] By the following morning, he messaging was back on brand. His first tweet of the day proclaimed, "The 75,000,000 great American Patriots who voted for me, AMERICA FIRST, and MAKE AMERICA GREAT AGAIN, will have a GIANT VOICE long into the future. They will not be disrespected or treated unfairly in any way, shape or form!!!" At 10:44 a.m. on January 8, Trump tweeted, "For those who have asked, I will not be going to the Inauguration on January 20." That ended up being his last tweet. Twitter permanently suspended his account that evening. The company said the tweet concerning the inauguration "could be viewed as a further statement that the election was not legitimate" and that the tweet about American patriots suggested that "he plans to continue to support, empower, and shield those who believe he won the election."[103] Facebook had already banned him indefinitely the previous day.[104] So, while Trump was back to form, the result was the loss of his preferred method of communicating with his followers.

In another big blow to Trump's brand, Shopify shut down the online merch stores of the Trump Organization and the Trump campaign for violating their "Acceptable Use Policy." The company's press release noted that the policy "prohibits promotion or support of organizations, platforms or people that threaten or condone violence to further a cause. As a result, we have terminated stores affiliated with President Trump."[105] Given that official Trump merch was a major fundraising arm of the campaign, the store closures forced Trump supporters to purchase from third-party sellers, taking away profits from Trump.

But other e-commerce sites were also wary of Trump-affiliated sellers in the wake of the riots. For example, eBay deactivated pages selling merch related to the Capitol riots, including a site selling shirts emblazoned with "MAGA Civil War January 6, 2021." The company claimed the shirts violated their policy against products promoting "hate and discrimination," adding, "While we are not removing politically affiliated merchandise from the site, we will remove any merchandise glorifying the violence incited on Capitol Hill."[106]

The social media ban forced Trump to release videos and statements through the news media, official press releases, and the White House Twitter account, which had just twenty-six million followers, less than a third of Trump's audience on his personal account. Not surprisingly, Trump was rarely heard from after January 8 even as he was charged by the House of Representatives with "incitement of insurrection" and impeached for a second time.[107] Without his social media megaphone, Trump seemed to be, for the first time, at a loss for words. He stayed relatively quiet until his farewell speech at Joint Base Andrews before boarding Air Force One for the final time as president.

Joe Biden started January 6 by celebrating the runoff election wins in Georgia that gave Democrats control of the Senate and anticipating congressional certification of the Electoral College results making him the forty-sixth president. That afternoon, Biden was supposed to hold a press briefing focused on economic recovery. But as the events at the Capitol unfolded, Biden and his team quickly composed a different speech. At 4:05 p.m., he delivered a brief address from his Delaware headquarters condemning the "assault on democracy." He blamed the events on a "small number of extremists" and insisted they halt their attack: "This is not dissent. It's disorder. It's chaos. It borders on sedition, and it must end now. I call this mob to pull back and allow the work of democracy to go forward." He called out Trump for encouraging the insurrection while also asking him to address the mob, saying, "The words of a President matter, no matter how good or bad that President is. At their best, the words of a President can inspire. At their worst, they can incite. Therefore, I call on President Trump to go on national television now, to fulfill his oath and defend the constitution and demand an end to this siege." In spite of everything, Biden remained true to his brand by staying positive and calling for unity, saying that the "scenes of chaos at the Capitol do not reflect a true America, do not represent who we are." Biden called for a renewal of a politics that doesn't stoke "the flames of hate and chaos." He also voiced support for the democratic process, but noted that "democracy is fragile" and requires leaders "who are devoted, not to the pursuit of power or their personal interests, pursuits of their own selfish interest at any cost, but for the common good."[108] This thinly veiled reference to Trump juxtaposed the key difference in their postelection brand strategies, with Biden dedicated to promoting the institution and the greater good while Trump focused on his individual brand and personal interests.

The events of January 6, although shocking and alarming, were completely on-brand for Trump. His public comments reflected the anger, divisiveness, and conspiracy-mongering central to his brand since he entered politics by wading into the Obama birther debate. According to the *New York Times*, "The convulsion in Washington capped 1,448 days of Twitter storms, provocations, race-baiting, busted norms, shock-jock governance and truth-bending prevarication from the Oval Office that have left the country more polarized than in generations."[109] The *Washington Post* commented, "He exhorted his followers, he spoke falsehoods, he took to Twitter, he attacked the media, and he confronted the Constitution of the United States. It was as if four years of the Trump presidency were squeezed into one day. In the twilight of his presidency, Trump was where he always yearns to be—in the middle of the vortex, at the center of attention in a broken nation."[110] Yet in the days that followed, Trump began to fade from public view after being stripped of his most powerful communication platform, Twitter. Meanwhile, for Biden, the events helped bolster his brand. In particular, his calls for unity took on new meaning. The storming of the Capitol may have "lent some new urgency to [Biden's] calls to back away from the bitter politics of the last few years," according to the *Wall Street Journal*.[111] More Republicans in Congress backed away from Trump and seemed open to the idea of working across the aisle again. But the insurrection also underscored the troubling fact that Trump's most die-hard supporters still believed Biden's election was illegitimate.[112] Hence, Biden's inauguration took on additional meaning as not only a ceremonial event but a significant symbolic moment in the peaceful transition of power.

INAUGURATION: JANUARY 20, 2021

Like most things in the 2020 presidential campaign, Biden's inauguration differed from past events. COVID safety protocols and heightened security following the Capitol insurrection meant that there were no massive crowds, inaugural parade, or glitzy balls. But the day's events represented Biden's brand by focusing on unity, inclusiveness, and respect for the traditions of the presidency.

The inaugural events kicked off the evening of January 5 with a somber vigil at the Lincoln Memorial. Four hundred lights representing the over four hundred thousand American lives lost to COVID-19 surrounded the Reflecting Pool. In his brief remarks, Biden said, "To heal we must remember."[113]

The following day, the pandemic's impact was felt again in the limited audience for the inaugural ceremony. Instead of being filled with onlookers, the National Mall was covered in nearly two hundred thousand flags representing the people who could not attend because of the pandemic and tight security. Biden's team said the display was intended to represent all fifty states, Washington, D.C., and the five U.S. territories and reflect a "commitment to an inclusive and safe event that everyone can enjoy from their home."[114] During the evening, the installation was lit by a symbolic fifty-six pillars of light.

The official inaugural theme was "America United," making it a true culmination of Biden's brand messaging. He noted that America can only overcome its challenges through unity, proclaiming, "My whole soul is in this: bringing America together. Uniting our people. And uniting our nation. I ask every American to join me in this cause." He addressed skeptics by saying, "I know speaking of unity can sound to some like a foolish fantasy. I know the forces that divide us are deep and they are real." As he did throughout the postcampaign period, he called for an end to divisive rhetoric: "We must end this uncivil war that pits red against blue, rural versus urban, conservative versus liberal. We can do this if we open our souls instead of hardening our hearts, if we show a little tolerance and humility, and if we're willing to stand in the other person's shoes." These traits of kindness, empathy, and understanding are hallmarks of Biden's brand. While the speech had an optimistic tone, Biden did not ignore what transpired in the previous weeks that culminated in an angry mob storming the very platform where he stood. "We face an attack on our democracy and on the truth," he said. "Recent weeks and months have taught us a painful lesson. There is truth and there are lies. Lies told for profit and for power," arguing that all Americans, but especially its leaders, have a duty "to defend the truth and to defeat the lies." He called on Americans to "reject a culture in which facts themselves are manipulated and even manufactured." These comments were a direct response to Trump's campaign of disinformation aimed at undermining the election results and our democratic institutions. Biden concluded by pledging to always level with the American people, to defend democracy, to serve the country "not thinking of power, but of possibilities, not out of personal interest, but of the public good," noting that "together, we shall write an American story of hope, not fear. Of unity, not division. Of light, not darkness."[115] In his closing, Biden once again presented himself as the anti-Trump and showcased himself as a humble leader aware of the challenges ahead and willing to work to unite the nation.

Despite the pandemic and unprecedented security measures, the ceremony was largely able to follow the traditional format. There were several symbolic moments that highlighted the differences between the outgoing and incoming presidents. Performances during the ceremony very consciously represented diversity. *ABC News* observed, "The celebration of diversity was unlike anything seen from the country's leadership in recent years," noting that it was less about what Biden said than "about the people he put center stage."[116] This included breakout star Amanda Gorman, a twenty-two-year-old black poet and activist whose work focuses on issues of race, feminism, and marginalization. Selected by Dr. Jill Biden, she was the youngest poet to perform at an inauguration and largely unknown prior to reciting her poem "The Hill We Climb," which focused on themes of hope and unity.[117] Other notable moments included the Pledge of Allegiance delivered simultaneously in spoken language and American Sign Language, Supreme Court Justice Sonia Sotomayor swearing in Vice President Kamala Harris, Jennifer Lopez addressing the audience in Spanish during her performance, a dramatic national anthem from LBGTQ+ advocate Lady Gaga, and Garth Brooks—a registered Republican—singing "Amazing Grace" in blue jeans and a cowboy hat.[118] Notable Democrats and Republicans commingled on the platform, including Barack and Michelle Obama, George and Laura Bush, Nancy Pelosi and Mitch McConnell, and Mike and Karen Pence, while Senator Bernie Sanders became an instant Internet meme as he huddled in his homemade mittens.[119]

Rather than attending multiple presidential balls, Biden's team stayed committed to inclusivity and safety by producing the inaugural special "Celebrating America" that aired and streamed on multiple channels that night. *Variety* declared that the "earnest inauguration special perfectly encapsulates President Joe Biden."[120] The program was relatively subdued, focused on unity rather than an all-out celebration. Biden explained that he and Harris "wanted to make sure our inauguration was not about us, but about you the American people."[121] Tributes were paid to frontline workers and teachers who bore the brunt of the pandemic, and star-studded performances expressed themes of unity and optimism for better days ahead. One prerecorded segment featured former presidents Barack Obama, George W. Bush, and Bill Clinton in a bipartisan show of support for Biden and display of working together despite not always agreeing.[122] This segment felt particularly powerful after an inauguration ceremony that the outgoing president refused to attend.

Biden's brand messaging was reflected throughout the inaugural events. He respected the traditions of the presidential transfer of power and once again called for unity. He recognized the symbolism of taking the oath of office on the Capitol steps that just two weeks prior had been overrun by insurrectionists. He celebrated the diversity of America and signaled that he'd be an inclusive leader. And he acknowledged the challenges facing a nation still grappling with a pandemic, economic hardships, and an extremely acrimonious political culture.

CONCLUSION

While the Trump and Biden brands are almost polar opposites, the one trait shared by both candidates was consistency in messaging that stayed on-brand throughout the tumultuous postcampaign period. Even though the circumstances of the 2020 race were unique, the communication strategies of both Trump and Biden were predictable when viewed from a political branding perspective, especially with candidates so deeply committed to their brand personality. So, what can we learn from examining such dedicated devotion to branding during the 2020 postelection campaign?

First, focusing on branding illuminates the tensions between the personal and the political in presidential politics. Candidates have long been sold to the public based on their personal characteristics, which is how they differentiate themselves from their competitors. However, candidates have traditionally cultivated brand personalities that include qualities considered to be presidential. We saw this with Biden, who stressed his experience, competence, sincerity, and a willingness to be a president for all Americans. Because most candidates want to be viewed as presidential, their personal brand is easily fused with the political brand of their party, which is more ideological and targets specific demographics, and the more generic brand of the presidency that attempts to speak to a broader audience. After the election was called in his favor, Biden's messaging quickly shifted from appealing primarily to Democrats and anti-Trump voters to targeting all Americans with a specific emphasis on reaching Trump supporters. Because his personal brand was focused on unity and inclusion, this shift in strategy was not a stretch and came off as authentic.

One of the many ways Trump differs from other politicians is that his personal brand is everything. Trump never relinquished any part of his personal brand, even though it did not appeal to a wide audience. He eschewed most of the brand traits of the presidency and instead made the presidency part of Brand Trump, using presidential symbols like the White House and Air Force One as props in his reelection campaign. He relied on the strength of his cult brand, drawing upon his celebrity status and promoting himself as the antipolitician superhero to his loyal base. While this strategy worked in 2016, it was not enough to win reelection. But it was enough to incite an insurrection and convince a sizable portion of the American public to believe the election was stolen. A CNN poll from late April 2021 found that 30 percent of Americans said Biden did not legitimately win enough votes to win the presidency, including 70 percent of Republicans.[123] Like most followers of cult brands, Trump supporters remain blindly loyal. For many, their devotion has intensified due to Trump's relentless claims that his election win was stolen by a corrupt political system. He's now calling Biden's win "THE BIG LIE," a clear attempt to rebrand a phrase that Democrats used during the second impeachment trial to compare Trump's false claims of election fraud to a Nazi propaganda technique.[124] Support of the "Big Lie," however defined, is now impacting the GOP as fealty to Trump is seen as a litmus test. Trump has vowed to use his influence with his base to unseat any Republicans who aren't supporting his allegations of election fraud, which could have a major impact on the 2022 midterms. This is another example of Trump privileging his personal brand and vendettas over party interests. He's even told the Republican National Committee and other GOP campaign organizations they can't use his name or likeness for fundraising, a claim the groups have rejected, while he continues to raise money through his Save America PAC.[125]

The centrality of branding to campaigns also shows the importance of having a clear communication strategy. Authenticity and consistency are important to voters. Both Trump and Biden were consistent in the messaging and emotional appeals in their speeches and social media statements. Biden's communication strategy, with his relaxed and reassuring tone, seemed to be a modern take on the WWII British slogan "Keep Calm and Carry On." Being presidential was part of Biden's brand from the start. This consistency aided Biden's transition from candidate to president and helped to underscore the legitimacy not only of his election but of the electoral process. Through his message of unity, Biden also attempted to restore faith in the presidency as an institution serving all Americans.

Meanwhile, Trump almost exclusively used divisive, paranoid-style rhetoric to rage against the system. His rogue, antipolitician style appealed to his supporters, who were psychologically primed to accept that the election was stolen without evidence because Trump had been telling them for years the system was rigged. For Trump, this was a way to explain a loss and maintain his brand as a winner, a strategy developed in 2016 as an election loss safeguard. The attack on the Capitol was an ugly, but unsurprising, result of Trump's relentless attacks against democratic institutions and his ability to persuade his most devoted followers to take action. For these voters, it's no longer about party loyalty, it's about loyalty to the cult brand Trump continues to promote. However, the potency of Trump's brand has been diluted by the loss of his social media platforms, especially Twitter. Without them, he's struggled to attract attention online with social media interactions about Trump dropping 91 percent since January.[126] He's been relegated to releasing statements and selling merch through his nearly identical "Donald J. Trump" and "Save America" websites. But these sites don't have the same audience as his banned Twitter account, and most news organizations no longer report on his every move. If Trump decides to run in 2024, it will be interesting to see what impact his limited access to social media has on his campaign. In the meantime, these personal sites are a way for Trump to control his messaging and promote his brand.[127]

In closing, while Biden's political branding in the 2020 postelection campaign was more traditional, it's still a powerful reminder of the importance of consistent brand messaging to promote both individuals and institutions, particularly in such a divisive political climate. Meanwhile, many questions remain about the consequences of Trump's style of political branding, both on himself and on our democratic institutions. Was Trump's presidency an anomaly? Many pundits and scholars seem to think so, but with the emergence of many Trump-styled antipoliticians, it's too soon to tell. Was Trump's personal brand tarnished by the events of the 2020 postelection period? In the eyes of many Americans and some Republican leaders, yes. But for true believers, their faith in the Trump brand persists, and he still has a strong hold on the Republican base. We'll have to wait to see whether his influence impacts the 2022 midterms and the next presidential race.

NOTES

1. "Branding & Marketing in Politics: How Visuals and Media Influence Elections," *Design in Mind*, October 15, 2020, https://www.designim.com/blog/branding -marketing-in-politics-how-visuals-and-media-influence-elections/.

2. Francisco Guzmán, Audhesh K. Paswan, and Eric Van Steenburg, "Self-Referencing and Political Candidate Brands: A Congruency Perspective," *Journal of Political Marketing* 14, no. 1–2 (2015): 176.

3. Robert Reich, *Locked in the Cabinet* (New York: Alfred A. Knopf, 1997), 261.

4. Jennifer Lees-Marshment et al., *Political Marketing* (New York: Taylor and Francis, 2019), 86, 88.

5. "How Political Branding Can Win or Lose an Election," *Network 9*, accessed April 1, 2021, https://network9.biz/how-political-branding-can-win-or-lose-an -election/; Carly Stec, "Brand Strategy 101: 7 Essentials for Strong Company Branding," *HubSpot*, October 11, 2017, https://blog.hubspot.com/blog/tabid/6307/bid /31739/7-components-that-comprise-a-comprehensive-brand-strategy.aspx.

6. Richard Nathan Rutter, Chris Hanretty, and Fiona Lettice, "Political Brands: Can Parties Be Distinguished by Their Online Brand Personality?" *Journal of Political Marketing* 17, no. 3 (2018): 196.

7. Sorin Nastasia, "Political Branding of Candidates," in *Encyclopedia of Social Media and Politics,* Vol. 1, ed. Kerric Harvey (Thousand Oaks, CA: Sage Reference, 2014), 225.

8. Jennifer L. Aaker, "Dimensions of Brand Personality," *Journal of Marketing Research* 34, no. 3 (1997): 352; Lees-Marshment et al., *Political Marketing*, 89.

9. Andrea Schneiker, "Telling the Story of the Superhero and Anti-Politician as President: Donald Trump's Branding on Twitter," *Political Studies Review* 17, no. 3 (2019): 212.

10. Chase Lovett, *Grocery Store Politics: How Political Brands Manipulate Voters* (Self-Published: Amazon Kindle, 2018), 1285.

11. Richard Hofstadter, *The Paranoid Style in American Politics and Other Essays* (Cambridge, MA: Harvard University Press, 1996), 29.

12. "Trump as Troll: Personae and Persuasive Inoculation in the 2016 Presidential Campaign," in *The 2016 US Presidential Campaign: Political Communication and Practice*, ed. Robert E. Denton (New York: Palgrave MacMillian, 2017), 168; "How Political Branding Can Win or Lose an Election."

13. Adam Hayes, "Cult Brand," *Investopedia*, November 4, 2020, https://www.investopedia.com/terms/c/cult-brand.asp.

14. Bolivar J. Bueno and Scott Jeffrey, "The Power of Cult Branding," *Global Cosmetic Industry* 176, no. 12 (2008): 17.

15. Bueno and Jeffrey, 17.

16. Jonathan Karl, "Front Row at the Trump Show Book Talk" (presentation, AEJMC History Division, virtual, April 6, 2021).

17. Jonathan Allen, "Trump Chose His Political Brand over His Presidency," *NBC News*, October 9, 2020, https://www.nbcnews.com/politics/2020-election/trump-chose-his-brand-over-his-presidency-n1242743.

18. Mary E. Stuckey, "'The Power of the Presidency to Hurt': The Indecorous Rhetoric of Donald J. Trump and the Rhetorical Norms of Democracy," *Presidential Studies Quarterly* 50, no. 2 (2020): 384.

19. Karl, "Front Row at the Trump Show Book Talk."

20. "Brand Biden vs. Brand Trump," *Ipsos,* October 21, 2020, https://www.ipsos.com/en/brand-biden-vs-brand-trump.

21. Susan Hennessey and Benjamin Wittes, *Unmaking the Presidency: Donald Trump's War on the World's Most Powerful Office* (New York: Farrar, Straus and Giroux, 2020), 13.

22. Mary E. Stuckey, "The Rhetoric of the Trump Administration," *Presidential Studies Quarterly* 51, no. 1 (2021): 143.

23. Stuckey, "The Rhetoric of the Trump Administration," 125.

24. Stuckey, "'The Power of the Presidency to Hurt,'" 369.

25. Stuckey, "'The Power of the Presidency to Hurt,'" 385.

26. Stuckey, "'The Power of the Presidency to Hurt,'" 384.

27. Matt Vasilogambros and Lindsey Van Ness, "States Expanded Voting Access for the Pandemic. The Changes Might Stick," *Pew Trusts*, November 6, 2020, https://www.pewtrusts.org/en/research-and-analysis/blogs/stateline/2020/11/06/states-expanded-voting-access-for-the-pandemic-the-changes-might-stick.

28. Curt Merrill et al., "Mail-In Ballots: When Every State Starts Counting," *CNN*, October 27, 2020, https://www.cnn.com/interactive/2020/politics/mail-in-voting/.

29. Miles Parks, "Ignoring FBI and Fellow Republicans, Trump Continues Assault on Mail-In Voting," *NPR*, August 28, 2020, https://www.npr.org

/2020/08/28/906676695/ignoring-fbi-and-fellow-republicans-trump-continues
-assault-on-mail-in-voting.

30. Ken Thomas and Andrew Restuccia, "In Election Night Remarks, Trump, Biden See Victory in Touching Distance," *Wall Street Journal*, November 4, 2020, https://www.wsj.com/articles/in-election-night-remarks-trump-biden-jockey-for-po sition-11604475526.

31. Karissa Bell, "Twitter Labels Trump Tweet for 'Making a Potentially Mislead-ing Claim,'" *Engadget*, November 4, 2020, https://www.yahoo.com/finance/news /twitter-labels-trump-tweet-election-night-061539034.html.

32. "Donald Trump 2020 Election Night Speech Transcript," *Rev*, November 4, 2020, https://www.rev.com/blog/transcripts/donald-trump-2020-election-night -speech-transcript.

33. Elise Viebeck et al., "Trump Campaign Mounts Challenges in Four States as Narrow Margins Raise Stakes for Battles over Which Ballots Will Count," *Wash-ington Post*, November 4, 2020, https://www.washingtonpost.com/politics/trump -supreme-court-election-votes/2020/11/04/4f528162-1ea1-11eb-90dd -abd0f7086a91_story.html.

34. "Trump Tries to Claim Victory Even As Ballots Are Being Counted in Several States—NBC Has Not Made a Call," *CNBC*, November 4, 2020, https://www.cnbc .com/2020/11/04/trump-tries-to-claim-victory-even-as-ballots-are-being-counted-in -several-states-nbc-has-not-made-a-call.html.

35. Susan B. Glasser, "Trump Is the Election Crisis He Is Warning About," *New Yorker*, July 30, 2020, https://www.newyorker.com/news/letter-from-trumps-wash ington/trump-is-the-election-crisis-he-is-warning-about.

36. Richard Hasen, "Trump's Relentless Attacks on Mail-In Ballots Are Part of a Larger Strategy," *New York Times*, August 19, 2020, https://www.nytimes.com /2020/08/19/opinion/trump-usps-mail-voting.html.

37. Stuckey, "'The Power of the Presidency to Hurt,'" 384; Hasen, "Trump's Re-lentless Attacks on Mail-In Ballots."

38. Roderick P. Hart, "Trump and the Return of Paranoid Style," *Presidential Studies Quarterly* 50, no. 2 (2020): 350.

39. Morgan Chalfont and Brett Samuels, "Trump Challenges Electoral Process as Hopes for Victory Fade," *The Hill*, November 5, 2020, https://thehill.com/homenews /administration/524731-trump-challenges-electoral-process-as-hopes-for-victory-fade.

40. Jane C. Timm, "Trump Told One Falsehood after Another about the Presi-dential Race. Here Are the Facts," *NBC News*, November 5, 2020, https://www .nbcnews.com/politics/2020-election/trump-told-one-falsehood-after-another-about -presidential-race-here-n1246701.

41. Meghan Graham and Salvador Rodriguez, "Twitter and Facebook Race to Label a Slew of Posts Making False Election Claims Before All Votes Counted," *CNBC*, November 6, 2020, https://www.cnbc.com/2020/11/04/twitter-and-facebook -label-trump-posts-claiming-election-stolen.html.

42. Ted Johnson and Dominic Patten, "The Moment When Networks Called the Presidential Race for Joe Biden," *Deadline*, November 7, 2020, https://deadline .com/2020/11/joe-biden-president-cnn-1234610930/.

43. Morgan Chalfant, "Trump Refuses to Accept Biden Victory, Promises Legal Challenges," *The Hill*, November 7, 2020, https://thehill.com/homenews /campaign/524935-trump-refuses-to-accept-biden-victory-promises-legal-challenges.

44. "Joe Biden 2020 Election Night Speech Transcript," *Rev*, November 4, 2020, https://www.rev.com/blog/transcripts/joe-biden-2020-election-night-speech -transcript.

45. Brian Welk, "Joe Biden Urges Supporters to 'Stay Calm,' Says 'Democracy Is Sometimes Messy,'" *The Wrap*, November 5, 2020, https://www.thewrap.com/joe -biden-urges-supporters-to-stay-calm-says-democracy-is-sometimes-messy/.

46. Grace Segers, "Joe Biden Urges Unity in Speech as His Lead Grows in Presidential Race," *CBS News*, November 6, 2020, https://www.cbsnews.com/news/joe -biden-kamala-harris-2020-election-remarks-watch-live-stream-today-2020-11-06/.

47. "Joe Biden November 6 Speech Transcript: 'We're Going to Win This Race,'" *Rev*, November 6, 2020, https://www.rev.com/blog/transcripts/joe-biden-november -6-speech-transcript-were-going-to-win-this-race.

48. "Joe Biden November 6 Speech Transcript."

49. Seger, "Joe Biden Urges Unity in Speech."

50. Johnson and Patten, "The Moment When Networks Called the Presidential Race."

51. Ruby Cramer and Henry J. Gomez, "Joe Biden's Long Wait Is Over: Relief and Celebration in a Painful Year," *BuzzFeed News*, November 7, 2020, https://www .buzzfeednews.com/article/rubycramer/joe-biden-victory-speech-president-family.

52. "Joe Biden and Kamala Harris Election Acceptance & Victory Speech Transcripts," *Rev*, November 7, 2020, https://www.rev.com/blog/transcripts/joe-biden -kamala-harris-address-nation-after-victory-speech-transcript-november-7.

53. George C. Edwards III, "The Bully in the Pulpit," *Presidential Studies Quarterly* 50, no. 2 (2020): 313.

54. "Joe Biden and Kamala Harris Election Acceptance & Victory Speech Transcripts."

55. "Joe Biden and Kamala Harris Election Acceptance & Victory Speech Transcripts."

56. "Donald Trump Thanksgiving Call to Troops Transcript 2020," *Rev*, November 26, 2020, https://www.rev.com/blog/transcripts/donald-trump-thanksgiving-call -to-troops-transcript-2020-addresses-possibility-of-conceding-election.

57. Franco Ordonez and Roberta Rampton, "Trump Is in No Mood to Concede, But Says Will Leave White House," *NPR*, November 26, 2020, https://www.npr.org /sections/biden-transition-updates/2020/11/26/939386434/trump-is-in-no-mood-to -concede-but-says-will-leave-white-house.

58. Philip Rucker, "Trump Escalates Baseless Attacks on Election with 46-Minute Video Rant," *Washington Post*, December 2, 2020, https://www.washingtonpost.com /politics/trump-election-video/2020/12/02/f6c8d63c-34e8-11eb-a997 -1f4c53d2a747_story.html.

59. "Donald Trump Speech on Election Fraud Claims Transcript December 2," *Rev*, December 2, 2020, https://www.rev.com/blog/transcripts/donald-trump-speech -on-election-fraud-claims-transcript-december-2.

60. Michael D. Shear, "Trump, in Video from White House, Delivers a 46-Minute Diatribe on the 'Rigged' Election," *New York Times*, December 2, 2020, https://www.nytimes.com/2020/12/02/us/politics/trump-election-video.html.

61. "Donald Trump Speech on Election Fraud Claims Transcript December 2."

62. Rucker, "Trump Escalates Baseless Attacks on Election."

63. Aamer Madhani and Kevin Freking, "In Video, Trump Recycles Unsubstantiated Voter Fraud Claims," *Associated Press*, December 2, 2020, https://apnews.com/article/joe-biden-donald-trump-media-social-media-elections-71d5469ac0bbccbfe601528a2517b239.

64. Susan Milligan, "Trump Promotes Voter Fraud Claims in Unusual 45-Minute Video Address," *U.S. News & World Report*, December 2, 2020, https://www.usnews.com/news/elections/articles/2020-12-02/trump-promotes-voter-fraud-claims-in-unusual-45-minute-video-address.

65. Jonathan Easley, "Trump Rants against Election Results for 46 Minutes in New Video Post," *The Hill*, December 2, 2020, https://thehill.com/homenews/campaign/528469-trump-rants-against-election-results-for-45-minutes-in-new-video-post.

66. Stuckey, "The Rhetoric of the Trump Administration," 144.

67. "Donald Trump Georgia Rally Transcript before Senate Runoff Elections December 5," *Rev*, December 5, 2020, https://www.rev.com/blog/transcripts/donald-trump-georgia-rally-transcript-before-senate-runoff-elections-december-5.

68. Aaron Rupar, "Trump's Georgia Rally Was Supposed to Pump Up Loeffler and Perdue. It Ended Up As a Grievance Fest," *Vox*, December 5, 2020, https://www.vox.com/2020/12/5/22156585/trump-valdosta-georgia-rally-loeffler-perdue-grievances.

69. Astead W. Herndon and Michael D. Shear, "Trump, in Georgia before Tuesday's Election, Can't Let Go of the Last One," *New York Times*, January 4, 2021, https://www.nytimes.com/2021/01/04/us/politics/trump-georgia-rally.html.

70. "Donald Trump Rally Speech Transcript Dalton, Georgia: Senate Runoff Election," *Rev*, January 4, 2021, https://www.rev.com/blog/transcripts/donald-trump-rally-speech-transcript-dalton-georgia-senate-runoff-election.

71. Brett Samuels, "Biden's Big Difference? Diversity," *The Hill*, March 17, 2021, https://thehill.com/homenews/senate/543539-bidens-big-difference-diversity.

72. Marc Fisher et al., "The Four-Hour Insurrection: How a Trump Mob Halted American Democracy," *Washington Post*, January 7, 2021, https://www.washingtonpost.com/graphics/2021/politics/trump-insurrection-capitol/.

73. Dan Barry and Sheera Frenkel, "'Be There. Will Be Wild!': Trump All but Circled the Date," *New York Times*, November 6, 2021, https://www.nytimes.com/2021/01/06/us/politics/capitol-mob-trump-supporters.html.

74. Philip Bump, "When Did the Jan. 6 Rally Become a March to the Capitol?" *Washington Post*, February 10, 2021, https://www.washingtonpost.com/politics/2021/02/10/when-did-jan-6-rally-become-march-capitol/.

75. Matthew Rosenberg and Jim Rutenberg, "Key Takeaways from Trump's Effort to Overturn the Election," *New York Times*, February 1, 2021, https://www.nytimes.com/2021/02/01/us/politics/trump-election-results.html.

76. Barry and Frenkel, "'Be There. Will Be Wild!'"

77. "Donald Trump Speech 'Save America' Rally Transcript January 6," *Rev*, January 6, 2021, https://www.rev.com/blog/transcripts/donald-trump-speech-save -america-rally-transcript-january-6.

78. Maggie Haberman, "Trump Told Crowd 'You Will Never Take Back Our Country with Weakness,'" *New York Times*, January 6, 2021, https://www.nytimes .com/2021/01/06/us/politics/trump-speech-capitol.html?action=click&auth=login -email&login=email&module=RelatedLinks&pgtype=Article.

79. Anne Gearan and Josh Dawsey, "Trump Issued a Call to Arms. Then He Urged His Followers 'To Remember This Day Forever!,'" *Washington Post*, January 6, 2021, https://www.washingtonpost.com/politics/trump-election-capitol -building/2021/01/06/3e9af194-5031-11eb-bda4-615aaefd0555_story.html.

80. "Donald Trump Speech 'Save America' Rally Transcript January 6."

81. Gearan and Dawsey, "Trump Issued a Call to Arms."

82. "Donald Trump Speech 'Save America' Rally Transcript January 6."

83. Marc Fisher et al., "The Four-Hour Insurrection."

84. Barry and Frenkel, "'Be There. Will Be Wild!'"

85. Gearan and Dawsey, "Trump Issued a Call to Arms."

86. Martha Mendoza and Juliet Linderman, "Officers Maced, Trampled: Docs Expose Depth of Jan. 6 Chaos," *Associated Press*, March 10, 2021, https://apnews.com /article/docs-expose-depth-january-6-capitol-siege-chaos-fd3204574c11e453be8f b4e3c81258c3.

87. Fisher et al., "The Four-Hour Insurrection."

88. Lauren Leatherby et al., "How a Presidential Rally Turned into a Capitol Rampage," *New York Times*, January 12, 2021, https://www.nytimes.com/interactive /2021/01/12/us/capitol-mob-timeline.html.

89. Shelly Tan, Youjin Shin, and Danielle Rindler, "How One of America's Ugliest Days Unraveled inside and outside the Capitol," *Washington Post*, January 9, 2021, https://www.washingtonpost.com/nation/interactive/2021/capitol-insurrection -visual-timeline/?itid=hp-top-table-main-0106.

90. Fisher et al., "The Four-Hour Insurrection."

91. Tan, Shin, and Rindler, "How One of America's Ugliest Days Unraveled."

92. Clare Hymes, Cassidy McDonald, and Eleanor Watson, "What We Know about the 'Unprecedented' U.S. Capitol Riot Arrests," *CBS News*, April 22, 2021, https://www.cbsnews.com/news/capitol-riot-arrests-2021-04-22/.

93. Fisher et al., "The Four-Hour Insurrection."

94. Gearan and Dawsey, "Trump Issued a Call to Arms."

95. Barry and Frenkel, "'Be There. Will Be Wild!'"

96. Haberman, "Trump Told Crowd."

97. Ashley Parker, Josh Dawsey, and Philip Rucker, "Six Hours of Paralysis: Inside Trump's Failure to Act after a Mob Stormed the Capitol," *Washington Post*, January 11, 2021, https://www.washingtonpost.com/politics/trump-mob-failure /2021/01/11/36a46e2e-542e-11eb-a817-e5e7f8a406d6_story.html.

98. Parker, Dawsey, and Rucker, "Six Hours of Paralysis."

99. Gearan and Dawsey, "Trump Issued a Call to Arms."

100. Gearan and Dawsey, "Trump Issued a Call to Arms."

101. Tan, Shin, and Rindler, "How One of America's Ugliest Days Unraveled."

102. Parker, Dawsey, and Rucker, "Six Hours of Paralysis."

103. Brian Fung, "Twitter Says Trump's Final Tweets Violated Its Glorification of Violence Policy," *CNN*, January 8, 2021, https://www.cnn.com/politics/live-news /washington-dc-riots-trump-news-friday/h_9a8e6e454dec8fdb394b86269949c95c.

104. Tony Romm and Elizabeth Dwoskin, "Trump Banned from Facebook Indefinitely, CEO Mark Zuckerberg Says," *Washington Post*, January 7, 2021, https:// www.washingtonpost.com/technology/2021/01/07/trump-twitter-ban/.

105. Jonathan Shieber, "Shopify Pulls Donald Trump Stores Off Its Platform," *TechCrunch*, January 7, 2021, https://techcrunch.com/2021/01/07/shopify-pulls -donald-trump-stores-off-its-website/.

106. Jason Del Rey, "Shopify Hits President Trump Where It Hurts: His Wallet," *Vox*, January 7, 2021, https://www.vox.com/recode/22218863/shopify-bans-trump -store-merch-capitol-facebook-twitter.

107. Dylan Byers, "How Facebook and Twitter Decided to Take Down Trump's Accounts," *NBC News*, January 14, 2021, https://www.nbcnews.com/tech/tech-news /how-facebook-twitter-decided-take-down-trump-s-accounts-n1254317.

108. "Joe Biden Speech Condemning Capitol Protest Transcript," *Rev*, January 6, 2021, https://www.rev.com/blog/transcripts/joe-biden-remarks-condemning-capitol -protest-transcript.

109. Peter Baker, "A Mob and the Breach of Democracy: The Violent End of the Trump Era," *New York Times*, January 6, 2021, https://www.nytimes.com /2021/01/06/us/politics/trump-congress.html?action=click&module=RelatedLinks &pgtype=Article.

110. Gearan and Dawsey, "Trump Issued a Call to Arms."

111. Gerald F. Seib, "A Single Day Shakes Two Presidencies, Two Parties and One Nation to the Core," *Wall Street Journal*, January 6, 2021, https://www.wsj .com/articles/a-single-day-shakes-two-presidencies-two-parties-and-one-nation-to -the-core-11609971164?mod=wsjtwittertest19.

112. Michael D. Shear and Jim Tankersley, "Biden Denounces Storming of Capitol as a 'Dark Moment' in Nation's History," *New York Times*, January 6, 2021, https://www.nytimes.com/2021/01/06/us/politics/biden-capitol-congress.html.

113. Bill Barrow and Aamer Madhani, "Biden Marks Nation's Covid Grief before Inauguration Pomp," *Associated Press*, January 19, 2021, https://apnews.com/article /biden-inauguration-joe-biden-donald-trump-capitol-siege-philadelphia-aa7d5101f 28c4792ccd4752795d0b968.

114. Elissa Nadworny, "Nearly 200,000 Flags on National Mall Represent Those Who Cannot Attend Inauguration," *NPR*, January 20, 20201, https://www .npr.org/sections/inauguration-day-live-updates/2021/01/20/958726800/nearly-200 -000-flags-on-national-mall-represent-those-who-cannot-attend-inaugura.

115. Aaron Blake and Eugene Scott, "Joe Biden's Inauguration Speech Transcript, Annotated," *Washington Post*, January 20, 2021, https://www.washingtonpost.com /politics/interactive/2021/01/20/biden-inauguration-speech/.

116. Kiara Brantley-Jones and Robert Zepeda, "How Inauguration Day Celebrated Firsts and Historic and Inclusive Moments," *ABC News*, January 23, 2021, https://abcnews.go.com/Politics/inauguration-day-celebrated-firsts-historic-inclusive-moments/story?id=75407756.

117. Todd Spangler, "Poet Amanda Gorman Goes from Inauguration Star to Internet Sensation," *Variety*, January 21, 2021, https://variety.com/2021/digital/news/amanda-gorman-poet-amazon-biden-inauguration-1234889368/.

118. Heidi Stevens, "Joe Biden and Kamala Harris' Inauguration Day Was the Most American Yet," *Chicago Tribune*, January 20, 2021, https://www.chicagotribune.com/columns/heidi-stevens/ct-heidi-stevens-inauguration-day-looks-like-america-0120-20210120-wbv44kvp5zcstbmnyx7kjg66va-story.html.

119. "A Closer Look at Who Attended President Biden's Inauguration," *New York Times*, January 20, 2021, https://www.nytimes.com/interactive/2021/01/21/us/politics/biden-inauguration-attendees.html.

120. Caroline Framke, "'Celebrating America': Earnest Inauguration Special Perfectly Encapsulates President Joe Biden," *Variety*, January 20, 2021, https://variety.com/2021/tv/news/celebrating-america-inauguration-special-tv-review-biden-1234889202/.

121. Framke, "'Celebrating America.'"

122. Biden Inaugural Committee, "Celebrating America," *YouTube* video, 1:30:34, January 20, 2021, https://www.youtube.com/watch?v=RkRLaS9P8r8.

123. Ashley Parker and Marianna Sotomayor, "For Republicans, Fealty to Trump's Election Falsehood Becomes Defining Loyalty Test," *Washington Post*, May 2, 2021, https://www.washingtonpost.com/politics/republicans-trump-election-falsehood/2021/05/01/7bd380a0-a921-11eb-8c1a-56f0cb4ff3b5_story.html?utm_campaign=wp_politics_am&utm_medium=email&utm_source=newsletter&wpisrc=nl_politics&carta-url=https%3A%2F%2Fs2.washingtonpost.com%2Fcar-ln-tr%2F322779c%2F608fde279d2fdae30241e465%2F5b2e6f76ae7e8a6f6d36dd7c%2F16%2F58%2F608fde279d2fdae30241e465.

124. Steve Benen, "'The Big Lie' Is Not a Phrase in Need of a New Definition," *MSNBC*, May 4, 2021, https://www.msnbc.com/rachel-maddow-show/big-lie-not-phrase-need-new-definition-n1266244.

125. Adam Brewster and Kathryn Watson, "RNC Says It Has the Right to Use Trump's Name and Likeness for Fundraising," *CBS News*, March 9, 2021, https://www.cbsnews.com/news/trump-rnc-name-likeness-fundraising/.

126. Thomas Colson, "Trump's Widely-Mocked New Blog Shows He Is Now Just 'Shouting into the Void,' Say Social Media Experts," *Business Insider*, May 8, 2021, https://www.businessinsider.com/donald-trump-widely-mocked-new-blog-social-media-ban-2021-5.

127. Colson, "Trump's Widely-Mocked New Blog."

Chapter 2

Argumentation in an Era of Ascending Partisanship

Benjamin Voth

I know that everyone here will soon be marching over to the Capitol building to peacefully and patriotically make your voices heard.

— President Donald Trump, January 6, 2017

The postelection era of the 2020 presidential election is among the most turbulent of the past hundred years. At the apex of these irregular and hyperpartisan events is the date of January 6, when the electoral votes resulting from the November balloting were to be finalized by Congress. A record number of Americans turned out to vote for the opposing candidates of Joe Biden and Donald Trump in November. More than 150 million ballots were cast in the midst of a pandemic. This chapter provides an argumentation analysis regarding political events taking place primarily after November 3, 2020. Comparisons are made between the political rhetoric of summer 2020 and the Trump rally of January 6, 2021, to contextualize how political arguments are understood through a partisan and arguably reactionary lens.

THE IMMEDIATE ELECTION AFTERMATH AND THE JANUARY 6, 2021, VIOLENCE

Polling of the election turned out to be overwhelmingly skewed in favor of candidate Biden, while the actual voting results were closer. The state of Texas brought legal action against several other states favoring Biden, including Arizona and Pennsylvania. That legal suit was joined by more than a dozen other states that challenged the unusual adaptations to voting that accompanied the election conducted during the acute difficulties of the

COVID-19 pandemic.[1] Voting reports on election night came to an abrupt end around midnight across the nation as six states—Pennsylvania, Arizona, Nevada, Georgia, Michigan, and North Carolina—tried to complete their counting. Those states constituted a margin of victory electorally. Ultimately in the early morning hours of the next day, counting resumed and began to favor Biden decisively. Final results would take weeks to complete along with recounts. Legal challenges also mounted by the dozens in states and localities. The Supreme Court refused to accept the Texas case challenging election changes that were not put in place by state legislatures but often implemented by localities on an emergency basis. These emergency procedures tended to encourage voting my mail and a broader range of dates for accepting such ballots. In the weeks that followed the election, it became apparent that Biden won the popular vote by a margin of approximately 81 million votes to 74 million. He won an electoral count of 306 to 232.[2] The electoral vote was scheduled to be counted in the House of Representatives on January 6, 2021. President Trump and his supporters argued that some or all of the six states primarily close on the night of the election should not be counted since they employed irregular voting procedures. The president staged a rally on January 6 prior to the electoral vote count in the House. In that speech, the president made the following arguments to a large crowd numbering in the tens of thousands:

> All of us here today do not want to see our election victory stolen by emboldened radical-left Democrats, which is what they're doing. And stolen by the fake news media. That's what they've done and what they're doing. We will never give up, we will never concede. It doesn't happen. You don't concede when there's theft involved.[3]

The president argued that the election had been stolen by the media and Big Tech companies. He identified the Democrats as "radical left." He explained that the pollsters had failed to accurately predict the results of the election:

> And I was told by the real pollsters—we do have real pollsters—they know that we were going to do well and we were going to win. What I was told, if I went from 63 million, which we had four years ago, to 66 million, there was no chance of losing. Well, we didn't go to 66, we went to 75 million, and they say we lost. We didn't lose.
>
> And by the way, does anybody believe that Joe had 80 million votes? Does anybody believe that? He had 80 million computer votes. It's a disgrace. There's never been anything like that. You could take third-world countries. Just take a look. Take third-world countries. Their elections are more honest than what we've been going through in this country. It's a disgrace. It's a disgrace.[4]

Pollsters would later acknowledge that presidential polling was exception-
ally bad and continuously suggested that Biden enjoyed a larger lead nationally and within individual states than was ultimately true to the results
of state and national elections.[5] President Trump told the highly supportive
crowd that he was urging Vice President Pence to allow a revote in contested
states:

> States want to revote. The states got defrauded. They were given false informa-
> tion. They voted on it. Now they want to recertify. They want it back. All Vice
> President Pence has to do is send it back to the states to recertify and we become
> president and you are the happiest people.
>
> And I actually, I just spoke to Mike. I said: "Mike, that doesn't take courage.
> What takes courage is to do nothing. That takes courage." And then we're stuck
> with a president who lost the election by a lot and we have to live with that for
> four more years. We're just not going to let that happen.

Trump repeatedly expressed the hope in the speech that Vice President Pence
might disallow some of the electoral votes of contested states. The most critical portion of the speech was offered midway through:

> Now, it is up to Congress to confront this egregious assault on our democracy.
> And after this, we're going to walk down, and I'll be there with you, we're
> going to walk down, we're going to walk down. Anyone you want, but I think
> right here, we're going to walk down to the Capitol, and we're going to cheer
> on our brave senators and congressmen and women, and we're probably not
> going to be cheering so much for some of them. Because you'll never take
> back our country with weakness. You have to show strength and you have to
> be strong. We have come to demand that Congress do the right thing and only
> count the electors who have been lawfully slated, lawfully slated. I know that
> everyone here will soon be marching over to the Capitol building to peacefully
> and patriotically make your voices heard. Today we will see whether Republi-
> cans stand strong for integrity of our elections. But whether or not they stand
> strong for our country, our country. Our country has been under siege for a
> long time. Far longer than this four-year period. We've set it on a much greater
> course. So much, and we, I thought, you know, four more years. I thought it
> would be easy.

Upon these remarks, the House of Representatives, controlled by the
Democratic party members, would vote to impeach President Trump for a
second time in a year. This set up an instant trial in the Senate for which
only one Republican senator voted to convict: Senator Mitt Romney. The
primary argument for impeachment was that the president was inciting
an insurrection. Incitement is defined by the *New Oxford Dictionary* as
"the action of provoking unlawful behavior or urging someone to behave

unlawfully."[6] Insurrection is defined as "a violent uprising against an authority or government."[7] The president's argument on January 6 did not encourage violence and in fact textually urged "peace." Moreover, the president argued for patriotism, which is the rhetorical antithesis of an insurrection. The president called for obedience to the Constitution and congressionally measured instructions on the counting of electoral ballots from the states. The most problematic aspect of the president's argument was the implication that Vice President Pence could essentially set aside state electoral votes without debate. This caused some public frustration and anger at Mike Pence for failing to carry out the president's wishes that day. Nonetheless, by the evening of January 6, *Washington Post* editorial writer Dana Milbank argued that the president had committed treason by encouraging a violent mob to attack the Capitol.[8]

As the votes were counted that day after violent disruptions, Senators Cruz and Hawley sponsored objections to the electoral votes of Pennsylvania and Arizona. Other challenges to electoral votes failed for lack of sponsorship by a senator. For this, many public advocates argued that Senators Cruz and Hawley were guilty of some dimension of treason. This was in fact precisely what the Constitution called for in the presidential election process and had been hammered out by congressional authorities more than a century before. In 2005, Senator Barbara Boxer challenged the electoral votes of Ohio because she believed the president of Diebold machines had promised that his voting machines would secure victory for President Bush in Ohio. Much like 2000, the vote in Ohio was close for the 2004 election. In 2005 and 2021, these sponsored motions on state electoral votes precipitated congressional debate about the legitimacy of the electoral votes produced by the individual state procedures. In all three cases, Congress voted to approve the electoral votes of Ohio, Arizona, and Pennsylvania after more than an hour of debate by members for and against the electoral votes. Senator Cruz reported in the midst of this: "Yesterday . . . I had multiple, multiple Democrats urging that I should be arrested and tried for the crimes of sedition and treason."[9] Alexandria Ocasio Cortez called for Cruz to resign from the Senate. Cruz responded on Twitter: "Leading a debate in the Senate on ensuring election integrity is doing our jobs, and it's in no way responsible for the despicable terrorists who attacked the Capitol yesterday."[10] The essential argument leading to the counting of the electoral votes as offered by Democrats was that there should be no congressional debate over the electoral votes of various states. In fact, following procedures comparable to numerous other Democratic challenges like those in 2005 should be compared to "treason."

THE "MOSTLY PEACEFUL" VIOLENT
INSURRECTION OF SUMMER 2020

In the summer of 2020, the nation witnessed the brutal murder of George Floyd by Minneapolis police officer Derek Chauvin. Cell phone video showed Chauvin kneeling on the back of Floyd for more than eight minutes as he pleaded for relief. He died shortly after being taken into custody. The graphic violence precipitated riots across the nation and the reinvigoration of the movement known as "Black Lives Matter." The movement primarily offered a social movement argument against the abuse of black men in police custody. Protests and riots took place across the nation. Though many of the protests were violent, deadly, and destructive, most major media employed a clever fantasy theme[11] language recognized ironically by the public as "mostly peaceful protests." In a fantasy theme, rhetorical vision guides the formation of ongoing arguments that continually reenforce the original vision. Journalists tried to discount images that contradicted the peaceful vision such as burning buildings and violent destruction of property. These protests were particularly pronounced and destructive in Washington, D.C. "Trump not only needs to not be in office in November, but he should resign now," Black Lives Matter Global Network cofounder Patrisse Cullors told CNN. "Trump needs to be out of office. He is not fit for office. And so, what we are going to push for is a move to get Trump out." She continued, "While we're also going to continue to push and pressure Vice President Joe Biden around his policies and relationship to policing and criminalization. That's going to be important. But our goal is to get Trump out now."[12] Later that summer a local D.C. area Black Lives Matter advocate further explained the argument: "I'm at the point where I'm ready to put these police in a f***ing grave," he said. "I'm at the point where I want to burn the f***ing White House down." He said he wanted to "take the fight" to senators and members of Congress—and if they "don't hear us," they will "burn them the f**k down."[13] These arguments were genealogical heirs to the argument made by Stokely Carmichael in 1966 in Greenwood, Mississippi, where he urged the new adherents of Black Power: "Every courthouse in Mississippi ought to be burned tomorrow to get rid of the dirt."[14] In that famous speech, Carmichael wrested the civil rights movement away from peaceful protestors such as Martin Luther King, James Farmer Jr., and James Meredith. The paradigm of "Beloved Community" was now being publicly resisted. Beloved Community is an important alternative to Afro-pessimism, having a grounding both in past and future orientations. Beloved Community is an organizing telos to the civil rights movement.[15] Drawn from the Christian teachings of Jesus urging his followers to "love one another," civil rights advocates argued that we "love" each other when we meet one another's needs. The particular problem of racism was broadly confronted in the civil rights movement. The role of debate in forming successful advocates against the human problem of racism was an important justification for further drawing upon argumentation to address the broader array of human injustices. Despite these prior successes, Carmichael believed that new threats of violence would reduce the problem of racism in the United States. The empirically successful movement of the Beloved Community was cast aside. These calls for violence were also echoes of the pre-Mecca persona of Malcolm X. Malcolm X prior to his pilgrimage to Mecca saw the task of nonviolent integration as hopeless and meaningless.[16] Famous speeches such as "The Ballot or the Bullet" implicated the impending necessity of violence as argument. Malcolm had a profound change of heart after Mecca and came to urge collaboration with King, Farmer, and Meredith.[17]

But in 2020, the idea of violently forcing President Trump from the White House was a dominant argument and was played out on the streets of D.C. and in the immediate vicinity of the White House. The violence on the streets of D.C. was so close to and explicitly aimed at the White House that dozens of secret service members were injured and President Trump was taken to a secure bunker.[18] The president was described in the press as a coward: "So naturally, as protesters congregated outside the White House to demand justice for the murder of George Floyd, the Coward-in-Chief ran and hid in the White House's underground bunker. You know, like Adolf Hitler and Saddam Hussein did. Trump received quite a bit of mockery on social media and expansive news coverage of the incident."[19] The major media did not generally describe these events as a violent unpatriotic insurrection against the government of the United States. The term of *treason* was not prominently suggested in any analysis of violence at the White House.

In late May, what is popularly known as the president's church, St. John's Episcopal Church was set on fire by Black Lives Matter protesters.[20] When President Trump walked out of a White House press conference to stand in front of the church with a Bible, he was derided by popular media. The fire was set in the church nursery. The *Washington Post* concluded with this description of events: "The bishop said she does not condone the destruction of property, but also doesn't want to lose sight of what the protests are calling for in the wake of Floyd's death: necessary change. 'It's a building. No one's life is gone, but we have work to do and we'll do it,' she said. 'Cleaning up, rebuild and focus on the rebuilding of our country which is more important.'"[21] Prominent leader of the Beloved Community John Lewis criticized Black Lives Matter leaders for refusing to forswear violence in protest. Movement leaders refused to yield to Lewis's arguments and continued to threaten the destruction of government facilities and urge the abolition of police. In a posthumous editorial, Lewis continued to ring the argumentation bell for nonviolence: "In my life I have done all I can to demonstrate that the way of peace, the way of love and nonviolence is the more excellent way. Now it is your turn to let freedom ring."[22] Lewis explained the importance of nonviolence in another interview with the *Washington Post* earlier in the summer: "Mr. President, the American people are tired and they cannot and will not take it anymore. They have a right to organize the unorganized. They have a right to protest in a peaceful, orderly, nonviolent fashion."[23] Both Lewis and Trump urged peaceful protest as their means of political argument.

THE JANUARY 6 INSURRECTION AT THE CAPITOL

As the president was speaking on the morning of January 6, Jacobin radicals were already moving toward the Capitol building. It was a forty-five-minute walk from the location of the speech to the legislative chambers. Jacobins were already attacking the chamber before the president finished his remarks. Among the protesters was activist Jayden X (aka John Sullivan), who would prove to be an important figure in the larger drama of violence at the Capitol. Sullivan filmed the death of Ashli Babbitt, an Iraq War veteran protesting the election results and angry enough upon entry to the Capitol to try to climb through a broken window toward the House chamber. As she climbed through that window, Babbitt was shot by an unknown police officer. To this date, no one has been identified as shooting and killing Ashli Babbitt; there is no reason to expect that charges will ever be filed for her killing. Activist Jayden X caught all of the event on tape, and it became some of the most viral video surrounding the event.[24] Sullivan was paid tens of thousands of dollars for his sensational video.[25] He was able to secure entry to the Capitol by falsely telling police that he was a journalist.[26] The video also caught Sullivan making some other important arguments, as explained by *Rolling Stone* magazine: "Sullivan does more than join in shouts of 'USA!' At one point in the footage, he can be heard yelling, 'It's a motherfucking revolution, let's take this shit.' In another, he claims he has a knife that might be useful in opening a locked Capitol door.'"[27] Additional reports about his remarks on January 6 provide: "We gotta get this s—t burned. It's our house, motherf—kers. We are getting this s–t."

Sullivan was indicted by the Justice Department for his actions at the Capitol. The FBI report provides the following account of his arguments made prior to January 6 when he was supporting the summer protests in D.C.:

"We about to burn this sh@t down," "we got to rip Trump out of office . . . f@%#ing pull him out of that shit . . . we ain't waiting until the next election . . . we about to go get that motherf@%#er."[28] The recorded arguments of Sullivan are consistent with prior activities supporting the Black Lives Matter movement and opposing the Trump administration. Sullivan reported that other protesters in the Capitol often accused him of being Antifa but he repeatedly denied such a connection, believing that the protesters would violently harm him if they understood his true political convictions. John Sullivan's alias of Jayden X is consistent with an activist pattern derived from Malcolm X, who changed his given name of Malcolm Little to repudiate the name given to him by "colonizers." Contemporary activists often use *X* as a surname to bolster their persona as a revolutionary. The call to "burn this shit down" is an enduring legacy of Carmichael's call to burn down courthouses in Mississippi.[29] Sullivan worked with intense preparation and deception to encourage as much violence at the Capitol on January 6 as he possibly could. His arguments were an important rhetorical force in achieving that injustice.

More than four hundred people have been arrested by the federal government for their presence and connection to protests at the Capitol on January 6, 2021.[30] Dozens have been charged with serious felonious crimes involving violent destruction of property and breaking and entering. No weapons have been uncovered as part of this intensive federal investigation into an alleged insurrection against the U.S. government. There remain no clear answers as to why more police and national guard were not called to the Capitol to control the potential risks of violent protests like those that took place in the summer of 2020. There are no clear answers as to why Capitol police apparently encouraged some protesters to enter the capitol at around the same time police were fighting to keep individuals out.[31] Analysis of video, officer accounts, and protestor accounts consistently confirm that protesters were sometimes allowed or even encouraged to enter while at other points Capitol police were fighting to prevent forced entry. Moreover, calls or prescription for more support from forces such as the National Guard went unheeded.

One of the most confusing details of the day's events is the death of officer Brian Sicknick. According to original journalistic accounts, officer Sicknick was killed by pro-Trump protesters who violently assaulted him with a fire extinguisher. A brief video of an officer being struck by a fire extinguisher was often offered as evidence. Later it was posited that he had been harmed by bear spray and tear gas. Not until a few days before the verdict in the George Floyd trial in late April 2021 did the federal government clarify that Sicknick was not killed by protesters but died of unrelated strokes shortly after the Capitol riots.[32] For days, weeks, and months, Sicknick was regularly offered as proof that Trump supporters were violently committed to their cause. Ironically, Sicknick was a Trump supporter[33] and his family pleaded with the media not to use his death to sensationalize events on January 6. Three other people died on Capitol grounds that day from medical emergencies that have not been tied to actions of protesters.[34]

CAPITOL INSURRECTION REDUX APRIL 2, 2021

On Friday April 2, 2021, Noah Green mounted another violent attack on the Capitol.[35] As a sympathizer of the Nation of Islam, Green also offered himself publicly under the alias Noah X.[36] Green's arguments mirrored the same arguments fed to Malcolm X by Elijah Muhammad and now fed to Green by Louis Farrakhan. The attack came at an unprecedented time when the Capitol was surrounded by fencing and razor wire to limit public access to major federal institutions. Local D.C. news provided this account of the killing: "The crash and shooting happened at a security checkpoint near the Capitol typically used by senators and staff on weekdays, though most are away from the building during the current recess. The attack occurred about 100 yards (91 meters) from the entrance of the building on the Senate side of the Capitol. Video shows the driver of the crashed car emerging with a knife in his hand and starting to run at the pair of officers, Pittman told reporters. Authorities shot the suspect. The U.S. Capitol Police officer who died Friday was identified as an 18-year veteran of the force."[37] Shortly before the attack, in late March, *Newsweek* reported that Green indicated this content on his social media account: "Green posted a 'Nation of Islam Certificate of Completion' given to him in 'recognition of your sacrifice in making your word bond and completing your 2021 saviors' day gift in the amount of $1,085.'" Another March 17 post saw him share a video link to a lecture from Farrakhan titled "The Divine Destruction of America."[38] Green blamed the U.S. government for his issues and wrote that he believed federal law enforcement agencies were trying to conduct mind-control experiments on him, according to CNN.[39] Green lunged at two police officers with a knife before being shot and killed. Popular media dismissed Green's killing of the Capitol police officer as the by-product of "mental delusions" and not a conspiracy to overthrow the government. The dismissal was similar to the FBI decision to dismiss the June 2017 shooting of Republican congressional members at baseball practice in Virginia. Despite government conclusions regarding the political animus of shooter James Hodgkinson against Republicans, the FBI concluded that the killings were not politically motivated and were rather "suicide by cop" ambitions of the mentally incapacitated shooter.[40] James Hodgkinson, a Bernie Sanders supporter, came to a baseball field eager to settle a political grudge surrounding his deeply held aspirations for universal health care that he believed were being unjustly obstructed by congressional Republicans.[41] Hodgkinson's animus was rhetorically coded in a manner similar to that for Noah Green: "mental derangement." Noah Green's death as a text argument[42] was a continuation of arguments made in the summer of 2020 for the killing of police officers.

ARGUMENTATION IMPLICATIONS FOR THE PARTISANSHIP AND POSTELECTION INTERVAL OF VIOLENCE

The violence at the Capitol on January 6 was penultimate to juggernauts of rhetorical arguments made in the 2020 election. The November presidential election was going to leave either the Biden side or the Trump side deeply politically grieved. The long-standing tradition of challenging electoral votes was not new. Republicans were relatively new to the argument, but the populist zeal of President Trump ensured a dramatic finish to the final approval of the election of President Joe Biden in Congress on the evening of January 6. Our intellectual culture composed of key epistemological figures ranging from journalists to FBI agents has not provided the clearest indications of how the violence transpired on that day among more than four hundred arrested protesters. In a video published in April 2021, CNN concedes that their journalistic mission in 2020 was subordinate to a partisan political goal of removing President Trump from the White House.[43] That argumentation goal was also explicit in the local and national ambitions of the Black Lives Matter movement of the summer 2020.

By the end of January 6, 2021, tech giant Jack Dorsey removed President Trump from the media platform of Twitter.[44] This dramatic act of censorship galvanized a public sense that Republicans, conservatives, and particularly Trump supporters do not deserve equal treatment in the public sphere—especially within privately held tech firms such as Twitter and Facebook. The justification for this censorship was predicated on the false argument that the president was urging violence at the Capitol in his speech to supporters on January 6, 2021. Though the American public sphere is replete with calls for violence against American sovereignty like those observed in the cases of Noah Green and local Black Lives Matter leaders in Washington D.C., epistemological agents such as CNN and the FBI characterize Republican threats of violence as salient and anti-Republican threats of violence as not rhetorically salient. This epistemological poisoning contributes to the ongoing cycle of political cynicism that creates mounting damage to American civic life—including the events of January 6, 2021. In the rhetorical framework of Kenneth Burke, Republican animus in politics is a realm of "action" whereas anti-Republican animus is a realm of "motion."[45] Anti-Republican agents do not "know" what they are doing. They are mentally ill and without argumentation coherence. The four hundred protesters arrested in relation to January 6, 2021, were coherent orchestrated agents who were not directed by the anti-Trump agent of Jayden X shouting "burn this shit down," but rather the words of President Trump uttered while the attack was already underway on the Capitol.

The antihermeneutic dominating argumentation study of Republican presidents makes the understanding of events surrounding the transition period between November 2020 and January 20, 2021, elusive if not impossible. The misunderstanding of President Trump was a partisan goal of the House impeachment hearings. The misunderstanding was furthered in the Senate trial as prosecutors sought to remove the president from office mere days before President Biden would be sworn in as the next president. Future understanding of presidential argumentation and rhetoric must recognize the reactionary premise that guides the current study of the presidency in the United States. President Trump's selection as the Republican nominee in 2016 was indicative of this painful antihermeneutic pattern. Trump's confrontational argument pattern sought to disrupt the conventional patterns of even Republican primary politics. This confrontational pattern was so well recognized by media interpolators that Trump enjoyed record positive media coverage from sources as diverse as CNN, the *Los Angeles Times*, the *Washington Post,* and the *New York Times*. The Shorenstein study documents the overwhelming preference of the media for President Trump throughout a primary process evaluating more than sixteen nominees.[46] Journalism so enjoyed the spectacle of candidate Trump confrontationally ridiculing Republican nominees like Jeb Bush and Ted Cruz that they granted him extra speaking time in presidential primary debates—an unprecedented maneuver that helped Trump consistently have the highest amount of speaking time in primary debates watched by ten to twenty million viewers per debate. Once Trump secured the nomination in the summer of 2016, his positive media coverage disappeared and Hillary Clinton received net positive coverage during one week of October 2016. Again this unprecedented singular preference for a candidate versus the rapid and complete reversal of the media against Trump betrays a deep motive of cynicism: Trump was the *worst* nominee for the Republicans so the journalistic outlets measured by Shorenstein *preferred* his candidacy.[47] Once this nomination was secured, an unabashed exposure designed to portray candidate Trump as a sexist and racist boor ensued in the fall of 2016. The public decision to reject this rhetorical media framing and put candidate Trump into the White House outraged America's intellectual epistemological culture and unleashed another intense rhetorical wave of reactionary arguments against now President Donald Trump. He was impeached twice and investigated intensely for allegations of colluding with the government of Russia. No independent reviews of the accusation about Russia could confirm it, and internal documents suggest that the Justice Department knew the allegations were untrue early on in the investigation.

The public preference for rhetorical disruption shows little sign of abating. Surveys continue to suggest that Trump is a probable nominee for the presidency in 2024. Surveys of partisanship continue to show that it is worsening within the public, despite promises that Biden's election would ensure its decline.[48] Special elections in Georgia flipped the U.S. Senate to Democratic control. The House and Senate controlled by Democrats along with the presidency ushered in an era of uniform one-party control. Dramatic immigration policies of President Trump were reversed along with most distinct measures of the previous administration. The COVID crisis continues to diminish as a threat. The political future of the United States remains unclear, and probability of impending political outcomes appears to tend toward former norms. In 2022, the most serious test of the new political order will commence in the midterm elections of Congress. The balance of the House and Senate will be on the table since the House paradoxically lost Democratic members in the 2020 election and the Senate is held by the slender margin of one. A conventional midterm result would likely flip the House and perhaps the Senate into Republican control. These results would press a presidential challenge to Biden more robust than most incumbent presidencies.

The painful yet fascinating arguments of the post–2020 election era provide ongoing lessons today. The reactionary hermeneutic of misunderstanding Republicans in epistemological communities as diverse as journalism and the Justice Department ensures that more public pain is ahead as political elections offer the public a choice between the well-intentioned Democrats and the ill-intentioned Republicans. This plainly partisan framing of arguments foments frustration in the public that manifested profoundly in the outsider election of Trump in 2016. The exceptional frustrations and violence of summer 2020 and January 6, 2021, suggest that violence as an extreme response remains possible in American politics. Hopefully, a renewed sense of Beloved Community like that so masterfully lived by advocates like James Meredith, Charles Evers, John Lewis, Fannie Lou Hammer, and James Farmer will restore an argumentation goal of understanding one another rather than trying to sabotage that necessary hermeneutic process essential to all good societies.

NOTES

1. Nicholas Rowan, "Seventeen States Throw Support Behind Texas in Election Lawsuit," *The Washington Examiner*, December 9, 2020, https://www.washington examiner.com/news/seventeen-states-throw-support-behind-texas-in-election-lawsuit.

2. "PRESIDENTIAL RESULTS," CNN, March 11, 2021, https://www.cnn.com /election/2020/results/president.

3. Brian Naylor, "Read Trump's January 6 Speech: A Key Part of the Impeachment Trial," *NPR*, February 10, 2021, https://www.npr.org/2021/02/10/966396848 /read-trumps-jan-6-speech-a-key-part-of-impeachment-trial.

4. Brian Naylor, "Read Trump's January 6 Speech."

5. Katelyn Carralle, "GOP Pollster Calls Profession Systematic Failure," *The Daily Mail*, November 4, 2020, https://www.dailymail.co.uk/news/article-8914929 /GOP-pollster-calls-profession-systematic-failure-APOLOGIZES-rival-Trump -ahead.html.

6. "Incitement," *New Oxford Dictionary*, 2021.

7. "Insurrection," *New Oxford Dictionary*, 2021.

8. Dana Milbank, "Opinion: President Trump Has Committed Treason," *The Washington Post*, January 6, 2021, https://www.washingtonpost.com/opinions/2021/01/06 /president-trump-has-committed-treason/.

9. Valerie Richardson, "Sen. Cruz to Democrats Calling for His Arrest for Treason: Calm Down," *The Washington Times*, January 3, 2021.

10. Ted Cruz, *Twitter*, January 7, 2021, https://twitter.com/tedcruz/status /1347243715182661633?ref_src=twsrc%5Etfw%7Ctwcamp%5Etweetembed %7Ctwterm%5E1347243715182661633%7Ctwgr%5E%7Ctwcon%5Es1_&ref _url=https%3A%2F%2Fthehill.com%2Fhomenews%2F533173-cruz-hits-back-after -aoc-calls-for-his-resignation.

11. Ernest Bormann, "Fantasy and Rhetorical Vision: The Rhetorical Criticism of Social Reality," *Quarterly Journal of Speech* 58 (1972): 396–407.

12. Mark Miller, "Black Lives Matter Co-Founder Says Groups Goal Is to Get Trump Out," *Washington Examiner*, June 20, 2021, https://www.washingtonexaminer .com/news/black-lives-matter-co-founder-says-groups-goal-is-to-get-trump-out.

13. Kassidy Vavra, "BLM Leader Threatens to Burn the White House and Put Police in Graves," *The Sun*, August 30, 2020, https://www.the-sun.com/news/1392855 /blm-leader-threatens-burn-white-house-police-graves/.

14. Simon Hall, "The NAACP, Black Power, and the African American Freedom Struggle, 1966–1969," *Historian* 69 (2007): 49–82, https://doi.org/10.1111/j.1540 -6563.2007.00174.x.

15. "The Beloved Community," *The King Center*, Accessed March 1, 2016, http:// www.thekingcenter.org/king-philosophy#sub4.

16. Robert Denton and Benjamin Voth, "Making Black Lives Matter," *Social Fragmentation and the Decline of American Democracy: The End of the Social Contract* (New York: Palgrave Macmillan, 2016): 138.

17. Denton and Voth, "Making Black Lives Matter," 127–149.

18. Kaitlan Collins and Noah Gray, "Trump Underground Bunker White House Protests," *CNN*, June 1, 2020, https://www.cnn.com/2020/05/31/politics/trump-underground-bunker-white-house-protests/index.html.

19. Chelsea Steiner, "Donald Trump Claims He Is Only Inspecting the Bunker," *MSN* June 1, 2020, https://www.msn.com/en-us/news/politics/noted-coward-donald-trump-claims-he-only-e2-80-98inspected-e2-80-99-bunker-didn-e2-80-99t-hide-in-it/ar-BB14ZBvO.

20. Peter Hermann, Sarah Pulliam Bailey, and Michelle Boorstein, "Fire Set at Historic St. Johns Church during Protests of George Floyd's Death," *Washington Post,* June 1, 2020, https://www.washingtonpost.com/religion/fire-set-at-historic-st-johns-church-during-protests-of-george-floyds-death/2020/06/01/4b5c4004-a3b6-11ea-b619-3f9133bbb482_story.html.

21. Hermann, Pulliam Bailey, and Boorstein, "Fire Set at Historic St. Johns Church."

22. John Lewis, "Civil Rights America," *The New York Times*, June 10, 2020, https://www.nytimes.com/2020/07/30/opinion/john-lewis-civil-rights-america.html.

23. Jonathan Capehart, "Black Lives Matter Protestors: Give Until You Cannot Give Anymore," *Washington Post*, June 10, 2020, https://www.washingtonpost.com/opinions/2020/06/10/john-lewis-black-lives-matter-protesters-give-until-you-cannot-give-any-more/.

24. Tim Dickinson, "I Don't Think She Deserved to Die: Black Activist Who Filmed Ashli Babbitt Shooting Speaks Out," *Rolling Stone*, January 14, 2021, https://www.rollingstone.com/culture/culture-features/ashli-babbitt-shooting-video-jayden-x-maga-riot-interview-1112949/.

25. Jerry Dunleavy, "Insurgence USA Leader Paid Tens of Thousands by CNN and NBC for Capitol Riot Footage," *Washington Examiner*, February 16, 2021, https://www.washingtonexaminer.com/news/insurgence-usa-cnn-nbc-capitol-riot-footage.

26. Dickinson, "I Don't Think She Deserved to Die."

27. Dickinson, "I Don't Think She Deserved to Die."

28. "Utah Resident John Sullivan Charged in Federal Court Following Civil Disorder at the United States Capitol, Examination of YouTube Channel JaydenX," *Arlington Cardinal*, January 14, 2021, https://www.arlingtoncardinal.com/2021/01/utah-resident-john-sullivan-charged-in-federal-court-following-civil-disorder-at-the-united-states-capitol-examination-of-youtube-channel-jaydenx/.

29. Hall, "The NAACP, Black Power, and the African American Freedom Struggle, 1966–1969."

30. Pete Williams, "Justice Department Now Expected to Charge More than 500 in Capitol Riot Probe," *NBC News*, April 23, 2021, https://www.nbcnews.com/politics/justice-department/justice-dept-now-expected-charge-more-500-capitol-riot-probe-n1265095.

31. Cara Kelly, Daphne Duret, Ramon Padilla, Erin Mansfield, Stephen J. Beard, and Jayme Fraser, "Capitol Riot Law Enforcement Failure Analysis," *USA Today*, January 13, 2021, https://www.usatoday.com/in-depth/news/investigations/2021/01/13/capitol-riot-law-enforcement-failure-analysis/6601142002/.

32. "Brian Sicknick Died of Natural Causes after Capitol Riot Medical Examiner Rules," *CNBC* April 19, 2021, https://www.cnbc.com/2021/04/19/brian-sicknick -died-of-natural-causes-after-capitol-riot-medical-examiner-rules.html.

33. Grace Hauck, Courtney Subramanian, Michael L. Diamond, Susan Loyer, and Paul Davidson, "Capitol Police Officer Brian Sicknick, Who Died Veteran War Critic," *USA Today,* January 8, 2021, https://www.usatoday.com/story/news /nation/2021/01/08/capitol-police-officer-brian-sicknick-who-died-veteran-war -critic/6595549002/.

34. Hauck et al., "Capitol Police Officer Brian Sicknick."

35. Michael Balsamo, Nomaan Merchant, and Eric Tucker, "Noah Green, Man Who Rammed Car into Capitol Police Officers, Suffered Delusions: Sources," *ABC7 News*, April 4, 2021, https://abc7news.com/capitol-attack-noah-green-suspect-delu sions-police-officer-killed/10483389/.

36. Aila Sisco, "Noah Green's Facebook Posts about Nation of Islam, Losing His Job," *Newsweek*, April 3, 2021, https://www.msn.com/en-us/news/world/noah -greens-facebook-posts-about-nation-of-islam-losing-his-job/ar-BB1ffwYV.

37. "What We Know about Capitol Attack Suspect Noah Green," *WKBN News*, April 2, 2021, https://www.wkbn.com/news/washington-dc/what-we-know-about -the-capitol-attack-suspect/.

38. Sisco, "Noah Green's Facebook Posts."

39. Craig McCarthy, "Facebook Admits to Pulling Capitol Suspect Noah Green's Accounts," *New York Post*, April 2, 2021, https://nypost.com/2021/04/02/facebook -admits-to-pulling-capitol-suspect-noah-greens-accounts/.

40. Jake Dima, "FBI Determined 2017 GOP Baseball Shooting Was 'Suicide by Cop,' Lawmaker Says," *Washington Examiner*, April 21, 2021, https://www.washington examiner.com/news/fbi-gop-baseball-shooting-suicide-by-cop.

41. Dima, "FBI Determined 2017 GOP Baseball Shooting Was 'Suicide by Cop.'"

42. Ben Voth, *The Rhetoric of Genocide: Death as a Text* (Lanham, MD: Lexing-ton Books, 2014).

43. Andrew Mark Miller, "CNN Director Shown on Undercover Video Boasting about Removing Trump from Office and Admitting to Spreading Propaganda," *The Washington Examiner*, April 13, 2021, https://www.washingtonexaminer.com/news /cnn-director-boasts-removing-trump-from-office-spreading-propaganda.

44. Haley Messenger, "Twitter to Uphold Permanent Ban against Trump, Even If He Were to Run for Office Again," *NBC News*, February 10, 2021, https://www.nbcnews .com/business/business-news/twitter-uphold-permanent-ban-against-trump-even-if -he-were-n1257269.

45. Kenneth Burke, *A Grammar of Motives* (New York: Prentice-Hall, 1945).

46. Thomas E. Patterson, "Research: Media Coverage of the 2016 Election," *Sho-renstein Center*, Harvard University, September 7, 2016.

47. Patterson, "Research: Media Coverage of the 2016 Election."

48. Gregory Skelley, "Few Americans Who Identify as Independent Are Actu-ally Independent. That's Really Bad for Politics," *538.com*, April 15, 2021, https:// fivethirtyeight.com/features/few-americans-who-identify-as-independent-are-actu ally-independent-thats-really-bad-for-politics/.

Chapter 3

Media Coverage and the Postelection of 2020

Robert E. Denton Jr.

As noted in the preface, the 2020 presidential election certainly did not end on election day. Up until the inauguration of Joe Biden, the election was contested nationally across states, in courts, and among public opinion. This chapter provides an overview of some of the issues and characterizations of how primarily the news media covered the postelection through the inauguration. I surveyed news articles and opinion pieces focusing on how the media covered the events, activities, and "drama" of this period. It is important to note that I do not argue for the validity of any of the issues or characterizations of coverage, per se. Rather, major observations and concerns raised by the media themselves are identified. As you can imagine, there are rather stark differences of coverage between mainstream media and partisan outlets, from cable media organizations and social media platforms. I purposely note the stark contrasts of coverage.

Collectively the media, broadly defined, serves as the primary way citizens learn from and follow campaigns. Historically, the news media influences the political attitudes, knowledge, and voting behaviors of citizens. And what citizens see and hear influences what they think, what they believe, and how they act. What has become crystal clear is that the media, broadly defined, are equal partners in the growing division and polarization of America. It is also my opinion that contemporary journalism is not serving our democracy. Thus, to understand the issues raised by media coverage, it is essential to recognize the transformation of the practice of journalism.

TRANSFORMATION OF THE PRACTICE OF JOURNALISM[1]

With the proliferation of news outlets, especially within the last decade, the practice of journalism has undergone a drastic transformation. It was primarily in the aftermath of the 2016 presidential election that the news media became an object of criticism. There are deep divides among media outlets in terms of coverage, bias, and partisanship, not unlike the political and ideological differences among the general public. In the words of Michael Delli Carpini, today's media regime consists of "a mix of legacy, partisan, and online actors and media institutions, [and as such] this regime has blurred distinctions between fact and opinion, news and entertainment, information producers and consumers, and mass mediated and interpersonal communication."[2] The notions of accuracy, neutrality, and independence from the people and organizations subject of presentations are relics from the past. "Objective reporting" as the process of gathering facts and information and presenting them as they exist is no longer the norm. Contemporary journalists even reject the notion of objective reporting. The Internet and social media have exacerbated the problem by creating audiences and consumers of news of like-minded folks who attune to news that reinforces their specific beliefs, attitudes, and values. Identity politics has influenced media consumption, not based on information but content based upon political identities. According to Ezra Klein, "In today's media sphere, where the explosion of choices has made it possible to get the political media you really want, it's expressed itself in polarized media that attaches to political identity, conflict, and celebrity."[3] In essence, news and information are framed to reinforce or persuade viewers to specific issue positions and political or ideological attitudes.

There is also an economic reality to the transformation. With so much choice and sources of news and information, to generate revenue depends upon audience. To increase audience does not mean provide consumers what they need but what they want. More choice of outlets means more targeted and narrow audiences. With the tribalism and polarization of media content clearly enhanced, the trend toward tribalism and polarization of public and politics also continues.

Social media have contributed to not only the decline of trust in the practice of American journalism but also to the spread of misinformation and even lies. Highly partisan and ideological websites release false, speculative, and sensational materials.[4] Algorithmic filter "bubbles" and "echo chambers" increase exposure to fake news. The Pew Research Center reports that those who obtain political news primarily from social media are less knowledgeable about issues and actually do not closely follow news and current events.[5] As local and even national newsrooms shrink, journalists move to new online websites. These websites may focus on special topics, issues, or industries. Not only does their content fill news vacuums, but it may find its way into traditional news sources. Also problematic, the websites give the appearance of "legitimate" news organizations. For example, Metric Media has a network of 1,300 websites that appear to be locally based—in this case, names like "Illinois Valley Times" or "Lansing Sun." The sites cover local government, schools, and events. It turns out this group is funded and directed by PR firms and partisan political groups. This occurs from both the left and the right, Democrat and Republican groups. The content is propaganda, slanted, strategic, persuasive, and sometimes borderline false and misleading.[6]

There has been a tremendous growth of news websites. Many of these websites are not what they appear to be. The funding sources of some of the websites dictate story content and perspective. As suggested by Elahe Izadi of the *Washington Post*, such an arrangement "unnerves transparency advocates who have been keeping tabs on a proliferation of unconventional news sites and watchdog outfits that may be blurring the lines between PR and journalism."[7]

Finally, not surprising, there are major differences between Democrats and Republicans in the use of media and sources for political news. The distribution of sources among Democrats and Independents who lean Democrat was much larger. Not surprising, 53 percent went to CNN on a weekly basis, 40 percent to NBC News, 37 percent to ABC News, 33 percent to CBS News, 33 percent to MSNBC, 30 percent to NPR, 31 percent to *The New York Times*, 26 percent to the *Washington Post*, and 22 percent to PBS. (Note: Numbers total more than 100 percent because individuals within a group may get news from multiple sources within a one-week period.) Even the *Wall Street Journal* pulled in 15 percent. Interestingly, a sizable percentage of members of both parties regularly went to primary sources of the opposition party. Twenty-four percent of Republicans and leaners checked in with CNN on at least a weekly basis and 23 percent of Democrats with Fox News.[8]

It is rather obvious that the impact of our sources of information influences our beliefs, attitudes, and values as well as electoral behavior. We may well be aware of our bias/preference of sources for news, but how attuned are we to the cumulative effects of exposure? A study by Kalev Leetaru, senior fellow at George Washington University Center for Cyber & Homeland Security, found that the degree of similarities across the networks in story coverage has varied the most during the Trump administration and especially during the first two quarters of 2020. "Since Donald Trump's election, the tone of news coverage has become darker and the media has fractured, with parallel universes that extend even to the pronouns each outlet uses."[9] The three major networks (NBC, CBS, ABC) were closely parallel in coverage from 2010 through Barack Obama's reelection in 2012. Upon the election of Trump, the networks became less and less similar. Thus, as Leetaru asserts, the study "remind[s] us just how different the view can be depending on what station we tuned into."

ISSUES AND CHARACTERIZATION OF POSTELECTION MEDIA COVERAGE

In surveying news articles and opinion pieces focusing on how the media covered the general election, I discovered several major observations, concerns, and characterizations of coverage. Interestingly, many of the concerns were raised by the media themselves. The general themes that emerged included lack of trust in news media, bias, press censorship, press hostility, and use of faulty polls to suppress the Trump vote.[10] While many of these themes also emerged in postelection coverage, additional considerations were press and corporate censorship, rushing to judgment, systemic election fraud, and what happened on and the meaning of January 6. Space does not allow the full fleshing out of each theme. However, in each case, there are multiple perspectives and arguments to be made about the validity of influence upon citizen attitudes and behavior. The primary purpose here is identify the major topics raised about the news media coverage of the postelection period.

Lack of Trust in Media

There continues to be a decline in the trust of news media. According to Gallup, a record number of Americans have no trust in the media. In fall 2020, they found only 9 percent of survey respondents said they trust the media "a great deal" while 60 percent said they have "little" to "no trust at all."[11] Perhaps most alarming is a total of 41 percent of Americans think the media is "unfriendly to" and even "an enemy of" the American citizenry.[12] Ironically, during the election, cable news ratings were at an all-time high and online news subscriptions increased.[13] There is a deep partisan divide in perceptions of trust and media. In the fall of 2020, Democrats' "great deal" or "fair" amount of trust in media was 73 percent and just 10 percent for Republicans. Independents' trust was at 36 percent.[14] Finally, younger Americans are significantly less trustful of media than middle-age and older Americans. "Very" or "somewhat" favorable views of media for those under thirty was just 19 percent.[15]

Bias

The intent focus on audience by media and platforms implies bias of content. Likewise, the partisan and ideological slant of self-selected audiences by definition reflects some degree of content bias. According to Gallup, in the fall of 2020, 49 percent of Americans see "a great deal" and 37 percent "a fair amount" of political bias in news coverage. Even 56 percent of U.S. adults see "a fair amount" of bias in their own selected news sources.[16] Ironically, according to the Knight Foundation, 69 percent of Americans are concerned about the news bias *other people* are getting compared to just 29 percent of the bias to which they may be exposed. And 73 percent of Americans acknowledge that bias in reporting of news that is supposed to be objective is "a major problem."[17] In fact, 61 percent of Democrats and 77 percent of Republicans view media bias or reporting from a specific point of view "a major problem."[18]

During the postelection period, there were articles comparing the contrast in coverage of Trump with that of Biden. Rasmussen found 55 percent of likely U.S. voters thought the news media was less aggressive in questioning Biden than they were in questioning Trump. As with most polls, there was a major partisan difference in opinion. Seventy-seven percent of Republicans thought the media was less aggressive with Biden compared to just 33 percent of Democrats. In line with the decline of cable news audiences across the board after Biden's inauguration, 28 percent indicated they followed political news less than they did when Trump was president.[19]

During Biden's first one hundred days, Biden's news coverage was 32 percent negative and 23 percent positive. Among right-leaning outlets, the coverage of Biden was 78 percent negative compared to 19 percent of left-leaning outlets. For Trump's first one hundred days, he received 44 percent negative and 11 percent positive coverage. Fifty-six percent of left-leaning media was negative; it was just 14 percent for right-leaning outlets. Another interesting difference was in the framing of the news stories during this period. For Biden, 65 percent were framed around his policy agenda and ideology and 35 percent on character and leadership. In contrast, 74 percent of stories were framed around Trump's character and leadership and 26 percent on his policy agenda and ideology.[20]

The general partisan and ideological bias were consistent across left- and right-leaning media, websites, and platforms. And program content went well beyond just news and talk shows. As an example, CNN aired an hour-long special entitled "A Radical Rebellion: The Transformation of the GOP." The host concluded the show characterizing the GOP as "a band of ideological warriors with apocalyptic visions that fuel the end of days, see opponents as traitors and devils, and believes that all methods are sanctioned in its battle to save civilization and itself. . . . In short, the Republican Party needs to have a political exorcism, drive out its demons, and come to terms with the modern world." On the same night, CNN had an episode of "United Shades of America" where the protesters of Portland, Oregon, were celebrated and the protests characterized as "mostly peaceful." The accounts of millions of dollars of damage, burning, and looting of property, of hundreds of protesters taking over the federal courthouse breaking windows and setting fires, and of nineteen officers seriously injured were never mentioned.[21]

Of course, right-leaning outlets focused more on contrasting views about Biden, Democrats, and the hypocrisy of the left. The simple reality is that with the transformation of the practice of journalism and the proliferation of news outlets, there is a wide range of bias. The implications are straightforward and alarming. And Americans are well aware. The Pew Research Center found that 89 percent of Trump voters and 84 percent of Biden voters recognize that the news sources they view influence the tone and content of presentations that will widely differ.[22]

Press and Corporate Censorship

Related to media bias are the notions of press censorship. During the campaign there were essays and stories about how the media would simply not report or would avoid certain stories that ran counter to audience beliefs or perspectives. The allegations of censorship went both ways in the media debates. In terms of Trump, they involved the lack of reporting on the historic Middle East diplomacy, the decline of Iran, the various successes against terrorist groups, and NATO members finally meeting financial obligations, to name only a few. Of course, as mentioned above, there were continued heightened criticisms of the coverage of George Floyd's death and the portrayal of summer protests. There were controversies surrounding various reporters and editors terminated for "counter reporting" on stories. Perhaps the most egregious allegation of nonreporting and investigation was that of Hunter Biden soliciting help from his father involving deals with China and other nations. The more mainstream and left-leaning media dismissed the accounts and did not investigate nor widely report the story. After the election, it become known that the Justice Department had indeed been investigating Hunter Biden since 2018 related to tax issues, money laundering, and Chinese business dealings. Jack Dorsey, CEO of Twitter, acknowledged at a congressional hearing on misinformation and social media that Twitter made a "total mistake" to block users from access to the *NY Post* stories on the subject.[23] As of this writing, there does appear to be a major investigation with conflicting details coming from Biden.

Also most notable were the collective social medias' attempt to "manage" misinformation resulting in tagging, removing, and banning of individuals, videos, and entities from access to the platforms. Kalev Leetaru of Real Clear

Politics observed that "Silicon Valley silenced the president."[24] During the postelection period, especially after January 6, Trump was banned by Twitter, Facebook, Instagram, YouTube (deleting videos), Snapchat, Reddit, and Twitch. Apple and Google got in on the act by banning the sale of Parler, a rival of Twitter, from their app stores and banished it from mobile devices. For some, the concerted effort to censor Trump was a means of preventing him from communicating with his seventy-four million voters and millions of social media followers.

Some media outlets applauded efforts to stop the spreading of misinformation, hate, and public discord. But it also stimulated a debate across media on the issue of free speech. The private technology platforms argued that their actions are legitimate and follow clear policy guidelines as to content. Such platform actions were not First Amendment issues. Free speech applies only to government and not private entities. This debate will, and in my opinion should, continue. Supreme Court Justice Clarence Thomas expressed concerns about the censorship and power of social media. "Today's digital platforms provide avenues for historically unprecedented amounts of speech, including speech by government actors. Also unprecedented, however, is control of so much speech in the hands of a few private parties," Thomas wrote. "We will soon have no choice but to address how our legal doctrines apply to highly concentrated, privately owned information infrastructure such as digital platforms. . . . Although both companies are public, one person controls Facebook (Mark Zuckerberg), and just two control Google (Larry Page and Sergey Brin)."[25]

The Pew Research Center found that during the first sixty days of the Biden administration, about half of the news stories about Biden mentioned Trump in some way. Interestingly, the number was about the same across all news outlets. Not surprising, over time the references declined. From the earliest days until the end of March, Trump being mentioned in stories ranged from 72 percent to 42 percent.[26]

In stories where COVID-19 was mentioned in a major way, Trump was mentioned 34 percent of the time, compared to 61 percent when COVID-19 was mentioned in a minor way.[27] This suggests that the media in general portrayed the rollout of the COVID 19 vaccines as a major success of the Biden administration, failing to give some credit to Trump's Operation Warp Speed playing an important role in the fast rollout of vaccine. In addition, Biden is credited with reaching the one hundred million mark in vaccinations to Americans, while actually the United States was on target to meet that goal before Biden took office.[28]

Rushing to Judgment

Within twenty-four hours of the election, there were articles and commentary expressing concerns of the rush to judgment in declaring Biden the winner. As with all the other concerns, the distinctions were clear among the partisan media outlets. The first was rushing to judgment by calling the election over and for Biden when clearly several states were "too close to call." In addition to making early calls for Biden, Christopher Bedford accuses the mainstream media of "holding calls on Republican wins like Florida for hours, and North Carolina for days, while recklessly rushing calls on states like Arizona for Team Blue."[29] An editorial by the *New York Sun* posed the question, "Why would the country be irreparably harmed by waiting for official results as prescribed by law?"[30]

Systemic Election Fraud

The dominant media focus for months immediately following the election was on the allegations of "systemic voter fraud." There were numerous concerns raised about voting across the nation and especially among several states. Generally, the concerns include the following:[31]

- Statistical anomalies in vote counts early on November 4
- Hundreds of affidavits reporting all types of irregularities and legal violations
- Statistically abnormal absentee vote counts with high percentages favoring Biden, some over 90 percent
- Thousands of missing votes found across several states, days following the election
- Restrictions and limits of voting and vote count monitoring
- Numerous procedural issues and protocols such as matching signatures on mail-in ballots
- Historic low ballot rejection rates
- Missing votes
- Nonresident votes
- Votes counted twice, absentee and in-person
- Localities with over 100 percent voting
- States' constitutional issues questioning authorities of changing voting protocols in violation of state law

Media outlets tended to take one side or the other; there was no evidence of widespread voter fraud or too numerous irregularities that may well impact the outcome of the election in several states. The coverage became a battle over semantics. There certainly may not have been "nationwide systemic fraud," but there were certainly hundreds of "irregularities," some quite alarming. However, this is the case for every election. And sworn affidavits are indeed a form of evidence, perhaps weak or poor evidence, but some form of evidence nevertheless.

The Heritage Foundation has an Election Fraud Database that presents "sampling" of election fraud cases that have been found proven, not merely allegations. As of this writing, their database has 1,322 proven instances of election fraud, with 17 cases from Missouri from the 2020 presidential election.[32]

Some state courts in late spring 2021 were offering rulings relative to voting irregularities and fraud some seven months after the election. The State Court of Claims in Michigan ruled that the Democrat Secretary of State instructions on signature verification for absentee ballots violated state law.[33] The Supreme Court of Wisconsin ruled in December that local election officials violated state law in giving blanket permission allowing voters to declare themselves homebound and thus did not need to comply with voter ID requirements. The court stated that the governor and local officials did not have the authority to exempt all voters to get an absentee ballot without a valid ID. Court records indicate that about 200,000 voters declared themselves permanently homebound; Biden won Wisconsin by 20,000 votes.[34] After winning a court appeal, an audit of Missoula County in Montana found 4,592 votes out of 72,491 mailed-in ballots violated state law. In this case, those votes may well have impacted local races.[35] In Virginia, a ruling upheld the banning of accepting ballots without postmarks after Election Day. There are rulings in Georgia and Arizona to review ballots.[36] And there are numerous others.

Between covering the allegations of election fraud, there was coverage of all the litigation, especially from Republicans. On a daily basis there was reporting on the lawsuits brought by the Trump campaign and other groups challenging the election results in several states. Once again, there was a great divide in media coverage of the veracity of the lawsuits and reporting of the daily number of lawsuits dismissed by the courts. What was lacking was an understanding of the decisions of many of the lawsuits. Some were dismissed because of legal issues, technicalities, or lack of standing never addressing the key arguments or questions raised. This was certainly true of the Supreme Court's dismissal of the Texas suit that 18 Republican state attorneys general and 126 House Republicans supported. The Court dismissed the lawsuit because "Texas has not demonstrated a judicially cognizable interest in the manner in which another state conducts its elections."[37]

At end of December 2020, John Lott, who works for the Department of Justice, published an interesting study entitled "A Simple Test for the Extent of Vote Fraud with Absentee Ballots in the 2020 Presidential Election: Georgia and Pennsylvania Data" in the Social Science Research Network (SSRN).[38] SSRN, the world's largest open-access repository of academic and scholarly research across disciplines, is owned by Elsevier. Lott's analysis indicates between 70,000 and 79,000 "excess" votes in Georgia and Pennsylvania. In adding the analysis from the states of Arizona, Michigan, Nevada, and Wisconsin, the total amounts to 289,000 "excess votes." Lott concludes, "The precinct level estimates for Georgia and Pennsylvania indicate that vote fraud may account for Biden's win in both states. The voter turnout rate data also indicates that there are significant excess votes in Arizona, Michigan, Nevada, and Wisconsin as well."[39]

Now months after Biden's inauguration, the controversy continues, but more focus is on the larger concerns of election security and integrity. In the intervening months since the inauguration, states have introduced nearly three thousand election-related bills. Among those bills, the most common reviews are on absentee and mail-in voting. Democrats are pushing for national minimum standards for access to voting.[40] In general, states with Republican legislatures are creating legislation that limits rule changes instituted because of the pandemic, limiting early voting, universal mailing of absentee ballots, adding restrictions to mail-in voting, enhancing ballot certification, providing better access for poll watchers, and holding election officials legally liable for ballot integrity and security, to name a few. As expected, the partisan media presents the voting legislation as either voter suppression initiatives or actions to increase confidence in the electoral and voting process. As my colleague Cayce Myers concludes in chapter 8 on "Litigating Victory: An Analysis of 2020 Postelection Lawsuits," voting rules matter and have become part of the partisan calculations for the pending 2022 midterm elections and the presidential contest of 2024.

Once again, my straightforward point is that the collective news media broadly defined failed in its role in covering the various aspects of election fraud. Rather than exploring the strengths and weaknesses of the various state voting laws, regulations and protocols, statistical anomalies, issues related to mail-in ballots, absentee ballots, and perhaps the benefits of national expectations going forward, the partisan media (both sides) narrowly focused on an almost all-or-none perspective on the issue of election integrity. That is, either there was rampant voter fraud or none at all. Investigative journalism would have at least provided detailed information, research, and analysis of affidavit allegations, including consulting with voting experts, exploring the history of voter fraud, and explanations of voting concerns, to name a few. Most of the reporting was argumentative and not very informative.

January 6

The Pew Research Center found 37 percent of Americans expressed strong negative emotion of anguish, horror, and shock in response to the January 6 Capitol episode. Fourteen percent were surprised and felt concern for the country. In this survey, 13 percent blamed Trump and Republicans for the riot and only 9 percent criticized law enforcement for not being adequately prepared for the potential event. As the norm, there were partisan differences of views of the January 6 event. Forty-eight percent of Democrats expressed negative emotions of the event compared to 27 percent of Republicans. Among Democrats, 21 percent blamed Trump for inciting violence, compared to 19 percent of Republicans.[41]

In a Gallup survey, 29 percent of Americans cited government leaders and their behavior as the top problem facing America, ahead of the coronavirus at 22 percent. In addition, 12 percent of Americans cited national division and lack of unity as the top problem in America. That's the highest percentage of response for that problem in seventy years dating back to 1939. In terms of party, 37 percent of Republicans and 28 percent of Democrats cite government or leadership as top problems for the nation.[42]

In hindsight, it does appear that some of the rioters at the Capitol pre-planned their attacks days and even weeks in advance. In fact, the Capitol police had specific intelligence that an armed invasion of the Capitol was planned in late December and protesters were in fact bringing guns and weapons.[43] Actually, militia members began planning within days of the election. Some two hundred now-charged defendants were engaged in advanced planning on social media. The planning was anything but casual. Chats included training, casing sites, identifying commanders on the scene, and requests for cash, communication equipment, and gear.

There were just over 800 participants at the Capitol riot. As of May 2021, there are 440 indicted with over 2,000 individual charges. The federal prosecutors anticipate at least another one hundred indictments. Among the charges:[44]

- 125 charged with assaulting, resisting, or impeding officers or employees, with 35 of those charged with using a "deadly" or "dangerous" weapon. Only three have been accused of carrying firearms; other "dangerous" weapons include tasers, tomahawk axes, crowbars, flagpoles, knifes, baseball bats, wooden sticks or clubs, and chemical sprays, to name a few.
- 350 charged with entering or remaining in a restricted building or grounds.
- 25 charged with destruction of government property.

Rioters came from forty-five states, with the most from Texas (forty-four) followed by Pennsylvania and New York (thirty-seven each) and Florida (thirty-five). Most of the defendants will not face jail time. Nearly half are charged with low-level misdemeanors such as trespassing or disorderly conduct.

Semantic Debate in Characterizing the Event

From January 6 until inauguration there was an evolution of how the event of January 6 was labeled. Was it an occupation, rampage, uprising, riot, insurrection, coup, attack, siege, protest? Govind Bhutada of VisualCapitalist.com analyzed more than 180 articles from Alexa's top-ranked news websites in the United States to discover how media outlets described the event.[45] Although the term *coup* was used heavily on social media platforms, the term was not used on the news websites. Fox News and the BBC used the term *riot* the most frequently, followed by CNN, the *New York Times*, the *Washington Post,* and Breitbart. Overall, *riot* was the most common term used to describe the event across news websites. The website Business Insider was most likely to use the term *insurrection* than the others in the beginning. Among the terms used to describe the participants, the *New York Times* most consistently used the terms *mob* or *rioters*. Of the outlets, the *Washington Post* and the *New York Times* used the term *siege* the most. The *New York Times* also used the term *attack* by far the most among the news websites. Interestingly, the term *insurrection* was used only three times on the Yahoo and CNN news websites. The most common descriptions for participants were *mob* and *rioters*, followed by *protesters*. To describe the people who entered the Capitol building, Fox News, Breitbart, and Epoch Times used *protesters* more often than any other news media outlet. In fact, these three outlets account for twenty-eight of the thirty-seven news articles in which the term *protesters* appeared. Bhutada echoes an obvious point made throughout this chapter that speaks to the role media play in our current political culture: "From a *riot* caused by *rioters* to an *insurrection* by President Trump's *militant supporters*, the way different media outlets analyze the U.S. Capitol incident impacts what their respective audiences take away from it."[46]

By the inauguration, left-leaning partisan media were consistently referring to the event of January 6 as an "insurrection." Right-leaning partisan media tended to distinguish the "extremists" and "rioters" from the much larger number of "protesters." Initially, those who attended the rally where Trump spoke were characterized as "protestors." Then upon breach of the Capitol, virtually all the news media, including right-leaning outlets, characterized the day as a "riot." David Bauder notes that some news organizations were hesitant to use terms such as *rebellion, revolt,* or *uprising*, fearing that such characterizations might cast the participants in a heroic light. He also notes that news organizations were intentionally careful to avoid phrases such as "attempted coup" or "attempt to overthrow the government" because of the military implications.[47]

By five months after January 6, 2021, Rasmussen found that 44 percent of likely voters agreed with President Biden's characterization that the riot was "the worst attack on our democracy since the Civil War." Forty-one percent disagreed, with another 14 percent "not sure." Not surprising, 66 percent of Democrat voters agreed with Biden; 26 percent of Republicans and 38 percent of nonaffiliated voters agreed with him. Among Republican voters, 59 percent disagreed with Biden's characterization; 20 percent of Democrats and 48 percent of unaffiliated voters disagreed with him.[48]

Contrast in Coverage of January 6 and the Summer Riots of 2020

While there was virtually unanimous outrage of the violence and destruction within the Capitol, there was intermedia debate about the differences in not only characterizing the events of January 6 but also differences in coverage of the participants and the violence once again compared to the participants and events over the summer of 2020. Those of the right-leaning partisan media pointed out how the left-leaning partisan media were silent in rebuking the riots during the Black Lives Matter and Antifa protests that led to months of violence, deaths, injuries, looting, and destruction of billions of dollars' worth of public and private property in the cities of Minneapolis; Washington, D.C.; New York City; Los Angeles; Seattle; and dozens of other cities across America. As already mentioned, left-leaning media largely portrayed the summer riots as "mostly peaceful" compared to the portrayal of January 6 as an "insurrection" by a "mob," as noted above by Govind Bhutada. Again, five months later, Rasmussen found only 35 percent of voters agreed with the description of the summer events as "mostly peaceful protests" by the news media and 52 percent described them as "riots" while 13 percent were not sure.[49]

At the very least, there were stark differences in people's reactions to the events of January 6 compared to reaction to the months of summer rioting. In response to January 6, the Capitol was transformed into a virtual "Fort Knox," with fencing and barricades erected around the building and much of the Capitol grounds. More than two thousand National Guard troops came to Washington and remained nearly five months.

The Role of Trump and Impeachment

There were media debates about the role of Trump in inciting the insurrection and issues related to the right of assembly and free speech. According to estimates, well over one hundred thousand people attended Trump's speech on January 6, with fewer than a thousand going to the Capitol grounds. Trump's seventy-minute address to followers provided the basis for accounts of inciting the riot and impeachment considerations. Although Trump did not explicitly direct the crowd to break into the Capitol, some of his remarks did call for action. Among his comments include the following:[50]

- "We will stop the steal."
- "We will never give up. We will never concede. It doesn't happen."
- "You don't concede when there's theft involved. Our country has had enough. We will not take it anymore."
- "You will have an illegitimate president. That is what you will have, and we can't let that happen."
- "If you don't fight like hell, you're not going to have a country anymore."
- "I know that everyone here will soon be marching over to the Capitol building to peacefully and patriotically make your voices heard."
- "We are going to walk down to the Capitol and we're going to cheer on our brave senators and congressmen and women, and we're probably not going to be cheering so much for some of them."

There is a distinction between what constitutes legal definition of incitement and the very political process of impeachment. The attack on the West Front of the Capitol started twenty minutes before Trump's speech ended.[51] The FBI was quick to caution that "there is an important legal distinction between gathering like-minded people for a political rally, which is protected by the First Amendment, and organizing an armed assault on the seat of American government. The task now is to distinguish which people belong in each category, and who played key roles in committing or coordinating the violence."[52] Nevertheless, media outlets took very clear sides on both issues (as well as the rather quick impeachment of Trump, "for the record").

Inauguration

As inauguration approached, the Capitol was on high alert. Washington was militarized more than at any time since 9/11. There were over twenty-five thousand National Guard troops and law enforcement officers within the District of Columbia. The FBI warned of protests and potential violence in all fifty states. Governors issued declarations of states of emergency. Many state capitols were highly secured with barriers and National Guard troops as well. Media outlets focused for days on the pending danger of another assault on the Capitol and potential confrontations with militia groups. Coverage also included key battleground state capitols on heightened alert. To the nation's relief, nothing happened but the inauguration of Joe Biden as the forty-sixth president of the United States.

CONCLUSION

The primary purpose of this chapter is simply to survey the various themes and issues of media coverage of the postelection phase of the 2020 presidential campaign from election day to inauguration. The themes that emerged include the general lack of trust in media broadly defined, general right/ left bias, press and corporate censorship, rush to judgment, and the question of systemic election fraud. In terms of January 6, there was a wide-ranging debate in characterizing the events and participants of the day, with comparisons of coverage of the events of the day to those of the summer riots of 2020, the role Trump played in the events of the day, and the anticipation leading up to the inauguration of Joe Biden.

However, what also becomes clear are the troubling implications resulting from the transformation of the practice of journalism across platforms and media. Media coverage of the postelection period, as with the general election phase,[53] simply reflects the current media environment. Today's tribal and partisan journalism, with the self-appointed censors of social media, impacts who runs and who is elected and even the very nature of our democracy. Within each theme or issue of coverage there was a clear divergence of arguments and presentations. Yet, these same news and media outlets are quick to claim "truth," "sense of fairness," and "balance." The economic realities and new technologies have contributed to the transformation of journalism, which in turn has contributed to the formation of our political, partisan, and ideological divides and echo chambers.

As noted earlier, Americans do understand the necessity and value of journalism to the functioning of a democracy. For a democracy to thrive, citizens must have access to true, accurate, and adequate information. But it seems we now have blurring of fact and opinion, with less trust in what is truth or reality. And for some, reporting has become propaganda. Frank Miele observes, "Journalism starts with facts and allows people to reach their own conclusion. Propaganda starts with a conclusion and manipulates people into accepting it as fact. You can decide for yourself whether what we have today is journalism or propaganda."[54] John MacArthur concurs, "For there no longer appears to be a consensus about what role journalism plays either in a democracy or a dictatorship, or why anyone with a pluralistic, oppositional or reformist bent would want to make a career in newspapers or magazines."[55] Thus, we have the emergence of a partisan and fragmented media environment creating information bubbles that reinforce "audience" beliefs, attitudes, values, and even what is "true." There seems to be less persuasion in the classical sense of providing arguments with evidence to reach conclusions. Information has become a series of "pronouncements." Genuine persuasion takes time, critical thinking, knowledge, information, and "reasoned" judgment. Social media and associated platforms as sources of political information are key contributors to our state of social polarization and fragmentation. Chris Stirewalt, fired from Fox News for calling Arizona for Biden, has an interesting perspective: "Having worked in cable news for more than a decade after a wonderfully misspent youth in newspapers, I can tell you the result: a nation of news consumers both overfed and malnourished. Americans gorge themselves daily on empty informational calories, indulging their sugar fixes of self-affirming half-truths and even outright lies."[56]

There are growing concerns about the freedom of speech, especially in the current "cancel culture." For Hugo Gurdon, "free speech as both a principle and an operational element of Western democracy is more threatened today than in living memory. News media, cardinal beneficiaries of the First Amendment, are among the most vociferous voices demanding that dissenters be gagged."[57] Steve Coll, dean of Columbia's Graduate School of Journalism, recently lamented, "Those of us in journalism have to come to terms with the fact that free speech, a principle we hold sacred, is being weaponized against the principles of journalism."[58]

As I have argued in recent publications, issues of access, free speech, and censorship are real and threaten our democracy. And the practice of contemporary journalism is at a crossroads. I have also argued that the last four or five years are just a reflection and culmination of decades of political, cultural, and social fragmentation. Trumpism and the extremes of the left and right are not the larger issue. They are symptoms of the state of our polity. Thus, democratic government is a reflection of its citizens. In terms of journalism, it is essential that it provides the information needed for critical thinking and understanding of issues and events. The current practice is failing in its responsibilities and obligations to the nation and democracy.

NOTES

1. This was discussed at great length and provides the basis of some content for this chapter. See Robert E. Denton Jr., "Media Coverage and the Practice of Journalism in the 2020 Presidential Campaign," in *The 2020 Presidential Campaign: A Communication Perspective,* Robert E. Denton Jr., ed. (Lanham, MD: Rowman & Littlefield, 2021), 94–98, and "Introduction and Overview: The Historic and Tragic Presidential

Campaign of 2020," in *Studies of Communication in the 2020 Presidential Campaign,* Robert E. Denton Jr., ed. (Lanham, MD: Lexington Books, 2021), 22–29.

2. Michael Delli Carpini, "When Worlds Collide: Contentious Politics in a Fragmented Media Regime," in *U.S. Election Analysis 2020: Media, Voters and the Campaign,* Daniel Jackson et al., eds. (Center for Comparative Politics and Media Research, November 2020), 77.

3. Ezra Klein, "Why the Media Is So Polarized—and How It Polarizes Us," VOX, January 28, 2020, https://www.vox.com/2020/1/28/21077888/why-were-polarized-media-book-ezra-news, retrieved January 29, 2020.

4. See Denton, "Media Coverage," pp. 94–98.

5. Amy Mitchell et al., "Americans Who Mainly Get Their News on Social Media Are Less Engaged, Less Knowledgeable," Pew Research Center, July 30, 2020, https://www.journalism.org/2020/07/30/americans-who-mainly-get-their-news-on-social-media-are-less-engaged-less-knowledgeable/, retrieved July 30, 2020.

6. Ibid.

7. Elahe Izadi, "The New Journalism—and the PR Firms behind It," *The Washington Post,* June 4, 2021, https://www.msn.com/en-us/news/us/the-new-journalism-and-the-pr-firms-behind-it/ar-AAKIjgD, retrieved June 8, 2021.

8. Mark Jurkowitz et al., "Americans Are Divided by Party in the Sources They Turn to for Political News," Pew Research Center, January 24, 2020, https://www.journalism.org/2020/01/24/americans-are-divided-by-party-in-the-sources-they-turn-to-for-political-news/, retrieved December 2, 2020.

9. Kalev Leetaru, "Visual Narratives: A Fracturing of the Nightly News," Real Clear Politics, February 13, 2020, https://www.realclearpolitics.com/articles/2020/02/13/visual_narratives_a_fracturing_of_the_nightly_news_142385.html, retrieved February 14, 2020.

10. See Denton, "Media Coverage and the Practice of Journalism in the 2020 Presidential Campaign," 100–111.

11. "How U.S. Media Lost the Trust of the Public," Canadian Broadcast Corporation, March 28, 2021, https://www.cbc.ca/news/world/media-distrust-big-news-1.5965622, retrieved April 6, 2021.

12. Jeffrey McCall, "News Media Take Losing Streak into 2020," January 2, 2020, https://thehill.com/opinion/technology/476470-news-media-take-losing-streak-into-2020, retrieved January 5, 2020.

13. "How U.S. Media Lost the Trust of the Public."

14. Megan Brenan, "Americans Remain Distrustful of Mass Media," Gallup, September 9, 2020, https://news.gallup.com/poll/321116/americans-remain-distrustful-mass-media.aspx, retrieved September 30, 2020.

15. "American Views 2020: Trust, Media and Democracy," Knight Foundation, August 4, 2020, https://knightfoundation.org/reports/american-views-2020-trust-media-and-democracy/, retrieved August 8, 2020.

16. Megan Brenan and Helen Stubbs, "News Media Viewed as Biased but Crucial to Democracy," Gallup, August 4, 2020, https://news.gallup.com/poll/316574/news-media-viewed-biased-crucial-democracy.aspx?utm_source=alert&utm

_medium=email&utm_content=morelink&utm_campaign=syndication, retrieved August 4, 2020.

17. "American Views 2020: Trust, Media and Democracy."

18. Ibid.

19. "Media Less Aggressive with President Biden Than They Were with Trump Voters Say," Rasmussen Reports, February 4, 2021, https://www.rasmussen reports.com/public_content/politics/biden_ad...campaign=RR02042021DN&utm _source=criticalimpact&utm_medium=email, retrieved February 4, 2021.

20. "At 100 Day Mark: Coverage of Biden Has Been Slightly More Negative Than Positive, Varied Greatly by Outlet Type," Pew Research Center, April 28, 2021, https://www.journalism.org/2021/04/28/at-100-day-mark-coverage-...01&utm _medium=email&utm_term=0_3e953b9b70-f6ef56ee84-399745905, retrieved May 5, 21.

21. Tim Graham, "CNN's View of Rioters Depends on Its Politics," Daily Signal, May 19, 2021, https://www.dailysignal.com/2021/05/19/cnns-view-of-rioters-de pen...9fYRGjK9OZn5FZqwnCViRB7zD_I2jCI_p-GrLW7IuJiiBDKk_3VQ_JTJJd dCUN1c, retrieved May 20, 2021.

22. Elisa Shearer, "Two-Thirds of U.S. Adults Say They've Seen Their Own News Sources Report Facts Meant to Favor One Side," Pew Research Center, November 2, 2020, https://www.pewresearch.org/fact-tank/2020/11/02/two-thirds-of-u-s-a ...ve-seen-their-own-news-sources-report-facts-meant-to-favor-one-side/, retrieved November 24, 2020.

23. Noah Manskar, "Jack Dorsey Says Blocking *Post*'s Hunter Biden Story was 'Total Mistake'—But Won't Say Who Made It," *New York Post*, March 25, 2021, https://nypost.com/2021/03/25/dorsey-says-blocking-posts-hunter-b... _medium=SocialFlow&utm_campaign=SocialFlow&utm_source=NYPTwitter, retrieved March 26, 2021.

24. Kalev Leetaru, "The Great Social Silencing," Real Clear Politics, January 12, 2021, https://www.realclearpolitics.com/articles/2021/01/12/the_great_social_silenc ing_145014.html, retrieved January 12, 2021.

25. Josh Gerstein, "Justice Thomas Grumbles over Trump's Social Media Ban," Politico, May 5, 2021, https://www.politico.com/news/2021/04/05/justice-clarence -thomas-trump-twitter-ban-479046, retrieved April 5, 2021.

26. Kirsten Worden and Amy Mitchel, "Trump Mentioned in about Half of Biden Stories during Early Weeks in Office, But Less So over Time," Pew Research Center, May 24, 2021, https://www.pewresearch.org/fact-tank/2021/05/24/trump-mentioned -in-a...of-biden-stories-during-early-weeks-in-office-but-less-so-over-time/, retrieved May 30, 2021.

27. Ibid.

28. Ben Johnson, "The Media Can't Quit Trump," DailyWire.com, May 26, 2021, https://www.dailywire.com/news/the-media-cant-quit-trump-nearly-40-of-all-stories -about-joe-biden-mention-donald-trump, retrieved May 30, 2021.

29. Christopher Bedford, "Saturday's Media Declaration Is a Naked Attempt to Silence Republicans, and Nothing Has Changed," *The Federalist*, November 7,

2020, https://thefederalist.com/2020/11/07/saturdays-media-declaration-is-a-naked -attempt-to-silence-republicans-and-nothing-has-changed/, retrieved November 11, 2020.

30. "Vainglory of the Press," *New York Sun, November 20, 2020*, https://www .nysun.com/editorials/vainglory-of-the-press/91341/, retrieved November 23, 2020.

31. "Anomalies in Vote Counts and Their Effects," Vote Integrity, November 24, 2020, https://votepatternanalysis.substack.com/p/voting-anomalies-2020, retrieved December 17, 2020; Julie Kelly, "Will This Texas Lawsuit Overturn the 2020 Election?" American Greatness, December 8, 2020, https://amgreatness. com/2020/12/08/will-this-texas-lawsuit-overturn-the-2020-election, retrieved December 10, 2020; Fred Lucas, "7 Takeaways from a Senate Panel's Hearing on Election Fraud," @FredLucasWH, December 16, 2020, https://www.dailysignal .com/2020/12/16/7-takeaways-from-a-s...w4dm9YZW9XTXVUdTZENVZDSE-plQzFYWWRyVUQwRFBcL1ppOWN5Z0xhNCJ9, retrieved December 17, 2020; Patrick Basham, "Reasons Why the 2020 Presidential Election Is Deeply Puzzling," Spectator USA, November 30, 2020, https://spectator.us/reasons-why-the-2020-pres idential-election-is-deeply-puzzling/, retrieved November 30, 2020; "Anomalies in Vote Counts and Their Effects on Election 2020," Voter Integrity Project, November 24, 2020, https://votepatternanalysis.substack.com/p/voting-anomalies-2020, retrieved December 1, 2020; David Catron, "Legitimacy of Biden Win Buried by Objective Data," *The American Spectator*, November 30, 2020, https://spectator.org /legitimacy-of-biden-win-buried-by-objective-data/, retrieved December 1, 2020.

32. John Malcolm, "No One Knows Full Extent of Election Fraud. That's Why We Track It," Daily Signal, May 25, 2021, https://www.dailysignal.com/2021/05/25 /no-one-knows-full-extent...VPgyFMzxDbeCUR6xygfvCftzGgp_HYfF9DI_Pm JlMDPd3QfcLDFMgXgspANiRt4, retrieved May 26, 2021.

33. "Months after Trump Complaints, Some Courts Are Finding Irregularities in 2020 Elections," Just the News.Com, March 18, 2021, https://justthenews.com /politics-policy/elections/thumonths-after-trump-complaints-some-courts-are-finding -illegalities, retrieved March 18, 2021.

34. Ibid.

35. "A River of Doubt Runs through Mail Voting in Montana," *Real Clear Politics*, March 24, 2021, https://www.realclearinvestigations.com/articles/2021/03/24/a _river_of_doubt_runs_through_mail_voting_in_big_sky_country_769321.html, retrieved March 25, 2021.

36. Kate Brumback and Nicholas Riccardi, "It's Not Just Arizona: Push to Review 2020 Ballots Spreads," Associated Press, May 25, 2021, https://abcnews.go.com /Politics/wireStory/arizona-push-review-2020-...ots-spreads-77886569?cid=clicksou rce_4380645_5_film_strip_icymi_hed, retrieved May 26, 2021.

37. Cameron Jenkins, "Trump Slams Supreme Court Decision to Throw Out Election Lawsuit," *The Hill,* December 12, 2020, https://thehill.com/homenews /administration/529940-trump-slams-supreme-court-decision-to-throw-out-election -lawsuit, retrieved December 29, 2020.

38. John R. Lott, "A Simple Test for the Extent of Vote Fraud with Absentee Ballots in the 2020 Presidential Election: Georgia and Pennsylvania Data," Social

Science Research Network, December 29, 2020, https://papers.ssrn.com/sol3/papers.cfm?abstract_id=3756988, retrieved December 30, 2020.

39. Ibid.

40. Alexa Corse and Jon Kamp, "States' New Voting Laws: What You Need to Know," *Wall Street Journal*, May 11, 2021, https://www.wsj.com/articles/states-new-voting-laws-what-you-need-to-know-11619791761, retrieved June 2, 2021.

41. Hannah Hartig, "In Their Own Words: How Americans Reacted to the Rioting at the U.S. Capitol," Pew Research Center, January 15, 2021, https://www.pewresearch.org/fact-tank/2021/01/15/in-their-own-words-how-americans-reacted-to-the-rioting-at-the-u-s-capitol/, retrieved January 30, 2021.

42. "Americans' Concern Grows about Government, National Discord," Gallup, January 25, 2021, https://news.gallup.com/poll/328754/americans-concern-grows-government-national-discord.aspx?version=print, retrieved January 25, 2021.

43. Karoun Demirjian, "Capitol Police Had Intelligence Indicating an Armed Invasion Weeks before Jan. 6 Riot, Senate Probe Finds," *The Washington Post*, June 8, 2021, https://www.washingtonpost.com/national-security/january-6-senate-i...tigation/2021/06/08/a8cc5b1e-c7d4-11eb-81b1-34796c7393af_story.html, retrieved June 8, 2021.

44. Clare Hymes, Cassidy McDonald, Eleanor Watson, "What We Know about the 'Unprecedented' U.S. Capitol Riot Arrests," *CBS News*, June 1, 2021, https://www.cbsnews.com/news/capitol-riot-arrests-latest-2021-06-01/, retrieved June 2, 2021.

45. Govind Bhutada, "How News Media Is Describing the Incident at the U.S. Capitol," Visualcapitalist.com, January 16, 2021, https://www.visualcapitalist.com/how-news-media-is-describing-the-incident-at-the-u-s-capitol/, retrieved June 2, 2021.

46. Ibid.

47. David Bauder, "Riot? Insurrection? Words Matter in Describing Capitol Siege," Associated Press, January 14, 2021, https://apnews.com/article/donald-trump-capitol-siege-riots-media-8000ce7db2b176c1be386d945be5fd6a, retrieved January 16, 2021.

48. Rasmussen Reports, "Voters Don't Agree with Biden and Media on Riots," June 4, 2021, https://www.rasmussenreports.com/public_content/politics/current_events/terrorism/voters_don_t_agree_with_biden_and_media_on_riots, retrieved June 5, 2021.

49. Ibid.

50. Brian Naylor, "Read Trump's Jan. 6 Speech," National Public Radio, February 10, 2021, https://www.npr.org/2021/02/10/966396848/read-trumps-jan-6-speech-a-key-part-of-impeachment-trial, retrieved February 13, 2021.

51. Fred Lucas, "6 Highlights from Congress' First Hearing on Capitol Riot," DailySignal.com, February 23, 2021, https://www.dailysignal.com/2021/02/23/6-highlights-from-congre...Ph40q6xxHjnPaXWIMZyGzdc-SjVl9my59wbybSfwx4RPcafqbVdF0G7_drPUpZ0, retrieved February 24, 2021.

52. Devlin Barrett, Spencer Hsu, and Aaron Davis, "'Be Ready to Fight': FBI Probe of U.S. Capitol Riot Finds Evidence Detailing Coordination of an Assault," *The Washington Post,* January 30, 2021, https://www.washingtonpost.com/national

-security/fbi-capitol-riot-co...planning/2021/01/30/c5ef346e-6258-11eb-9430
-e7c77b5b0297_story.htm, retrieved January 31, 2021.

53. See Robert E. Denton Jr., "Media Coverage," 94–98.

54. Frank Miele, "Propaganda, Election Fraud and the Death of Journalism," Real Clear Politics, November 23, 2020, https://www.realclearpolitics.com/articles /2020/11/23/propaganda_election_fraud_and_the_death_of_journalism_144705 .html, retrieved November 23, 2020.

55. John MacArthur, "The Decline of American Journalism," *The Spectator*, February 18, 2021, https://spectator.us/topic/decline-american-journalism-new-york -times-donald-mcneil/, retrieved February 18, 2021.

56. Chris Stirewalt, "I Called Arizona for Biden on Fox News. Here's What I Learned," *Los Angeles Times*, January 28, 2021, https://www.latimes.com/opinion/story /2021-01-28/fox-news-chris-stirewalt-firing-arizona, retrieved May 25, 2021.

57. Hugo Gurdon, "Doubts Grow in Freedom's Last Redoubt," *Washington Examiner*, January 28, 2021, https://www.washingtonexaminer.com/opinion/doubts-grow -in-freedoms-last-redoubt, retrieved January 30, 2021.

58. Ibid.

Chapter 4

Trump's Address at the January 6, 2021, "Save America" Rally

Inciting Insurrection or Protected Speech?

W. Wat Hopkins

On January 6, 2021, Donald Trump began his third campaign to hold on to the presidency. His first ended in November 2020 when Joe Biden garnered 306 electoral votes to Trump's 232. His second ended when virtually all the lawsuits brought on his behalf to overturn election results failed.[1] His third campaign was designed to mobilize into action the radical right of his party to stop Congress from certifying the election. That campaign failed, too, even though Trump was successful in inciting a riot.

Speaking to possibly as many as ten thousand followers,[2] Trump rambled about a variety of topics. He touted his own accomplishments and attacked Democrats both generically and by name—President Joe Biden and his son, Hunter Biden, Hillary Clinton, Stacey Abrams, and former president and first lady Barrack and Michelle Obama. He also attacked the media, Twitter, and weak Republicans—Senators Mitch McConnell and Mitt Romney, Representative Liz Cheney, Georgia governor Brian Kemp, and former attorney general Bill Barr.[3]

The central focus of the speech was his claim that the election was rigged or fraudulent or stolen. He said so some fifteen times. Six times, he wondered whether Vice President Mike Pence would act to save the election or be complicit in its theft. Seven times he worried that the country would be lost or demanded that "we're not going to let it happen," because "we're going to fight like hell." His supporters, he said, should "be brave," "show strength," and "never forget." Once he suggested that the members of the audience be peaceful, and three times he suggested they walk down Pennsylvania Avenue to the Capitol—twice he said he was going to walk with them, though he didn't.[4]

Trump's words—as ink on paper, or as political rhetoric at a rally—are hardly incendiary and almost certainly would not rise to the level of incitement. Those words in context, however—before a rambunctious crowd whose anger had been stoked for weeks, if not months, a crowd whose members had been encouraged to violence and had planned violent activity, based in part on the president's tweets and speeches—constituted a spark that ignited a flame.

He was impeached for incitement of insurrection January 13, but the Republican-controlled Senate refused to receive the article until after Trump was out of office, then argued that a trial would be unconstitutional because Trump was no longer in office. He was acquitted February 13 when fifty-seven senators voted to find him guilty and forty-three voted not guilty—a two-thirds majority (sixty-seven) was required for conviction.

The Senate shenanigans did not escape a barrage of criticism. The *New York Times* wrote that evidence presented at the impeachment demonstrated that Trump convinced his loyalists that "the only way to save their nation was to 'fight like hell.'" Trump whipped them into a rage, the *Times* wrote, "summoned them to Washington, pointed them at the Congress and then retreated to the safety of the White House to enjoy the show."[5] The *Washington Post* wrote that Trump "fed his mob lies, told them they were losing their country and directed them to the Capitol when it was obvious they did not mean to conduct orderly protest." They began streaming toward the sitting Congress, the *Post* added, even before Trump finished speaking.[6] In calling for Trump's conviction, the *Post* likened his behavior to a fire chief who encouraged arsonists to light a blaze "then hardly lifted a finger to put it out." The town's leaders, the *Post* wrote, "would dismiss that fire chief and bar that person from ever again serving in the role."[7]

Even some Republicans joined in. Liz Cheney, Wyoming's lone member of Congress, said, "There's no question the president formed the mob. . . . He lit the flame."[8] And Senate Majority Leader Mitch McConnell, after voting to acquit Trump, said the former president was guilty of a "disgraceful dereliction of duty." There was no question, he said, that "President Trump is practically and morally responsible for provoking the events of the day."[9]

Twitter permanently suspended Trump's account two days after the attack on the Capitol "due to the risk of further incitement of violence." After the "horrific events this week," Twitter announced, it found that additional violations of the company's rules "would potentially result in this very course of action." Twitter cited as evidence Trump's announcement that he would not be attending the inauguration, a possible sign that "the Inauguration would be a 'safe' target, as he would not be there."[10]

Eventually, Trump was sued in federal court on allegations related to his role in the attack. Representative Eric Swalwell of California, one of the House managers in the impeachment, charged that "the horrific events of January 6 were a direct and foreseeable consequence of the Defendants' unlawful actions." Swalwell also named Rudolph Giuliani and Representative Mo Brooks in the suit, seeking compensatory and punitive damages to be determined at trial.[11]

Public criticism means as little to the law as it does to impeachment proceedings, however. Incitement to insurrection is not protected by the First Amendment because it constitutes words that are "no essential part of any exposition of ideas, and are of such slight value as a step to truth that any benefit that may be derived from them is clearly outweighed by the social interest in order and morality."[12] Specifically, the government may protect itself "against incitements to commit unlawful acts."[13] It is better, the Supreme Court held, to "discuss the public issues of the day . . . without incitement to violence or crime,"[14] and effect change through "attack by ballot."[15]

The evidence against President Trump was compelling,[16] but proving incitement is an onerous task. Incitement "blurs, if not obliterates, 'the fundamental distinction between speech and conduct,'"[17] which is sometimes difficult to demarcate. The Supreme Court has recognized the difficulty in determining "whether ambiguous speech is advocacy of political methods or subtly shades into a methodical but prudent incitement to violence," that is, when political rhetoric crosses the line to become inciteful speech. But the Court has found that "the Constitution enjoins upon us the duty, however difficult, of distinguishing between the two."[18]

Seventeen years after recognizing that responsibility, the Court established a test for determining whether speech constitutes incitement of illegal conduct or is protected by the First Amendment. In *Brandenburg v. Ohio*, the Court held that such a determination rests upon: (1) whether a speaker intended to incite violence, (2) whether such violence was imminent, (3) and whether it was likely.[19]

The ruling, scholars have asserted, was "a clear break" from First Amendment precedent because it added "imminence" and "likelihood" to the long-established element of criminal advocacy in determining whether speech crossed the threshold.[20] Until *Brandenburg,* the guidance in such cases grew primarily from Justice Oliver Wendell Holmes, who wrote:

> The character of every act depends upon the circumstances in which it is done. . . . The question in every case is whether the words used are used in such circumstances and are of such a nature as to create a clear and present danger that they will bring about the substantive evils that Congress has a right to prevent. It is a question of proximity and degree.[21]

The *Brandenburg* opinion was incomplete, however. It provided no guidance on the application of the elements;[22] the Court did not define either "imminence" or "likelihood," leaving that chore for another day.

INCITING VIOLENCE

Brandenburg was the first of three cases in which the Court delineated its incitement jurisprudence.[23] Clarence Brandenburg was convicted of advocating the use of violence to accomplish industrial or political reform and challenged the conviction on First Amendment grounds.[24] He was captured on film at a Ku Klux Klan rally saying, "We're not a revengent [*sic*] organization, but if our President, our Congress, our Supreme Court, continues to suppress the white, Caucasian race, it's possible that there might have to be some revengence [*sic*] taken."[25]

In an unsigned opinion, the Court reiterated its position that "the mere abstract teaching . . . of the moral propriety or even moral necessity for a resort to force and violence, is not the same as preparing a group for violent action and steeling it to such action."[26] The Court held that a state can only proscribe advocacy of force if "such advocacy is directed to inciting or producing imminent lawless action and is likely to incite or produce such action,"[27] thus delineating the three elements.

Four years later, in *Hess v. Indiana*,[28] the Court clarified the *Brandenburg* test only slightly. When civil rights activists in Bloomington were asked to disperse, a leader of the group told the protesters that "we'll take the fucking streets later."[29] The Court found that "later" did not mean "imminent." "At best," the Court held, "the statement could be taken as counsel for present moderation; at worst, it amounted to nothing more than advocacy of illegal action at some indefinite future time." Therefore, there was no intent "to incit[e] or produc[e] imminent lawless action" or speech that was "likely to incite or produce such action."[30] Intent, the Court suggested, could be determined "from the import of the language" that "words were intended to produce" imminent disorder.[31]

Put differently, *Brandenburg* featured a requirement that a speaker had the purpose to produce the disorder. The requirement, First Amendment scholar Clay Calvert wrote, marked a significant development in the evolution of the incitement doctrine because no previous test required intent.[32]

The Court's third incitement case, nine years later, was *NAACP v. Claiborne Hardware Co.*,[33] which had its origins during civil unrest in Claiborne County, Mississippi. White merchants filed a lawsuit against a number of Black defendants seeking compensation for revenue alleged to have been lost due to a boycott of their businesses.[34] The merchants, among other claims, alleged that Charles Evers, the field secretary for the NAACP in Mississippi, was liable because he threatened violence against residents who did not honor the boycott. Evers was clearly aggressive in his advocacy. In organizational meetings, he used strong language to warn residents that they were expected to participate in the boycott. "Store watchers" and "Black hats" would be watching,[35] he said, and, "if we catch any of you going in any of them racist stores, we're gonna break your damn neck."[36]

This kind of enthusiasm for the cause prompted Justice John Paul Stevens, writing for the Court, to characterize the debate as including "elements of criminality and elements of majesty."[37] He wrote: "Evidence that persuasive rhetoric, determination to remedy past injustices, and a host of voluntary decisions by free citizens were critical factors in the boycott's success presents us with the question whether the state court's judgment is consistent with the Constitution of the United States."[38]

It was not.

The judge in the case, called a "chancellor," awarded plaintiffs damages for all business losses sustained during a seven-year period, from 1966 to the end of 1972,[39] even though he did not find that any act of violence occurred after 1966.[40] The nonviolent elements of the boycott, Justice Stevens held, were entitled to First Amendment protection,[41] so the damage award could not be sustained.[42]

Justice Stevens also found, specifically, that Evers's speech "did not transcend the bounds of protected speech set forth in *Brandenburg*."[43] Some of Evers's language, including the references to broken necks, "in the passionate atmosphere in which the speeches were delivered, . . . might have been understood as inviting an unlawful form of discipline or, at least, as intending to create a fear of violence whether or not improper discipline was specifically intended." Justice Stevens wrote that neither violence nor words that create an immediate panic are protected by the First Amendment.[44] But Evers's language—though strong—did not reach the level of speech proscribed by *Brandenburg*: "If that language had been followed by acts of violence, a substantial question would be presented whether Evers could be held liable for the consequences of that unlawful conduct."[45]

Specifically, Justice Stevens held that "when such appeals do not incite lawless action, they must be regarded as protected speech."[46] Therefore:

> We conclude that Evers' addresses did not exceed the bounds of protected speech. If there were other evidence of his authorization of wrongful conduct, the references to discipline in the speeches could be used to corroborate that evidence. But any such theory fails for the simple reason that there is no evidence—apart from the speeches themselves—that Evers authorized, ratified, or directly threatened acts of violence.[47]

Claiborne Hardware, therefore, adds to the *Brandenburg* test for incitement. Adding to the intent, incitement, and likelihood elements, *Claiborne Hardware* requires the presence of violence. Without lawless action, the

Court held, the advocacy to violence "must be regarded as protected speech." Therefore, as Richard Ashby Wilson and Jordan Kiper write, had there been violence after Evers's remarks, the outcome of *Claiborne Hardware* may have been decidedly different.[48]

Also, as a result of *Claiborne Hardware,* the context of speech became more important to a determination of incitement. The context requirement grew out of a clear and present danger test enunciated by Justice Oliver Wendell Holmes in *Schenck v. United States.* The question in all cases, Justice Holmes wrote, is one of "proximity and degree."[49] In an earlier case, Justice Holmes had written that constitutional provisions "are not mathematical formulas having their essence in their form; they are organic, living institutions transplanted from England soil. The(ir) significance is vital, not formal; it is to be gathered not simply by taking the words and a dictionary, but by considering their origin and the line of their growth."[50]

The Court has supported that proposition by noting that the definition of "vagueness"—key to the question of the constitutionality of many restrictions on speech—was not always contingent upon dictionaries, but on context: "The applicable standard . . . is not one of wholly consistent academic definition of abstract terms. It is, rather, the practical criterion of fair notice to those to whom the statute is directed. The particular context is all important."[51]

In two later cases, the Court upheld the essence of the *Claiborne Hardware* rule, though it did not cite the case. The Court, in these two cases, emphasized the importance of context. In *Texas v. Johnson,*[52] the Court was called upon to determine the constitutionality of a state law prohibiting the burning of the American flag. Texas attempted to justify the law by arguing that it was necessary to prevent breaches of the peace.[53] In the case involving Gregory Lee Johnson, however, "no disturbance of the peace actually occurred or threatened to occur because of Johnson's burning of the flag."[54] The Court also noted that the context in which the flag burning occurred was important.[55] The government's interest in preserving the flag as a symbol "is directly related to expression in the context of activity."[56] The context of the flag burning was political protest, which receives the highest degree of First Amendment protection.

Similarly, in *Virginia v. Black,*[57] the Court found that Virginia's prohibition against cross burning "ignores all of the contextual factors that are necessary to decide whether a particular cross burning is intended to intimidate. The First Amendment does not permit such a shortcut."[58] The problem with the Virginia law was that it mandated that all cross burning be regarded as an intent to intimidate. Persons charged with the crime, therefore, were required to demonstrate that the context of their activity was not, in fact, for the purpose of intimidating any person or group of people, an unconstitutional requirement.

Finally, in finding the outrageous picketing of the Westboro Baptist Church at the funeral of a serviceman to be protected, the Court held that the context of the protest was as important as the content of the signs church members displayed.[59] In *Snyder v. Phelps,* Chief Justice John Roberts wrote for the Court, "In considering content, form, and context, no factor is dispositive, and it is necessary to evaluate all the circumstances of the speech, including what was said, where it was said, and how it was said."[60]

The Court made it clear, therefore, that in determining whether speech incites violent action, it would consider the context of the speech act along with the intent of the speaker and the likelihood of imminent illegal conduct. If the only evidence of incitement, the Court has said, is that speech "authorized, ratified or directly threatened acts of violence" was the speech itself, the charge of incitement fails.[61]

BRANDENBURG APPLIED

"Reciting *Brandenburg*'s elements is simple," one First Amendment scholar wrote, "but applying them is complicated."[62] Indeed, scholars have written that the legal system "does not possess a systematic framework to evaluate which speech causes the greatest risk of violence,"[63] in part because "*Brandenburg* provides no guidance on the three elements of the test."[64] Scholars Richard Ashby Wilson and Jordan Kiper have written that courts have spelled out to some degree the meaning of *advocacy* and *imminence* but have provided "very little direction regarding how likely crime must be."[65] Clay Calvert, on the other hand, writes that the Court has never explicitly explained its understanding of "imminence," except that "later" means absence of imminence.[66]

The ambiguity in the law is likely a key reason that First Amendment scholars disagree over whether Trump's speech cleared the *Brandenburg* hurdle or was tripped by it.[67] Adam Liptak, Supreme Court reporter for the *New York Times,* suggests that Trump's mixed message—his call to march peacefully juxtaposed against his vitriol about the election—might make the difference.[68] Catherine J. Ross, however, writes that incitement can be implicit as well as explicit. Context matters, she writes, and Trump's apparent calls for peace could have been undercut by his repeated claims that the election had been stolen in tandem with his earlier exhortations, like that of December 19, 2020: "Big protest. . . . Be there, will be wild."[69] Sending different messages is part of Trump's style, Fabiola Cineas writes. He sometimes denounces violence, but usually walks back those denunciations.[70] Suzanne Nossel writes that a court would likely find that the second two elements of *Brandenburg* were met: "Violent mayhem erupted right after Trump's fiery speech at the

Ellipse, meeting the requirements of both imminence and likelihood." That same court, however, might not find that Trump advocated the violence.[71]

The debate calls for a more detailed examination of Trump's speech to determine whether it was protected by the First Amendment or constituted incitement to illegal conduct. The speech must be weighed against the three-part *Brandenburg* within the context of its delivery.

Intent

Simple declarative statements demanding violent action are clear evidence of a speaker's intent. Incitement can be achieved in other ways, however. A speaker who understands the state of mind of an audience and who is familiar with past responses of that audience can intentionally incite violence with subtle language that plays on emotions and temperament.[72] Were members of an audience already riled up, for example? Did they arrive at a rally in a fervent state? Under those circumstances, Clay Calvert suggests, "more neutral sounding [words] would likely produce the same violent results."[73] Indeed, the Court has said as much. In *Hess,* for example, it suggested that intent can be determined by a "rational inference from the import of the language."[74] Context, the Court has said, "is all important."[75]

Trump's supporters at the "Save America" rally were clearly animated and showed up on January 6 expecting to engage in some kind of action.

Talk of a response to what they believed to be a stolen election began on social media outlets even before most major news organizations declared Joe Biden the winner. Trump was a party to the uproar. Early on the morning of November 4, he tweeted:

> This is a fraud on the American public. This is an embarrassment to our country. We were getting ready to win this election—frankly, we did win. . . . We want all voting to stop. We don't want them to find any ballots at 4 o'clock in the morning and add them to the list.[76]

Others joined the president's call. The first "Stop the Steal" movement began on Facebook the same day. It reached 320,000 followers before Facebook shut it down. On Fox News, Newt Gingrich, former House speaker, predicted that Trump's supporters would erupt in rage.[77] And supporters wrote that they were "awaiting direction." One wrote that the Biden presidency would mean that "our way of life as we know it is over. Our Republic would be over. Then it is our duty as Americans to fight, kill and die for our rights." Another wrote, "If Trump asks me to come, I will." And another, "War is on the horizon."[78]

By December, many of the radicals on social media were conversing in the language of insurrection, and Trump joined the discussion, tweeting, "Big protest in D.C. on January 6th. Be there, will be wild."[79] One supporter wrote that she was going to Washington for the rally because "Trump wants all able bodied Patriots to come."[80] In the meantime, followers were moving from state to state encouraging select senators to object to the congressional vote counting.[81] Radical groups were planning training sessions for "urban warfare" and appeared to be "awaiting direction" from Trump. One supporter tweeted that "POTUS has the right to activate units, too."[82]

As the rally date drew near, Trump continued to tweet about a stolen election. He was also tweeting about the upcoming rally—he tweeted about it five times on January 1. The same day, one supporter tweeted, "The calvary [*sic*] is coming, Mr. President." Trump responded, "A great honor!" And, the day before the rally, another tweeted, "If you are not prepared to use force to defend civilization, then be prepared to accept barbarism."[83]

There is little doubt, therefore, that Trump supporters arrived in Washington animated, even riled up. In addition, speakers stoked the fire during a rally the night before Trump's speech. One speaker told the crowd, "We are standing on the precipice of history, and we are ready to take our country back." Then, apparently addressing the president, she said, "We heard your call. We are here for you."[84]

The next day, before Trump spoke, Rudolph Giuliani told the waiting crowd that "trial by combat" against the Democrats was needed to win the election. And Donald Trump Jr. added that Republican members of Congress who did not back the pro-Trump efforts were also targeted. "We're coming for you," he said.[85]

The president's response to the attack is also a tell as to his intent. He did not heed the advice of White House counsel and others that he should attempt to quell the riot.[86] And when Representative Kevin McCarthy encouraged Trump to make a plea for the rioters to stop, Trump's reported response was, "Well, Kevin, I guess these people are more upset about the election than you are."[87]

A startling piece of evidence was the president's response to the plight of Vice President Mike Pence, whom Trump had previously attacked in tweets. Pence was rushed from the Senate floor about 2:12 p.m. while rioters were chanting, "Hang Mike Pence." About 2:34 p.m., shortly after live television coverage of Pence being escorted out of the chamber by security, Trump tweeted, "Mike Pence didn't have the courage to do what should have been done to protect our Country and Constitution. . . . USA demands the truth."[88]

Trump, therefore, must have understood the tenor of the crowd when he began his speech.

He also clearly understood the reaction his words could cause, based on a long history of provoking violence at rallies. That cause-and-effect dated to at least his first presidential campaign. Beginning in 2015, at rallies in Miami, Birmingham, Louisville, and Fayetteville, North Carolina, protestors were assaulted immediately after Trump's verbal assaults.[89] This was a continuing pattern. One observer wrote that Trump's campaign rallies "have always been incubation grounds for violence."[90] Indeed, *ABC News* reported finding fifty-four criminal cases in which Trump had direct connection with violent acts.[91]

One of those cases went to court. Kashiya Nwanguma and others alleged in a federal lawsuit that they were assaulted in response to Trump's verbal attacks at a rally in Louisville. The court refused to dismiss the lawsuit, holding that Trump's orders to "Get 'em out of here" were sufficient to make a claim for liability and, therefore, were not protected by the First Amendment.[92] An appellate court, however, reversed the holding. The U.S. Court of Appeals for the Sixth Circuit conceded that Trump's orders five times to "Get 'em out of here" resulted in members of the audience assaulting the plaintiffs. The court ruled, however, that the plaintiffs failed to make out a valid incitement-to-riot claim under Kentucky law.[93]

Trump could have learned two lessons from the lawsuit. First, his words have force—they result in his supporters taking action, often violent action, against persons perceived to be his opponents. As one commentator wrote, "Trump's messaging on January 6 is precisely in line with how he's historically addressed violence on the part of hate groups and his supporters. He emboldens it."[94] Second, Trump learned that he could get by without liability for the violence he invokes.

It was with this knowledge that President Trump took the podium on January 6.

Imminence

As Clay Calvert writes, the Supreme Court has never explained its understanding of imminence. What is clear, however, is that "later," it is not imminent. While First Amendment experts may be undecided about whether a court would find that Trump intended the riot, they are in general agreement that the speech met the *Brandenburg* elements of imminence and likelihood.

Catherine Ross writes, for example, that Trump's exhortations that the crowd should walk to the Capitol "more than satisfy the imminence requirement."[95] Suzanne Nossel agrees: "Violent mayhem erupted right after Trump's fiery speech at the Ellipse, meeting the requirements of both imminence and likelihood."[96] Indeed, the crowd started toward the Capitol even before Trump had finished his speech.[97] That seems the definition of imminence.

Likelihood

Justice Stevens wrote in *Claiborne Hardware* that the likelihood element of the *Brandenburg* test is satisfied when there is, in fact, a violent response to speech. The absence of lawless action means the appeals for violence "must be regarded as protected speech."[98] The presence, then, of lawless action means *Brandenburg*'s "likelihood" element was met. Trump's speech was a perfect example, and many of his supporters said so.

The day before the riot, one supporter wrote, "This is not a President that sounds like he is giving up on the White House. I truly believe that if we let them complete the steal we will never have a free election again. I really believe we are going to take back what they did on November 3."[99]

Dozens of supporters said they were in attendance because they were obeying Trump. A video captured one man screaming at a police officer, "We were invited by the president of the United States."[100] A woman who flew to Washington from Texas said she was present because the president said, "'Be there.' So I went and answered the call of my president," she continued.[101] Another woman had a similar story. "I thought I was following my president," she said. "I thought I was following what we were called to do. . . . He asked us to fly there. He asked us to be there. So I was doing what he asked us to do."[102]

There is more than anecdotal evidence. *The Atlantic* magazine reported, after examining records of 193 persons charged with being inside the Capitol or with breaking through barriers to enter the grounds, "The overwhelming reason for action, cited again and again in court documents, was that arrestees were following Trump's orders to keep Congress from certifying Joe Biden as the presidential election winner."[103]

Indeed, several attorneys reported that they were going to blame their clients' actions on the president. "The group had gone to the White House and listened to President Donald J. Trump's speech and then had followed the President's instructions and gone to the Capitol," one attorney said.[104] Another said, "What you've got here are people like my client who take the President seriously. . . . They were betrayed by somebody in whom they'd placed their faith."[105] And another lawyer reported that the only reason his client was in Washington was because of the president. "You're being told, 'You gotta fight like hell,'" he said. "Does 'fight like hell' mean you can throw stuff at people. Maybe."[106]

Court documents also indicated that members of the radical Proud Boys group interpreted Trump's comment from a campaign debate, "Stand back and stand by," as meaning, "Await orders from the Commander in Chief."[107]

CONCLUSION

Context is everything.[108] That's why, particularly in law, the precept *post hoc ergo propter hoc* is a fallacy. Its literal definition is "after this, therefore because of this."[109] More colloquially, it means that if incident A occurs *before* incident B, then incident A *caused* incident B. As Justice William O. Douglas wrote in another context, however, "Common sense revolts at the idea."[110] Cause and effect is not based upon chronological happenstance. Sometimes, however, incident A does, in fact, cause incident B. That occurred January 6, 2021, in Washington. And, in this case, common sense would so testify. But we have more than common sense to go on.

Trump's speech at the Ellipse on January 6 did not cause a riot because it was particularly powerful—it was not. Indeed, it was, as is typical of Trump's speeches, self-serving, rambling, and banal. Similarly, the speech did not cause the riot because it was particularly incendiary. It was a mundane, political screed on topics that Trump—as candidate and as president—enjoyed discussing: himself and his critics.

Placed within context, however, the speech was the spark that ignited the historic attack on the Capitol. President Trump intended to incite the riot within a context where violent activity was both likely and imminent.

Likelihood "ultimately depends on a contextual approach that accounts not only for the words used, but also the surrounding context in which those words are uttered."[111] Trump exhorted his supporters—who arrived in Washington after being primed for action, and dozens of whom indicated they were acting in response to Trump's call for action—to march to the Capitol, and, indeed, they began doing so before his speech was concluded.[112] Therefore, as Suzanne Nossel wrote, a court would likely find that the second two elements of the test were met: "Violent mayhem erupted right after Trump's fiery speech at the Ellipse, meeting the requirements of both imminence and likelihood."[113]

The remaining element—intent—is also met. President Trump began stoking the fires of violence even before the election was declared, complaining that it was stolen and that the democracy would be lost in the absence of action to keep him in office. In addition, he repeatedly tweeted about the January 6 rally. He was aware of the tenor of his supporters. It was "A great honor," he tweeted in response to a promise that "The calvary [*sic*] is coming."[114]

By the time the rally began, an aggressive, vitriolic demand for action was unnecessary. "More neutral sounding [words] would likely produce the same violent results,"[115] Clay Calvert wrote. Trump's inactivity during the riot was also telling—it suggests that things were going exactly as he wanted, and he would do nothing to inhibit the activity.[116]

Trump, therefore, satisfied the *Brandenburg* test requiring a speaker to have a purpose to produce violent disorder that was both imminent and likely. As Justice Holmes advised, "The character of every act depends upon the circumstances in which it was done. . . . It is a question of proximity and degree." [117] President Trump's words, spoken "in many places and in ordinary times," might have found themselves impotent, and certainly protected. The time, place, and context of his speech, however, were extraordinary and clearly outside the protection of the First Amendment.

NOTES

1. See chapter 8, Cayce Myers, "Litigating Victory: An Analysis of 2020 Post-election Lawsuits."

2. "It Is Difficult, if Not Impossible, to Estimate the Size of the Crowd That Stormed Capitol Hill," January 8, 2021, https://theconversation.com/it-is-difficult-if-not-impossible-to-estimate-the-size-of-the-crowd-that-stormed-capitol-hill-152889.

3. Transcript, "Donald Trump, Save America Rally," January 6, 2021, https://www.rev.com/blog/transcripts/donald-trump-speech-save-america-rally-transcript-january-6.

4. Ibid.

5. Editorial, "Trump Is Guilty," *New York Times*, February 12, 2021, available at https://www.nytimes.com/2021/02/12/opinion/trump-impeachment-guilty.html?smid=em-share.

6. Editorial, "Trump Trial Has Crystallized the Horror of Jan.6. The Senate Must Convict Him," *Washington Post,* February 10, 2021, available at https://www.washingtonpost.com/opinions/trumps-trial-has-crystallized-the-horror-of-jan-6-the-senate-must-convict-him/2021/02/10/b43dcff6-6be4-11eb-9f80-3d7646ce1bc0_story.html.

7. Ibid.

8. See Maggie Haberman, "Trump Told Crowd 'You Will Never Take Back Our Country with Weakness,'" *New York Times*, January 6, 2021, available at https://www.nytimes.com/2021/01/06/us/politics/trump-speech-capitol.html?action=click&module=RelatedLinks&pgtype=Article.

9. See Carl Hulse and Nicholas Fandos, "McConnell, Denouncing Trump after Voting to Acquit, Says His Hands Were Tied," *New York Times,* February 13, 2021, available at https://www.nytimes.com/2021/02/13/us/mcconnell-trump-impeachment-acquittal.html?smid=em-share.

10. Twitter, "Permanent Suspension of @realDonaldTrump," January 9, 2021, https://blog.twitter.com/en_us/topics/company/2020/suspension.html.

11. *Swalwell v. Trump et al.*, 2021 WL 841306 (D.D.C. Mar. 5, 2021).

12. *Chaplinsky v. New Hampshire,* 315 U.S. 568, 572 (1942). See also *Ashcroft v. Free Speech Coalition*, 535 U.S. 234, 246 (2002).

13. *American Commuc'ns Ass'n C.I.O. v. Douds*, 339 U.S. 382, 394 (1950).

14. *De Jonge v. State of Oregon*, 299 U.S. 353, 365 (1937).

15. *Harisiades v. Shaughnessy*, 342 U.S. 580, 592 (1952).

16. The *Washington Post* established a website on which it posted the evidence presented at the impeachment trial. See "All the Evidence Presented in Trump's Impeachment Trial," *Washington Post*, February 13, 2020, https://www.washingtonpost .com/politics/interactive/2021/evidence-trump-second-impeachment/.

17. Clay Calvert, "First Amendment Envelope Pushers: Revisiting the Incitement-to-Violence Test with Messrs. Brandenburg, Trump & Spencer," 51 *Connecticut Law Review* 111, 121 (2019) (quoting Martin H. Redish, "Fear, Loathing, and the First Amendment: Optimistic Skepticism and the Theory of Free Expression," 76 *Ohio St. L. J.* 691, 700 (2015)).

18. *Harisiades,* 342 U.S. at 592.

19. 395 U.S. 444, 447 (1969).

20. Richard Ashby Wilson and Jordan Kiper, "Incitement in an Era of Populism: Updating Brandenburg after Charlottesville," 5 *U. Pa. J.L.& Pub. Aff.* 189, 204 (2020).

21. *Schenck v. United States,* 249 U.S. 47, 52 (1919).

22. See Wilson and Kiper, supra note 20, at 202.

23. See Calvert, supra note 17, at 117; JoAnne Sweeny, "Incitement in the Era of Trump and Charlottesville," 47 *Cap. U. L.R.* 585, 592–93 (2019).

24. 395 U.S. at 445.

25. Ibid. at 446.

26. Ibid. at 448 (quoting *Noto v. United States*, 367 U.S. 290, 297–98 (1961)).

27. Ibid. at 447.

28. 414 U.S. 105 (1973).

29. Ibid. at 107.

30. Ibid. at 108 (quoting *Brandenburg,* 395 U.S. at 447).

31. Ibid. at 109.

32. Calvert, supra note 17, at 130.

33. 458 U.S. 886 (1982).

34. Ibid. at 888–93.

35. Ibid. at 903.

36. Ibid. at 902.

37. Ibid. at 888.

38. Ibid. at 888–89.

39. Ibid. at 920.

40. Ibid. at 906.

41. Ibid. at 915.

42. Ibid. at 921.

43. Ibid. at 928.

44. Ibid. at 916, 927.

45. Ibid. at 928.

46. Ibid.

47. Ibid. at 929.

48. Wilson and Kiper, supra note 20, at 218.

49. 249 U.S. 47, 52 (1919).

50. *Gombers v. United States*, 233 U.S. 604, 610 (1914).

51. *American Commc'ns Ass'n, C.I.O. v. Douds,* 339 U.S. 382, 412 (1950).

52. 491 U.S. 397 (1989).

53. Ibid. at 407.

54. Ibid. at 408. The Court found, "The only evidence by the State at trial to show the reaction to Johnson's actions was the testimony of several persons who had been seriously offended by the flag burning." Ibid.

55. Ibid. at 405.

56. Ibid. at 410.

57. 538 U.S. 342 (2003).

58. Ibid. at 367. See also *Clark v. Community for Creative Non-Violence*, 463 U.S. 288, 302 (1984) (Marshall, J., dissenting) ("A realistic appraisal of the competing interests at stake in this case requires a closer look at the nature of the expressive conduct at issue and the context in which that conduct would be displayed.").

59. *Snyder v. Phelps*, 562 U.S. 443, 454 (2011).

60. Ibid.

61. *Claiborne Hardware,* 485 U.S. 886, 929 (1982).

62. Calvert, supra note 17, at 126.

63. Wilson and Kiper, *supra* note 20, at 190.

64. Ibid. at 203. Wilson and Kiper suggest a ten-factor test to assist in determining when speech is inciteful. Another author suggests an eight-element test. David Crump, "Camouflaged Incitement: Freedom of Speech, Communicative Torts, and the Borderland of the *Brandenburg* Test," 29 *Ga. L. Rev*. 1, 51 (1994).

65. Wilson and Kiper, supra note 20, at 194.

66. Calvert, supra note 17, at 132–33.

67. See David L. Hudson Jr., "Does the First Amendment Protect Trump on Incitement to Riot?" *First Amendment Watch*, January 14, 2021, https://firstamendment watch.org/does-the-first-amendment-protect-trump-on-incitemebnt-to-riot?.

68. Adam Liptak, "Impeachment Trial May Hinge on Meaning of 'Incitement,'" *New York Times*, February 10, 2021, available at https://nytimes.com/2021/02/10/8s /incitement-court-senators-impeachment.html?smid=em=share.

69. See Catherine J. Ross, "What the First Amendment Really Says about Whether Trump Incited the Capitol Riot," *Slate*, January 19, 2021, https://slate.com /technology/2021/01/trump-incitement-violence-brandenburg-first-amendment-html.

70. Fabiola Cineas, "Donald Trump Is the Accelerant," *ABC News*, January 9, 2021, https://abcnews.go.com/Politics/blame-abc-news-finds-17-cases-invoking -trump/story?id=58912889.

71. Suzanne Nossel, "Don't Let Trump's Second Trial Change the First Amendment," *New York Times*, January 14, 2021, available at https://www.nytimes.com /2021/01/04/opinion/trump-trial-incitement-html?searchResultPosition=5.

72. See Calvert, supra note 17, at 140.

73. Ibid. at 142.

74. 414 U.S. 105, 109 (1973)

75. *American Commc'ns Ass'n, CIA v. Douds,* 339 U.S. 382, 412 (1950).

76. See Jim Rutenberg et al., "77 Days: Trump's Campaign to Subvert the Election," *New York Times*, January 31, 2021, available at https://www.nytimes.com/2021/01/31/us/trump-election-lie.html?action=click&module=Spotlight&pgtype=Homepage.

77. Ibid.

78. Alan Feuer, "Oath Keepers Plotting before Capitol Riot Awaited 'Direction' from Trump, Prosecutors Say," *New York Times*, February 11, 2021, available at https://www.nytimes.com/2021/02/11/us/politics/oath-keepers-trump-investigation.html?referringSource=articleShare.

79. Dan Barry and Sheera Frenkel, "'Be There. Will Be Wild!'": Trump All But Circled the Date," *New York Times*, January 6, 2021, available at https://www.nytimes.com/2021/01/06/us/politics/capitol-mob-trump-supporters.html?searchResultPosition=13.

80. Feuer, supra note 78.

81. See Rutenberg, supra note 76.

82. Feuer, supra note 78.

83. Barry and Fenkel, supra note 79.

84. Rutenberg, supra note 76.

85. Haberman, supra note 8.

86. See Maggie Haberman and Jonathan Martin, "After the Speech: What Trump Did As the Capitol Was Attacked," *New York Times*, February 13, 2021, available at https://www.nytimes.com/2021/02/13/us/politics/trump-capitol-riot.html?smid=em-share.

87. See Nicolas Fandos, "Trump Sided with the Capitol Mob, Herrera Beutler Says McCarthy Told Her," *New York Times*, February 13, 2021, available at https://www.nytimes.com/2021/02/12/us/mccarthy-trump-herrera-beutler.html?smid=em-share.

88. See Haberman and Martin, supra note 86; Rosalind S. Halderman and Josh Dawsey, "Mounting Evidence Suggests Trump Knew of Danger to Pence When He Attacked Him as Lacking 'Courage' amid Capitol Siege," *Washington Post*, February 11, 2021, available at https://www.washingtonpost.com/politics/trump-tweet-pence-capitol/2021/02/11/cc7d9f7e-6c7f-11eb-9f80-3d7646ce1bc0_story.html.

89. See Cineas, supra note 70.

90. Ibid.

91. Mike Levine, "'No Blame?' ABC News Finds 54 Cases Invoking 'Trump' in Connection with Violence, Threats, Alleged Assaults," *ABC News*, May 30, 2020, https://abcnews.go.com/Politics/blame-abc-news-finds-17-cases-invoking-trump/story?id=58912889.

92. *Nwanguma, et al. v. Trump*, 273 F. Supp. 3d 719, 726-27 (W.D. Ky. 2017).

93. *Nwanguma, et al. v. Trump*, 903 F.3d 604, 606-07, 609 (6th Cir. 2018).

94. Cineas, supra note 70.

95. Ross, supra note 69.

96. Nossel, supra note 71.

97. See "Editorial," supra note 6.

98. 458 U.S. 886, 982 (1982). See also discussion accompanying supra notes 44–47.

99. Rosalind S. Helderman, Spencer S. Hsu, and Rachel Weiner, "'Trump Said to do So'": Accounts of Rioters Who say the President Spurred Them to Rush the Capitol Could be Pivotal Testimony," *Washington Post*, January 16, 2021, available at https://www.washingtonpost.com/politics/trump-rioters-testimony/2021/01/16/01b3d5c6-575b-11eb-a931-5b162d0d033d_story.html

100. Ibid.

101. Alan Feuer and Nicole Hong, "'I Answered the Call of My President'": Rioters Say Trump Urged Them On," *New York Times*, January 17, 2021, available at https://www.nytimes.com/2021/01/17/nyregion/protesters-blaming-trump-pardon.html?searchResultPosition=1.

102. Helderman et al., supra note 99.

103. Robert A. Pape and Keven Ruby, "The Capital Rioters Aren't Like Other Extremists," *The Atlantic,* February 2, 2021, available at https://www.theatlantic.com/ideas/archive/2021/02/the-capitol-rioters-arent-like-other-extremists/617895/?utm_source=newsletter&utm_medium=email&utm_campaign=masthead-newsletter&utm_content=20210206&silverid-ref=NjY4NTQwMDIyNTU2S0.

104. Ibid.

105. Feuer and Hong, supra note 101.

106. Ibid.

107. Helderman et al., supra note 99.

108. Wilson and Kiper, supra note 20, at 216. See also *American Commuc'ns Ass'n C.I.O. v. Douds*, 339 U.S. 382, 394 (1950); Ross, supra note 69.

109. See https://www.merriam-webster.com/dictionary/post%20hoc%2C%20ergo%20propter%20hoc.

110. *United States v. Causby*, 328 U.S. 256, 261 (1946). The full quote is: "It is ancient doctrine that at common law ownership of the land extended to the periphery of the universe. . . . But that doctrine has no place in the modern world. The air is a public highway, as Congress has declared. Were that not true, every transcontinental flight would subject the operator to countless trespass suits. Common sense revolts at the idea." Ibid. at 260–61. See also Lawrence Lessig, *Free Culture* (New York: Penguin, 2003), 1–3, noting that "in a single paragraph, hundreds of years of property law were erased," ibid. at 2.

111. Calvert, supra note 17, at 135.

112. See "Editorial," supra note 6.

113. Nossel, supra note 71.

114. See Barry and Fenkel, supra note 79.

115. Calvert, supra note 17, at 142.

116. See supra notes 86–88 and accompanying discussion.

117. *Schenck v. United States*, 249 U.S. 47, 52 (1919).

Chapter 5

Rethinking the "Carnivalesque"

Trump's Co-opting of a Counterhegemonic, Counterdiscursive Rhetorical Strategy

Theodore F. Sheckels

As both a political progressive and a rhetorical critic intrigued by the ideas of Mikhail Bakhtin, I found that the events in Washington, D.C., on January 6, 2021, posed a dilemma. I certainly joined others in strongly denouncing them, but, as I watched, I *was* finding that, from a Bakhtinian perspective, I should be applauding. This chapter explains this dilemma and how I escaped it. It leads to what I think is an interesting refinement of Bakhtin's concept of the carnivalesque, plus a theory-rich way of describing these January 6 events. Calling them an "insurrection" may be legally accurate, but calling them "carnivalesque" reflects more accurately what they were like as a rhetorical phenomenon.[1]

BAKHTIN POLYPHONY

Bakhtin was a prolific writer. Because he continued to revise his works, because some of the works attributed to him might not be written by him, and because virtually nothing by him was published during his lifetime, editing his work has proven quite challenging. Much as in the case of Kenneth Burke, Bakhtin's canon, once established, poses another problem: what is the core text (if there is one)? Many would point to *The Dialogic Imagination* (1981), but this text poses two major problems: First, it is a collection of essays pulled from various points in Bakhtin's career, not a book he actually wrote; second, it is mainly about the novel, although both those studying dialogue and those studying discourse have appropriated the ideas and—arguably—applied them to matters Bakhtin simply did not have in mind. To the contrary, I would point to *Problems of Dostoevsky's Poetics* (1984)—mainly because it does deal with discourse, in fact much more than with Dostoevsky—as the core text.[2] But still others would point to *Rabelais and His World* (1968), and those who do make the carnivalesque Bakhtin's most compelling idea.

In the Dostoevsky book, Bakhtin distinguishes between univocal discourse (his villain) and polyphony (his hero); then he parses polyphony into four categories based on, first, the control the rhetor has and, second, whether the voices proceed in the same or in multiple directions. Thus, we get what Bakhtin terms passive varidirectional polyphony, and he cites parody as a crucial example. The rhetor controls things (thus the voices are passive), with the surface voice saying one thing and the beneath-the-surface one saying the opposite (thus varidirectional). Here, Bakhtin talks about parody per se, but throughout his canon he evinces an interest in the broader and undefined parodic spirit he delights in. Mockery, especially of authority, was very much something Bakhtin delighted in.

Bakhtin actually uses the terms *villain* and *hero* (in Russian, of course). On the surface, they may seem to be just metaphors, but, if one puts Bakhtin's work in context, they are more than metaphors. Bakhtin was writing at the time of the Soviet ascendancy, which he did not overtly fight against but nonetheless seemed opposed to. Thus, his period of exile in Kazakhstan; thus, his antipathy toward univocal discourse. It, stripped of any echoings, was the language that science and technology tried to create for the sake of stark objectivity *and* the language the Soviet government tried to create to silence dissent and control the people. So, when Bakhtin refers to it as "villain," he has its political villainy very much in mind (even though he cannot say so overtly).[3]

And polyphony is the "hero," the voice that can challenge that villainy. A rhetor might insinuate a dissenting voice into a text, the goal being to keep the double-voicing just beneath the surface (out of the reach of authorities). A rhetor might use parody, in which a text might praise on the surface but mock beneath it. These would be varidirectional. Or a rhetor might mock more directly, assembling disrespectful voices—probably just echoes, to be safe. This would be unidirectional. Either way, the polyphony is heroically challenging the controlling forces that are pushing the villainous univocal discourse on the people. This pushing affects one's life, but it also affects one's writing, for the ascendant Soviet regime was also pushing formal realism as the preferred—perhaps the required—style. As Bakhtin saw this style, it was perfect for univocal discourse, for it stuck to the surface, but he preferred a much richer one alert to the many and various dimensions of language. Polyphony, with its many, many echoes, was the essence of this richer style. So, the mission Bakhtin was on in advocating polyphony as heroic was literary as well as political.

COUNTERHEGEMONY

With this understanding of Bakhtin's mission (as he establishes it in the Dostoevsky book), let's superimpose it on the combined thoughts of Antonio Gramsci, Michel Foucault, and Stuart Hall. All three saw a hegemonic force controlling "things," although Foucault talks about it as the dominant "discourse" or "episteme." Gramsci sees the controlling force as capitalism and the victim as workers; Hall sees the controlling forces as colonialism and the victim as those who have been, one way or another—back then or now—colonized. Foucault's vision is perhaps the broadest, seeing an era and those with privilege in that era as the controlling, regulating force and the victim as those who transgress whatever norms the force has established and polices. The particulars do not matter here. What is relevant, from the perspective of rhetorical criticism, is that Bakhtin's polyphony fits the picture these other thinkers have painted because they insist that there will be counterhegemonic or counterdiscursive energy, manifested through rhetorical means (broadly defined to include writing, speaking, and demonstrating). Bakhtin's polyphony is, then, a tool to be used by those in a power-down position to challenge hegemony, the dominant "discourse," or whatever one might want to call it.

THE CARNIVALESQUE

So, how does Bakhtin's study of the carnivalesque fit in?

As he describes it, whether in its pure form in the medieval "carnival" or in Rabelais's French Renaissance satire, it is a subversive entity. In valorizing the carnivalesque, Bakhtin is valorizing an approach to expression that not only runs contrary to the Soviet push for a formal realistic style that can serve ideological ends but sets up the possibility of an alternative style or, more broadly, rhetorical approach, that could be used to question the preferred ideology. The carnivalesque, then, plays the same heroic role as polyphony, and, with its irreverent shouting, mock saluting, and singing, it is really just an example of polyphony. If one is trying to harmonize the Bakhtin canon, this is a key linkage between the core Dostoevsky book and the popular Rabelais one. If one is asking the broader question of what Bakhtin offers the rhetorical critic, this linkage reinforces one's sense of Bakhtin as one who believes that the resources of language must be mustered in order to challenge any and all attempts to abuse power. Polyphony is the key tool, of which the carnivalesque is a particular and particularly powerful instance.

So, let's briefly consider what characterized the carnivalesque as a genre or mode. This is important because it raises a question of definition crucial if one is to use Bakhtin's concept in rhetorical criticism.

The carnivalesque, at its base, is the power-down writing or speaking or in some other way acting against those with power who are arguably abusing it. In its medieval form, the carnivalesque mocked the church, it mocked the university, it mocked the elite. And one only needs to look at the long tradition of calypso performers in Trinidad to see that Carnival still mocks in this manner. Rabelais in the sixteenth century wrote in this spirit; so have some since. As a mode of expression, it is so compelling because of how it is used: it is used with exuberance; it is used with irreverence; and it is typically used by those power-down to challenge those power-up. I am here defining the carnivalesque in terms of its goal. And, quite clearly, Bakhtin had this power-focused goal in mind.

However, in discussing the carnivalesque as a popular mode and, then, a popular literary mode, Bakhtin also discusses its recurring traits. He explores several, but, as Bakhtin has been interpreted by many, the key trait seems to be attention to what Bakhtin (in translation) calls "the lower bodily stratum." This attention not only reduces all humans to the same basic functions—eating, drinking, excreting, fornicating—but reconnects humans to the earth. Humans had tried to deny that link by denying their bodies. The carnivalesque, in its authentic (according to Bakhtin) version, offered a kind of rebirth by calling attention to the bodily, earthy side of human beings by exaggerating it through excesses of eating, drinking, excreting, and fornicating. The excesses are there in the medieval festivals Bakhtin describes; the excesses are there in literary works Bakhtin believes are truly carnivalesque. Bakhtin laments how the form had become sanitized after Rabelais, but—and this is the question the critic must ask—is this focus on "the lower bodily stratum" essential to the role the carnivalesque might play as a type of subversive polyphony? An answer might be found in the other goal Bakhtin saw of using such references. They were present not just to prompt a kind of earthly rebirth, but to flip accepted societal structures. Turning people upside down, with "the lower bodily stratum" replacing where the head was, is but a metaphor for how the festivalgoers and carnivalesque writers wanted to reverse the rules, norms, and especially the hierarchies dominating society. Rabelais, understood in his day, was trying to effect his own reversals; Bakhtin, in his day, is trying to effect his. The essence of the carnivalesque, then, is not the traits of the popular manifestations (especially the focus on the "lower bodily stratum") but the goal.

Not all will agree with this interpretation of Bakhtin, so let me turn to Bakhtin's words to establish what I think is a proper reading of his study of Rabelais. I would argue that Bakhtin makes five crucial points.

First, the target of the carnivalesque is prevailing power. Bakhtin thus describes the prevailing discourse: "As opposed to laughter, medieval seriousness was infused with elements of fear, weakness, humility, submission, falsehood, hypocrisy, or on the other hand with violence, intimidation, threats, prohibitions. As a spokesman of power, seriousness terrorized, demanded, and forbade" (p. 94).[4]

Second, the goal of the carnivalesque is to undermine that very power. The carnivalesque is "degradation, that is the lowering of all that is high, spiritual, ideal, abstract" (p. 19); its goal is "to liberate from the prevailing point of view of the world, from conventions and established truths" (p. 34) and to lead "men out of the confines of the apparent (false) unity of the indisputable and stable" (p. 48). As such, it is "opposed to the intolerant, dogmatic seriousness of the Middle Ages" (p. 121). The carnivalesque "uncrowns intolerant seriousness" (p. 179). The carnivalesque has a "deeply revolutionary spirit" (p. 119)! It seeks "the complete destruction of the established hierarchy, social, political, and domestic" (p. 237). The result is not a mob but "the people as a whole, but organized in their own way, the way of the people. It is outside of and contrary to all existing forms of the coercive socioeconomic and political organization, which is suspended for the time of the festivity" (p. 255).

Third, the carnivalesque offers many techniques to accomplish this goal. As Bakhtin put it, "A boundless world of humorous forms and manifestations opposed the official and serious tone of medieval ecclesiastical and feudal culture" (p. 4). As Bakhtin notes, "Officially the palaces, churches, institutions, and private homes were dominated by hierarchy and etiquette, but in the marketplace a special kind of speech was heard, almost a language of its own, quite unlike the language of the Church, palace, courts, and institutions. It was also unlike the tongue of official literature or of the ruling classes— the aristocracy, the nobles, the high-ranking clergy and the top burghers" (p. 154). This language consists of "abuses, curses, profanities, and improprieties" and represents "a breach of the established norms of verbal address" (p. 187).

Fourth, reference to "the lower bodily stratum" is but one of the language or image categories the carnivalesque used, and it is used as a metaphor of sorts to represent how all must be flipped in the revolution the carnivalesque evokes. Note how Bakhtin describes the rhetoric of the "feast of fools": "Nearly all of the rituals of the feast of fools are a grotesque degradation of various church rituals and symbols and their transfer to the material bodily level; gluttony and drunken orgies on the altar table, indecent gestures, dis-robing" (pp. 74–75). Through these carnivalesque rituals and others, "the merry, abundant, and victorious bodily element opposes the serious medieval world of fear and oppression with all of its intimidating and intimidated ideology" (p. 226). "Down, inside out, vice-versa, upside down, such is the direction of all these movements. All of them thrust down, turn over, push headfirst, transfer top to bottom, and bottom to top, both in the literal sense of space, and in the metaphorical meaning of the image" (p. 370). This use of language and images did not begin with Rabelais: "For thousands of years the people have used these festive comic images to express their criticism, their deep distrust of official truth, and their highest hopes and aspirations. Freedom was not so much an exterior right as it was the inner content of these images" (p. 269). As Bakhtin puts it, "No dogma, no authoritarianism, no narrow-minded seriousness can coexist with Rabelaisian images" (p. 3). But these images are the tool the carnivalesque uses to undermine power, not the essence of carnivalesque.

Fifth, there is a tone to the carnivalesque both joyous and irreverent. Re-ferring to the laughter, Bakhtin says, "This laughter is ambivalent: it is gay, triumphant, and at the same time mocking, deriding" (pp. 11–12). Referring to those who have gathered to laugh, Bakhtin notes "the suspension of all hierarchic differences, of all ranks and status" (p. 246), for "in the world of carnival all hierarchies are canceled. All castes and ages are equal" (p. 251).

Consider the following four examples. Back in the period of protests against the Vietnam War, a popular poster depicted a nude fornicating couple while, with their bodies, assuming the shape of a peace sign. Around the same time, a popular poster depicted Richard Nixon sitting on a toilet. Fast-forward decades. In 1993, the women in the U.S. Senate claimed six hours of that body's time to protest the events at Tailhook in 1991 and question the four-star retirement rank being advocated for the admiral in charge at the time. Then in 2015, Georgia congressman John Lewis led a sit-in on the floor of the U.S. House of Representatives. All four events, I would argue, were carnivalesque insofar as they, with a degree of irreverence, offered challenges to prevailing authority structures. The first two called attention to "the lower bodily stratum"; the latter two did not. But that difference is inconsequential if one understands the carnivalesque in terms of its goal, not any specific traits. It questions what is presumed authoritative, and it does so with an exu-berance that might be out of place if the authoritative structures were allowed to exercise their normal power.

One might well wonder how Bakhtin in general and his concept of the carnivalesque has been treated within communication studies and especially rhetoric. Although this chapter is not the place to survey all of the extant literature, a few general comments are useful. First, Bakhtin has been unfortunately treated in a fragmentary manner, with discussions focusing on one Bakhtinian idea or another but not the theorist's work as a whole. As I noted earlier, we as a result tend to get different "Bakhtins" based on which idea—and which piece of writing—the critic turns to. Second, those who have focused on the carnivalesque have used it in three different contexts. It has quite often been applied to popular culture artifacts such as films (e.g., *Rocky*) and television shows (e.g., Jackie Gleason back in time, Stephen Colbert more recently);[5] it has occasionally been applied to freewheeling Internet environments;[6] and it has been a few times applied to political (and other) demonstrations.[7] The latter, obviously, is the most relevant to this chapter. These discussions have largely dodged the "lower bodily stratum" issue, which, I believe, has restrained the application of Bakhtin's idea, and focused on the energy, the irreverence, and the antiauthoritarian qualities of these rallies and marches. That emphasis is present in a discussion of the irreverent Sydney Gay and Lesbian Mardi Gras festivities and in a discussion of the irreverent Minnesota gubernatorial political campaign launched by Jesse "The Body" Ventura, but it recedes in the explorations of other demonstrations. It is in the spirit of these studies that this chapter on the events of January 6, 2021, proceeds; but do note that the events that have been discussed are most commonly challenges from the political left against what is presented as the excesses of the political "right." (Ventura's challenge against *both* "left" and "right" is an exception.)[8]

This discussion of Bakhtin and rhetorical theory is a lengthy but necessary prelude to establishing two jumping-off points for discussing the events in Washington, D.C., on January 6. First, the carnivalesque, as a type of polyphony, is a subversive rhetorical technique directed against those who possess power and are thought to be abusing power, a technique challenging their ideas, their norms, and their assumptions, especially those related to matters of privilege and power; second, the technique is usually thought of as one that the political "left" uses insofar as it becomes a counterhegemonic or counterdiscursive tool. Given how academic criticism typically valorizes such rhetoric, the events of January 6 pose a problem, for we are dealing with the carnivalesque, but it is being used in a manner that most certainly makes those who lean "left" very disconcerted. Thus, the dilemma I mentioned at the onset: accustomed to valorizing carnivalesque display, what does one do in a case such as this?

THE EVENTS OF JANUARY 6 AS CARNIVALESQUE

When watching the events on January 6, especially those at the U.S. Capitol, I immediately thought of the carnivalesque. What occurred was exuberant and irreverent, and it was framed as those power-down challenging those power-up. And, as is true of most instances of the carnivalesque, those exhibiting it were having fun. Now, I do not want anyone to think that I was not disturbed by what the demonstrators did, especially the violence, but when one reviews the videos, one must conclude that these demonstrators were less venting anger and more enjoying their irreverence. Classic carnivalesque!

One is, of course, dependent on media coverage in assessing what happened that day. In retrospect, we know there was vandalism, and there were, unfortunately, deaths. There were also threats of far worse actions than what transpired, and even though the insurrection was tame compared to what one sees in other countries, it was still sufficient to provoke considerable, enduring trauma for members of the Capitol police, legislators, and their staffs. Gradually, media coverage shifted toward the more violent aspects of the day, perhaps leaving one with a picture consonant with the term *insurrection*. But let's try to step back from the events and construct as full a picture as possible.

There was a chanting mob, with a line of police attempting to hold that mob back. Not an unusual picture for a demonstration. In fact, what made this one unusual was how quickly the line gave way. Then, what did the mob do? Some acted violently, but most meandered through Capitol spaces not usually accessible to the public. They did not think they would be there, so they delighted in the very fact that they had gained access to this space. Many of these meanderers did not look hostile; in fact, they looked more like happy tourists than terrorists. Truth be told, joy was seen on their faces as often as anger. That joy was because their irreverence was triumphing, their message was getting through just as they got through the rather poorly held police line. There was a "Yes, we did it" joy, not the angry one of people about to do any physical harm. There were undoubtedly some dangerous people in the mix—I am not disputing that. Rather, I am inviting critics to look at the big picture, which is very much in keeping with the concept of the carnivalesque.

Some people invaded the sacred spaces of the legislators. They sat in their chairs; they looked through their materials. In two of the most often reproduced images, a bare-chested man wearing a Viking helmet (Jacob A. Chansley, aka Jake Angeli) assumed a position of power and a somewhat more normally dressed man (Richard Barnett) sat at House Speaker Nancy Pelosi's Capitol office desk with his feet up. These are classic depictions of the out-of-power usurping the positions of the powerful and, thus, precisely in accord with the spirit of the carnivalesque. There were, in our picture, undoubtedly those bent on violence; but I would submit that most present had rather vague goals. They gathered to protest; they gathered to—maybe—stop the proceedings of Congress. But did they come to Washington to overthrow the elected government? Probably only a very few. Most were there to call into question how power was being used to suppress what they thought was the true vote in November. They were irreverent, but they were also joyous. And their more general goal was to put the people back in power, if only for the short term. In other words, they were seeking to flip the power structures that were about to, once again, validate an election result they believed to be invalid. What one sees in these events is a textbook example of the carnivalesque (if that spirit is understood in terms of its goals, not just its frequent "lower bodily stratum" trait).

Again, this interpretation is not ignoring or excusing the violence. Bakhtin looks at both medieval manifestations of the carnivalesque as well as Rabelais's adaptation of that spirit in the Renaissance in a literary form. There was violence in these, although tinged with comedy. But, to mention a coarse example, one being soaked in urine is likely to think he is being grossly assaulted, not joked with. So, the carnivalesque is not nonviolent protest; rather, it is a popular uprising against authority thought to be abusive. And, if the uprising gets a little rough, so be it: that is how Bakhtin depicts the carnivalesque as manifested in medieval festivals and in Rabelais. And what occurred on January 6 is very much in line with this depiction. If one honestly assesses demonstrations that could be characterized in Bakhtin's terms, one will find a continuum when it comes to violence. Some lean toward it; some avoid it entirely. But the presence or absence of violence is not the defining characteristic; rather, it is the mix of joyous irreverence and a desire to flip the prevailing power structure, putting those power-down power-up. Classic carnivalesque.

As already noted, mainstream media chose to emphasize the violence not on the 6th but on the days afterwards. They also began exploring social media posts, some very deep online, and located very some disturbing discussions. Some had plans on the 6th, and these plans were very much in keeping with the label "insurrection." However, what is not clear—and probably never will be—is how many who gathered were committed to violence and how many were in Washington to display their discontent and exhibit their irreverence. The more there might be of the latter, the more the events might seem to fit the carnivalesque, but, as Bakhtin's account makes clear, there is inherently more than just a touch of rebellion in carnival. Present-day calypso artists in Trinidad stick to words, but, as Bakhtin points out, post-Rabelais carnival lost a good bit of its edge. But for Bakhtin, the true carnivalesque very much has this edge.

THE CRITIC'S PROBLEM

The usual take on the carnivalesque is what one might term a "liberal" one. Back in the Middle Ages, carnival was when the peasantry celebrated the day before the penitential season of Lent began. It was a "blowout" featuring both sensual excesses and the mockery of the elite, be they civic, church, or educational. The tradition continues with Carnival in Brazil and Trinidad and Mardi Gras in New Orleans and elsewhere, with the sensual excess stressed and the mockery minimized (if not eliminated). But, on Trinidad, the calypso tradition is alive, featuring singers on floats singing the mocking songs they wrote. So, whether it be back in time or in Trinidad, there is very much what Gramsci and Hall would term an antihegemonic quality or what Foucault would term a counterdiscursive quality. In other words, the carnivalesque is typically directed against those with power who may well be using that power to oppress.

Let me return to a tame example to illustrate my point. In 2015, the Republican Speaker of the House, Paul Ryan, was not permitting several pieces of gun control legislation to come to the floor for a vote. So, the late representative John Lewis of Georgia, recalling his civil rights days, organized a sit-in. Members of Congress seized control of the House and sat down on the floor at the chamber's front, where supportive colleagues from the Senate joined them. Lewis and others spoke. Ryan ordered, as a hegemonic countermeasure, C-SPAN to stop telecasting the irreverent event. So, these demonstrators took out their cell phones, which (by the way) were prohibited in the House chamber, and began videostreaming. News media, including—ironically—C-SPAN, picked it up, and people were able to view these disgruntled legislators who were enjoying themselves as they challenged the rules and the authority structure of the House of Representatives.[9]

Another example: On January 21, 2017, women took to the streets in cities in this nation and abroad to protest Donald Trump's presidency. Their marches were irreverent and joyful, very much in the counterhegemonic or counterdiscursive spirit of the carnivalesque. Insofar as the marching women wore "pussy hats," they were evoking the "lower bodily stratum."

So, why wasn't the MAGA group's "invasion" of the U.S. Capitol on January 6 like these other events? Did the political flipping make it less carnivalesque or something other than carnivalesque? And, if the carnivalesque is to be ordinarily applauded as an irreverent challenge to abuses of power, how do we then, with consistency, not applaud what the demonstrators did? Put another way, is the carnivalesque "okay" as an embodied rhetorical strategy only when we agree with the politics?

SOLUTION: VARIETIES OF CARNIVALESQUE

These questions, together, lead me to suggest that there may be variants of the carnivalesque that we need to recognize. I'm calling them genuine, permitted, and co-opted. As I hope readers will see, these are rhetorically different phenomena, although they look much the same.

The genuine is what I described when I glanced at John Lewis's House sit-in or the women's march. In those cases, there was a target exercising hegemonic power to oppress the demonstrating group. So described, this carnivalesque is what Bakhtin describes and what most using the term rhetorically have in mind.

There has, however, been a long debate about the extent to which the carnivalesque is permitted and therefore invalidated. Back in the Middle Ages, the peasantry was allowed—so the argument goes—their day of mockery, and, as a result, the mockery was muted. And in Trinidad, the calypso artists are permitted to write and perform their satirical pieces, resulting in—arguably—the satire losing its bite. We can debate and debate about this permission and to what extent it weakens the antihegemonic thrust of the counterhegemonic. It is worth noting that Bakhtin wrote about the carnivalesque at a time when Stalin was oppressing all dissent in the Soviet Union. Why, at that point in time, look back to Rabelais and back further to medieval times? Arguably, Bakhtin saw in the carnivalesque the potential to respond to the emerging Soviet system with mocking irreverence, and he saw the potential to get away with doing so because, although authorities would say they were permitting parody and satire, they were really just trying to save face and not be the oppressors the carnivalesque discourse was presenting them as. In other words, the permission might be illusory. Bakhtin says that the carnivalesque was "a festival offered not by some exterior source but by the people to themselves." They were not "receiving something that they must accept respectfully and gratefully" (p. 246). The carnivalesque was "completely independent of Church and State but tolerated by them" (p. 221). That toleration, according to one of Bakhtin's most noteworthy interpreters, Michael Holquist, does not make carnival a permitted "safety valve for passions the common people might otherwise direct to revolution." Rather, it "is not only not an impediment to revolutionary change, it is revolution itself" (p. xiviii). However, post-Rabelais, carnival did lose its edge and, so, some later examples, including ones in our day, might fall into a permitted category, which weakens it—somewhat, but not entirely. The August 1963 March on Washington was permitted, but did that significantly reduce its counterhegemonic power? Having to get a permit does not necessarily reduce the carnivalesque's anti-authority force.

The third variant is the one not yet fully recognized. In it, the truly hegemonic forces use the carnivalesque to sustain their power by misleading the power-down into mocking, as if they are oppressors, those who are not. The carnivalesque power then becomes co-opted by those with power who mislead those who are power-down into participating in their own oppression.

The events on January 6 were an example of the co-opted carnivalesque. Let me explain. The demonstrators were self-proclaimed patriots fighting for democracy. However, they were not being allowed to see the workings of democracy from the election onward. On Election Day and after, officials of both political parties worked diligently to count all valid votes. They conducted recounts where appropriate, and they entertained all judicial challenges with appropriate circumspection, requiring standing, asking for evidence, citing the sacred text of the U.S. Constitution. Those convening electors and the electors themselves dutifully and carefully acted on December 14, and Congress was going to dutifully act to count the electors' votes and proclaim the official verdict on January 6. All of this was democracy, and the demonstrators, given their support for democracy and opposition to any and all forces trying to suppress it, should have been saluting these—and other—events, not mocking them by their words and actions.

Social media sites, some newspeople, and especially President Donald Trump and those who, for whatever reason, supported his baseless claim of a stolen election offered the demonstrators an alternative view of political reality. This view transformed the prodemocratic processes—and those enacting them—into antidemocratic oppressors. They were the agents of a vaguely defined supposed hegemony that the demonstrators felt compelled to treat irreverently and maybe even overcome.

So, in this drama, who are the truly hegemonic? Arguably, those who co-opted the carnivalesque display, directing it at not only the wrong target but one actually consonant with the demonstrating group's belief in democracy. Put another way, hegemonic forces transformed what is commonly an anti-hegemonic phenomenon into one that actually served the need—that is, to retain power—of the hegemonic. The hegemonic forces did so through various means—mainstream media, fringe social media, presidential statements, statements by those who, for whatever reason, supported the president's position and, by extension, his desire to maintain power.

Sorting the carnivalesque into types and, then, exploring the third type, the co-opted type, does three things. First, it eliminates the dilemma explained at this comment's beginning—generally supporting the carnivalesque as a tool of the power-down but not this instance. Second, it adds to the rhetorical critic's understanding of Bakhtin's concept. Third, it poses an interesting question, one I wish to close with.

As I have suggested, the carnivalesque, because it is seen as a tool of the power-down, is typically associated with progressive causes. It is a tool that has been used by some, such as those conducting a House of Representatives sit-in and the women who marched on January 21, 2017; it is a tool that could be easily used by Black Lives Matter. There are undoubtedly contexts in which conservative groups might be power-down: imagine that the United States has actually embraced socialism. These groups could exhibit carnivalesque energy, and their action would be what has been described as genuine carnivalesque. We tend to see the carnivalesque as a "left"-leaning phenomenon, but not necessarily so. The carnivalesque involves power, not political ideology.

But the events of January 6 show us that there exists a way that those power-up can co-opt the phenomenon. This leads to the question of whether this has happened before but has been off the critic's "radar screen." One's mind immediately goes to Nazi Germany. Were there examples there of the co-opted carnivalesque? The Soviet Union or Mao's China? Today in North Korea? Did we see on January 6 not an unusual example of the carnivalesque but a twist on it that had escaped critical attention?

The following example is not perfect and it is fictitious, but I will close this part of the chapter with it nonetheless. As a fan of Broadway musicals and as one who has critically studied them, I recall the eerie moment at the end of act I of *Cabaret*. We see people in a German beer garden, celebrating with drink and song—carnivalesque elements but not a perfect case. Then, we hear the lyrics of "Tomorrow Belongs to Me"; then, we see the swastikas and the heil salutes. The energy evoked and exhibited will not be directed against hegemonic forces but rather be in the evil service of them.

UNDERSTANDING THE CARNIVALESQUE, UNDERSTANDING JANUARY 6

This analysis leads to two conclusions: one about the carnivalesque that refines and advances, I think, our understanding of Bakhtin's contribution to rhetorical inquiry, and the other about the events of January 6 in Washington, D.C.

We should now understand the carnivalesque better by focusing on its goals, not on one of its striking traits (the focus on "the lower bodily stratum") back in medieval festivals and some medieval and early Renaissance writing. We also should recognize that there are versions of the carnivalesque. One, the co-opted, represents a largely unrecognized (in the Bakhtin literature) misappropriation of the spirit Bakhtin salutes. Bakhtin sees the carnivalesque as promoting the genuinely power-down over the genuinely oppressive power-up. On January 6, we saw the potential of redefining power-down and power-up through conventional (speeches) and unconventional (social media) communication to serve manufactured, not genuine, power imbalances and abuses. Bakhtin—and others—may have been naive not to recognize the possibility of such co-opting of a counterhegemonic, counterdiscursive tool, but, their naivete aside, we must now recognize it and not quickly associate the carnivalesque with the politics we want to applaud. Seen in its three variants, the carnivalesque is more of a neutral rhetorical tool than one of the political "left."

We should also, through the lens of the carnivalesque, see the events of January 6 more fully and, thus, more clearly.

As time passes, in a number of contexts, people will undoubtedly debate whether these events constituted an "insurrection." This will be an interesting legal debate to follow. Section Three of the Fourteenth Amendment to the U.S. Constitution has rarely been noted, let alone tested in the various courts as to what its terms precisely mean. We have less problem applying the term *carnivalesque* to the events. If what Bakhtin outlines in his study of Rabelais is correctly understood, the events of January 6 are a textbook example. The irreverence was present, the joy was present, the touches of violence were too, but they were more rallying cries than realities, more accidents than planned occurrences. And, crucially, the goal was to confront those power-up (and thought to be abusive) with the strongly held feelings and views of those power-down.

So, what does the understanding of the events as carnivalesque gain us? As I have noted several times already, I join others in deploring what occurred. However, understanding the events as carnivalesque puts them in a context that makes them both richer and more understandable.

In what ways can we see the events as richer? The crowd that stormed the Capitol did not have one voice; it had many. Some were angry; some were jubilant. Some believed in outlandish conspiracy theories; some, simply, that there had been a fraudulent election. There were indeed White supremacists there, but not all who demonstrated were. And many present probably, if interrogated, would not have been able to articulate their reason for being there in terms one might rightly judge as incoherent. Such is the case for any "carnivalesque" crowd. Were those back in medieval times who mocked the church, the state, and the academy all identical in their beliefs? Of course not. Were those women who marched on January 21, 2017, all identical? Again, of course not. So, the critic needs to shift focus from presenting the events of January 6 as if they were univocal and grant the polyphony present in the carnivalesque display that day. Doing so should not lead the critic away from noting what was dangerous, but it should keep the jubilant dimension of the demonstration in view too. Understanding the events as carnivalesque alerts the critic to the many, often contradictory characteristics of what occurred.

The media gravitate, unfortunately, to simple answers, and so do many critics. But the events of January 6, understood as carnivalesque, were far from simple. If one labels the events an "insurrection," then the next step is to paint all who marched and raised their voices as "insurrectionists." Understanding them as such, we quickly condemn them. But are we truly understanding them? The carnivalesque, as a critical lens, alerts us to, first, the polyphony and, second, to the inherent vagueness of the opposed position those exhibiting the carnivalesque assume. As already noted, there were multiple ideologies, multiple views, and multiple feelings on display on January 6. The critic—and the citizen—should not latch ahold of the most objectionable, apply it to all, and quickly condemn. Instead, the critic—and the citizen—should condemn the White supremacist while, maybe, feeling sorry for those who have been misled by wild and wildly inaccurate social media posts; should condemn those actually advocating the overthrow of the government while recognizing that most gathered probably just wanted their views heard and recognized. In other words, if asked, "Do you want to overthrow the U.S. government?" they would have said "Of course not."

The carnivalesque, whether at medieval festivals or in Rabelais's satire, was neither univocal nor thematically harmonious. It was, as a popular folk form, polyphonous and messy. And so, I would argue, were the events of January 6. Critics do need to escape the naive view that the carnivalesque, insofar as it is counterhegemonic, is always to be valorized. The events of January 6 demonstrate how it can be co-opted and used to purposes one would never applaud. Critics also need to grasp how carnivalesque events are not one thing, but many. Some are to be rightly condemned; others command critical—and civic—understanding, not condemnation.

Understanding the events of January 6 as carnivalesque, then, should simultaneously lead us to grasp a danger in the mode Bakhtin describes and salutes and produce a measure of tolerance for not so much what occurred as the people involved. There will, I am guessing, be a quick negative reaction to January 6 on the part of rhetorical scholars, regardless of their politics. The events are very difficult to defend. Seeing them as carnivalesque does not offer a broad defense, but it does prevent an overly simplistic understanding that leads to too-quick condemnation. Furthermore, it alerts the critic to how the events were multivoiced and multifaceted. Dangerous people stormed up the U.S. Capitol steps, but so did deluded people and people who were just seeking the exuberant jubilation of yet another Trump rally. Out of understanding the mix that makes up the carnivalesque comes a measure of tolerance that might help us get beyond the events of January 6.

NOTES

1. I am here enclosing "carnivalesque" in quotation marks, for it is often so inscribed in the critical literature, but, hereafter, I am dropping these marks for convenience.

2. Michael Holquist, ed., *The Dialogic Imagination: Four Essays by M. M. Bakhtin* (Austin: University of Texas Press, 1981); Mikhail Bakhtin, *Problems of Dostoevsky's Poetics*, edited by Caryl Emerson (Minneapolis: University of Minnesota Press, 1985).

3. For a fuller discussion of this context, see Michael Holquist's "Prologue" to Helene Iswolsky's translation/edition of *Rabelais and His World* published in 1968 by MIT and republished in 1984 by Indiana University Press.

4. All quotations of Bakhtin are from this edition of *Rabelais and His World*.

5. See, for example, Virginia Wright Wexman, "Returning from the Moon: Jackie Gleason, the Carnivalesque, and Television Comedy," *Journal of Film & Video*, 42.4 (1990), 20–32; Grant Wiedenfeld, "The Conservative Backlash Argument Controverted: Carnivalesque, Comedy, and Regret in *Rocky*," *Critical Studies in Mass Communication*, 33.2 (2016), 168–80; Melissa Zimdars, "Fat Acceptance Television?: Rethinking Reality Television and TLC's *Big Sexy* and the Carnivalesque," *Popular Communication*, 13.3 (2015), 232–46.

6. See, for example, Donald F. Theall, "The Carnivalesque, the Internet, and Control of Content: Satirizing Knowledge, Power, and Control," *Continuum: Journal of Media & Cultural Studies*, 13.2 (1999), 153–65; Polly Bugros McLean and David Wallace, "Blogging the Unspeakable: Racial Politics, Blogs, and the Carnivalesque," *International Journal of Communication*, 7 (2013), 1318–37.

7. See, for example, Peter Stallybrass, "'Drunk with the cup of liberty': Robin Hood, the Carnivalesque, and the Rhetoric of Violence in Early Modern England," *Semiotica*, 54.1/2 (1985), 113–45; Nour Halabi, "The Contingency of Meaning to the Party of God," *International Journal of Communication*, 11 (2017), 4032–45; and Svilen Veselinov Trifonov, "Twenty-Five Years of Democracy, Twenty-Five Years of Social Protest: The Role of the Carnivalesque in Bulgaria's 2013 Antigovernment Protests," *Journal of International & Intercultural Communication*, 10.3 (2017), 237–54.

8. For Sydney Gay and Lesbian Mardi Gras, see Steven Katz, "Producing Consuming Gendered Representations: An Interpretation of the Sydney Gay and Lesbian Mardi Gras," *Market & Culture*, 6.1 (2003), 5–22; for Jesse Ventura, see James A. Janack, "The Rhetoric of 'The Body': Jesse Ventura and Bakhtin's Carnival," *Communication Studies*, 57.2 (2006), 197–214.

9. For fuller discussion, see Theodore F. Sheckels, *Rhetorical Criticism* (San Diego: Cognella, 2019), pp. 172–74.

Chapter 6

Political Advertising in the Aftermath of the 2020 Postelection

John C. Tedesco and Scott W. Dunn

Donald J. Trump's term as U.S. president ended with the lowest approval rating for any U.S. president since Gallup polling started tracking presidential approval in 1938.[1] In fact, Gallup polling data reveals that Trump's 41 percent average approval rating over his four-year term is the lowest average approval rating for any U.S. president in more than eighty years of presidential approval polling conducted by the organization. Gallup's data also distinguish Trump as the only president in history whose job approval rating throughout his presidency never exceeded the 50 percent approval mark.[2] Even for the biggest polling skeptic, Trump's polling numbers were alarming and signaled trouble for his 2020 reelection chances. Combine the troubling polling numbers with the results from the 2018 midterm elections, where the Democrats gained a near fifty-year high of forty seats in the House of Representatives, and a Trump reelection appeared even less likely. In fact, the combined voting results for all 2018 House candidates showed that House Democratic candidates received ten million more votes than House Republican candidates, which is the largest margin of votes ever recorded between Democrat and Republican House candidates.[3] A Trump reelection looked like a long shot for most political observers, but the nation was in very uncertain times with the public health pandemic, social and racial unrest, large unemployment rates brought about by the pandemic, and some uncertain footing with our traditional allies.

To help assuage the impact of the pandemic on the 2020 elections, states began identifying strategies that would help the election go on as scheduled with safety measures in place. Many states passed laws prior to the election to increase the health and safety of poll workers and voters during the public health pandemic and to ensure that the state could manage the election. Since each state governs its own election procedures, changes to voting laws varied but included extension of the number of days after the election for which a postmarked ballot could be counted, removal of in-person requirements to demonstrate voting hardship to receive an absentee ballot, expansion of early voting dates and hours, permission for same-day voter registration, or distribution of absentee ballots to all registered voters. Voters were encouraged regularly by campaigns and advocacy groups to "make a plan" to vote to ensure that voters were aware of voting procedural changes in their state and deadlines to register, complete early voting, or mail election ballots. The laws that dictate how states count mail-in ballots also varied between the states, with some states allowing the processing and counting of ballots received prior to Election Day and other states requiring that mail-in ballots be processed beginning on Election Day. In states where ballots could not be processed until Election Day, states were aware that the large volume of mail-in ballots could not be counted in a single day and election officials and media warned that processing could take several days or even weeks to complete. Media organizations for several weeks prior to the election were informing viewers that it was unlikely the next president would be declared on Election Day.

Despite the fact that Trump submitted a mail-in ballot for his own vote, he repeatedly attacked mail-in voting as a "disaster" and "out of control."[4] In fact, several stories from FactCheck.org, a nonpartisan project of the Annenberg Public Policy Center at the University of Pennsylvania, spotlighted the deceptive messages Trump was using to undermine the safety, security, and fairness of mail-in ballots.[5] Among the many challenges to mail-in voting, Trump tweeted that universal mail-in voting would result in the most fraudulent election in history, suggested that mail-in ballots were being sent to noncitizens, that millions of people would have unlawful access to ballots, and that mailed ballots are corrupt. Trump even asserted that Republicans would never win another election if states supplied universal mail-in ballots to voters.[6]

Trump's criticism of mail-in ballots appeared to be without merit. In fact, Washington state signed vote-by-mail into law in 2011. Washington's Republican secretary of state Kim Wyman, elected to office in 2012, is arguably the nation's foremost expert on vote-by-mail since she has presided over years of statewide elections where registered Washington voters are sent a ballot via mail. Wyman is a vocal advocate for vote-by-mail as a secure and safe way to conduct elections. In fact, in an opinion piece she penned to share her observations about vote-by-mail in Washington, she asserted, "Restricting or hindering voter access is inexcusable, and falling short of our commitment to ensuring our elections are safe, secure and accurate is irresponsible."[7] Wyman added, "A national election—especially one that the whole world is watching, and particularly during a pandemic—is not the time to trumpet conspiracy theories and tweet our way into a frenzy. We cannot sit by and let political posturing undermine how we conduct our elections. It weakens the credibility of our election results. Worse, it erodes people's faith in our democracy."[8] Wyman was one of only a few Republican voices that advocated for vote-by-mail, which revealed partisan disparity on this issue. Her statement, which focused on voting rights and condemned attempts to obstruct voting, was a rare position among Republicans.

Another important disparity to acknowledge exists in voter behaviors— or how voters responded to Trump's fear appeals regarding vote-by-mail. In general, Democrats were more likely to encourage vote-by-mail, while Republicans speculated, without evidence, that vote-by-mail was ripe with fraud. In fact, FiveThirtyEight gathered data on the mail-in rates and showed that upward of 70 percent of voters in some states (e.g., New Jersey, Vermont) opted to use a mail-in ballot. Partisan differences were considerable, so Democratic states generally had higher percentages of mail-in or early voting. For example, 78 percent of Pennsylvania's mail-in ballots supported Biden and 23 percent supported Trump, while 34 percent of votes on Election Day supported Biden and 65 percent supported Trump. Similarly, the discrepancy in North Carolina was huge, with 70 percent of North Carolina mail-in ballots supporting Biden and 28 percent supporting Trump, whereas on Election Day 33 percent of votes supported Biden and 65 percent supported Trump.[9] The scenario that Trump would be ahead on Election Day and that Biden would catch up once the mail-in ballots were counted was speculated broadly among political observers. Despite all the indicators of a difficult reelection ahead, Trump created an alternate reality when he asserted, "The only way we lose is if the election is rigged."[10] This assertion, first made during an August 17, 2020, Trump rally in Wisconsin, foreshadowed the strategy Trump would use to allege a fraudulent election and to support the "big lie" that the election was stolen.

For many, it is not surprising that Trump prematurely declared himself the 2020 election winner during his election night speech. Trump claimed, "It's also clear that we have won Georgia. We're up by 2.5% or 117,000 votes with only 7% left. They're not going to catch us. They can't catch us."[11] A few minutes later in the speech, he stated, "We're up 690,000 votes in Pennsylvania. 690,000. These aren't even close. This is not like, 'oh, it's close. . . .' With 64% of the vote in, it's going to be almost impossible to catch. And we're coming into good Pennsylvania areas where they happen to like your president. I mean, it's very good. So, we'll probably expand that. We're winning Michigan, but I'll tell you, I looked at the numbers. I said, 'Wow.' I looked, I said, 'Wow, that's a lot.' By almost 300,000 votes and

65% of the vote is in and we're winning Wisconsin."[12] Toward the end of his election night speech, Trump asserted, "We were getting ready to win this election. Frankly, we did win this election. We did win this election. So, our goal now is to ensure the integrity for the good of this nation. . . . We want the law to be used in a proper manner. So, we'll be going to the US Supreme Court. We want all voting to stop. We don't want them to find any ballots at four o'clock in the morning and add them to the list. Okay? It's a very sad moment. To me, this is a very sad moment and we will win this. And as far as I'm concerned, we already won it."[13]

It is ironic that Trump's election night speech indicated that he would pursue an all-out effort to challenge voting procedures in states like Georgia, Pennsylvania, and Arizona to "ensure the integrity for the good of this nation." In fact, his strategy appeared to be the polar opposite, to stop hundreds of thousands of valid ballots from being counted despite the fact that voters completed those ballots in accordance with their state election laws. Trump was aware that his months-long campaign against mail-in ballots meant that most Republicans would vote in person. Trump was keenly aware that the overwhelming majority of mail-in ballots were from Democrats, so he could deduce easily that his campaign would be much more likely to lose in states that continued to count large amounts of mail-in ballots, particularly from heavily Democratic precincts.

In the ensuing days and weeks after Election Day, Trump and his supporters perpetuated a range of baseless claims of fraudulent ballots despite audits that confirmed vote tallies, then recounts that confirmed initial results and audited results. Georgia, for example, essentially counted ballots three times through audits and recounts. Despite losing more than eighty legal challenges or having them dismissed outright by courts, mostly due to insufficient evidence, Trump and many of his Republican party supporters continued to assert that voter fraud, faulty voting machines, irregularities in election procedures, or illegal vote certification were the reasons for his loss.

Conservative media, particularly Fox News, regularly went to sources that questioned the election outcome, supported the narrative of fraud, provided a venue for a range of conspiracy theories, and perpetuated the narrative created by the Trump campaign. Trump identified a legal team, and there were many lawsuits across several states in hopes to halt or overturn the election certification in places like Michigan, Pennsylvania, and Georgia, which were critical states for Trump to win if his plan to steal the election from voters was to succeed.

Trump, as sitting president, had the advantage of the bully pulpit. Despite the fact that most election lawsuits were dismissed by election officials and judges, many of whom were appointed by Trump, his campaign to overturn the election continued. When Trump's own attorney general reported that the Justice Department did not identify widespread fraud, Trump turned to others who would sing along with him. When his own director of the Cybersecurity and Infrastructure Security Agency, Chris Krebs, asserted that the election was the "most secure" in U.S. history, Trump fired Krebs. Though Krebs demonstrated ethical principles, sadly Trump was able to gain support from many Republican states' attorneys general in his attempt to appeal to the Supreme Court. Trump continued to find supportive voices on Fox News and among Republican legislators, and media and many of those voices continued to support Trump and his unsubstantiated claims.

Meanwhile, Trump was waging an aggressive fundraising campaign through social media to raise funds to support the many legal challenges. Trump also created ads to support his attempts to overturn the election. More than a month after Election Day, the Trump campaign was airing advertisements on cable television. One ad, directed toward Georgia, requested voters to contact their legislators and the Georgia governor to urge the governor to ensure that Georgia voters got to hear the evidence of fraud. The ad shows images of a suitcase being pulled from under a table and suggests that the suitcase is full of illegal ballots that were counted after observers left for the night. The narrator states,

> Election observers in Georgia thought they were done counting for the night. But, when they went home security footage shows poll workers pulling out trunks containing ballots from overwhelmingly Democratic precincts. The media won't admit it, but it's on video, and now heavily Democrat DeKalb County cannot find chain of custody documents. It's outrageous. Contact your legislators and Governor today. Text FRAUD to 88022. Demand they hear the evidence.[14]

Multiple fact checks revealed that the "suitcase" was actually the official carrying case for the ballots.[15, 16, 17] In this case, the fraud existed in the claims made by the Trump campaign in the ad. So, while much of the postelection wrangling was carried out through traditional and social media, paid advertising was also employed.

ADVERTISING IN THE POSTELECTION

There was considerable advertising in the aftermath of the 2020 election. Most of the advertisements focused on the Georgia Senate races as the two undecided seats would determine control of the U.S. Senate. While this chapter is focused on the postpresidential election, it is hard to ignore how some of the advertisements aimed toward Georgia voters addressed the presidential race and its impacts for Georgians. For example, a National Republican Senatorial Committee advertisement attempted to associate the Democratic Senate candidates Jon Ossoff and Raphael Warnock with New York representative Alexandria Ocasio-Cortez and Vermont senator Bernie Sanders. Since the battle for the Senate hinged on the outcome of the two Georgia Senate races, the advertising aimed at Georgia was unprecedented. The overwhelming arguments in the Georgia Senate ads focused on whether Senators Kelly Loeffler and David Perdue would be puppets for McConnell's agenda or whether Ossoff and Warnock would provide the liberal linchpin to the liberal agendas of New York's Congresswoman Alexandria Ocasio-Cortez or Vermont's Senator Bernie Sanders.

However, the postpresidential election advertising emanated mostly from The Lincoln Project. AdImpact, one of the leading ad tracking firms, revealed that more than $4 million was spent on advertising just in the first few weeks of January 2021, which was after the Georgia runoffs. AdImpact reported that a group called Science Moms, which is a collective of climate scientists and moms, launched a $10 million campaign during this time to educate mothers and engage them in the climate change movement.[18] While there were other groups advertising, the top spender seems to have been the anti-Trump super PAC The Lincoln Project. Specific amounts spent on advertising by The Lincoln Project are hard to find, but according to Federal Election Commission data reported by the Center for Responsive Politics, the organization spent more than $7 million during the first quarter of 2021.[19] While obviously not all of this money was spent on advertising, it is fair to assume that much of it was, since running advertising against Trump and like-minded Republicans is one of the primary goals of the group.

Political advertising has been shown to influence viewers' perceptions of candidate character or image,[20] to shape and reinforce attitudes toward policies and candidates,[21] to increase interest in elections, and to mobilize viewers to vote.[22] One particularly important benefit of advertising is that it has the power to overcome selective exposure.[23] Politically interested viewers typically catch a large amount of political ads in the context of news programs, as the news contexts help prime the viewer to receive the ad sandwiched between news segments, which fosters the credibility of the ads. But, even the most news averse television viewers get exposure to political ads as they appear in commercial breaks of all types of cable programming.

The Lincoln Project is a political action committee formed in 2019 by current and former Republicans intent on preventing the reelection of Donald Trump. The founders of The Lincoln Project include George Conway, Steve Schmidt, John Weaver, Rick Wilson, and several other Republicans or former Republicans, many of whom have worked on political campaigns. For example, Conway is husband to Trump advisor Kellyanne Conway, Schmidt managed John McCain's 2008 presidential campaign, Weaver managed McCain's 2000 presidential campaign, and Wilson is a prominent political strategist and media consultant. The founders named the organization in tribute to President Abraham Lincoln's unifying leadership to end the Civil War. The Lincoln Project created and aired ads during the presidential campaign, but Trump's postelection attempts to steal the election from the American voter resulted in some of the hardest-hitting Lincoln Project ads. The Lincoln Project encountered its own series of problems when it was revealed that Weaver engaged in inappropriate sexual chat with young men and questions arose about the group's goals and future plans.[24] However, these issues did not prevent the organization from continuing to raise money or from developing numerous hard-hitting advertisements that targeted Trump and his Republican supporters and enablers. While most super PACs are supported by wealthy donors, The Lincoln Project appealed to voters across the political spectrum turned off by Trump, and it was particularly successful at generating small donations online through its viral videos.

As a large and formal organization made up of prominent political actors opposing the candidate of their own party—or the party they spent much of their political careers promoting—The Lincoln Project fills a specific and rare niche in the political landscape. While there are voters who cross party lines in every election, it is unusual to have such an organized group. One of the few historical examples is the "Democrats for Nixon" organization started by former Texas governor John Connally to oppose Democratic candidate George McGovern in 1972.[25] While this group aired several ads attacking McGovern's defense[26] and welfare[27] policies, it remained a small organization made up of a handful of elected officials[28] that dissolved once the 1972 election ended.

The Lincoln Project's rhetorical strength likely comes from a similar ethos-based appeal as seen in the earlier Democrats for Nixon ads. Presumably, politicians or political operatives going against their party's nominee would be seen as more credible than political actors predictably supporting their own party's candidate. Thus, an undecided voter considering voting for Richard Nixon or Joe Biden would be more persuaded by a cross-party endorsement than by more typical intraparty endorsements. Furthermore, as communication scholar Dannagal Young has argued, The Lincoln Project takes this strategy even further by using a combative rhetorical style that tends to appeal more to Republican voters than to Democratic ones.[29] In fact, Young argues that the style used by the organization's ads echoes the rhetoric of Trump himself. Thus, The Lincoln Project fills a particular rhetorical niche with the potential to appeal to voters who lean Republican and respond to conservative arguments and rhetorical styles but may be persuaded to abandon their support for Trump.

While The Lincoln Project weighed in on the Georgia Senate races with several advertisements attacking Senators Kelly Loeffler and David Perdue, the first postelection advertisement about the presidential election was called "Dawn" and it was released on November 7. The ad ends by affirming Joe Biden as president, but it celebrates the end of the Trump era by asserting that America will be ready to move on, to grow, and to heal. The narrator asserts,

> The end is coming. The end of the noise and lies. The end of chaos and division. The end of the hate. In its place, a new America is ready to stand tall again, ready to restore the goodness in the heart of our nation, ready to put people before politics. Ready to lead, to innovate, to grow, to heal. It won't always be easy. There are tough times to come, COVID to be defeated, an economy to restore. But, that new day is coming. A day when words like caring, competent and professional won't be insults. A day when compassion and character mean more than celebrity. A day when every American's rights are respected and valued. That day is coming because of your hard work, your commitment, your energy and passion. That day is coming because of your vote. Joe Biden, our president![30]

For longtime political observers, "Dawn" is reminiscent of President Ronald Reagan's "Morning in America" ad, which was officially called "Prouder, Stronger, Better." The ad became known as "Morning in America" because the narrator begins by stating, "It's morning in America" before showing uplifting images of American families, workers, and communities. Like "Morning in America," "Dawn" depicts an America on the move. "Dawn" includes a racially diverse set of characters, shows the beauty of American landscapes and the importance of farming, industry, and productivity. The Statue of Liberty features prominently to depict America and its freedoms. The ad clearly celebrates a Biden victory and was released on the day when the major news networks and the Associated Press declared Biden the winner. "Dawn" was a full-circle moment for the organization. In fact, The Lincoln Project aired "Mourning in America," a play on Reagan's "Morning in America" early in the presidential election cycle. While Reagan's "Morning in America" paints an idyllic version of American life, "Mourning in America" focuses on Trump's mishandling of the COVID-19 pandemic and the resulting economic devastation. "Dawn" presents a very negative view of Trump's America as one that sowed lies, division, chaos, and hate while being void of care, compassion, and competence.

The Lincoln Project did not limit its attacks to Trump. In "Democracy," an ad released on November 13, ten days after Election Day, Republicans who did not accept the election outcome were equated with Russia, Iran, North Korea, and China. The narrator in "Democracy" states,

> First, they fought to birth a democracy. Then, generations fought and died to defend democracy. In 2020, Americans voted. Joe Biden was elected president with the most votes ever cast for a president in US history. But still, most Republican leaders are refusing to accept the outcome of the democratic process. It's shameful, cowardly, and un-American. Across the globe, our enemies attack America by saying we really aren't a democracy. Now, Republicans are acting like Russia, Iran, North Korea, China. Are these Republicans not Americans? If the president wasn't elected legally, then no one was elected legally. Call your Republican officials and tell them to start acting like Americans and support democracy. The question in 2020 was America or Trump. America won. It's time for Republicans to put America first.[31]

This advertisement included a warning that it could be disturbing to some viewers, and an age verification was necessary to view it on YouTube. Images in the ad contrast America under the Trump administration as one filled with protests and social unrest. There is a clip where Trump is shown with a live bald eagle and the bald eagle gets upset in Trump's presence. Senate Majority Leader Mitch McConnell, House Minority Leader Kevin McCarthy, and Georgia senators Kelly Loeffler and David Perdue are shown when the ad discusses cowardly and un-American behavior. Trump is associated with the world's most notorious despots as pictures of him with Russian president Vladimir Putin, China's Xi Jinping, North Korea's Kim Jong-Un, and Saudi Arabia's Mohammed bin Salman are presented to suggest that these are the leaders Republicans are empowering by supporting Trump.

Two additional advertisements focus on American democracy and Trump's presidency and reelection as a considerable threat to democracy. "Oath" shows senators taking their oath to defend the country against enemies foreign and domestic. At the end of the ad, the narrator announces, "You swore to this. Before God . . . and country. You took the oath . . . and you broke it. Your God and your country are watching."[32] When the narrator states that the oath was broken, pictures of Senators Josh Hawley, Ted Cruz, and Lindsey Graham and other prominent Republicans are shown. "Why We Fight" is an ad that addresses the failure of Republicans to acknowledge Joe Biden as president. It asserts that the failure of Republicans to acknowledge that Biden won fairly suggests that those Republicans do not believe in democracy. The fight depicted in the ad is the fight to save America from antidemocratic, autocratic leaders intent on stealing the country and suppressing votes. The transcript of "Why We fight" states,

America is starting to breathe again. A decent man as president—a plan to protect us.

It feels almost normal, but it's not. Republicans still will not admit that President Biden was legally elected, which means they don't believe in democracy. They believe an election is only legitimate if they win. That's not democracy. Their plan, pass voter suppression bills to block minorities from voting. Take back Congress, impeach president Biden. We refuse. We refuse to accept the end of the American experiment.

We refuse to allow anti-democratic autocrats to steal our country. We choose to fight and we will not lose. Join us.[33]

As Trump's strongest supporters and enablers became clear, The Lincoln Project directed its attacks toward the "weak, spineless, cowardly, and corrupt"[34] who aligned with Trump. The advertisement "Leaders" launched on November 19 and featured Florida senator Marco Rubio, Texas senator Ted Cruz, Arkansas senator Tom Cotton, Utah senator Mike Lee, Missouri senator Josh Hawley, and former U.S. ambassador to the United Nations Nikki Haley. "Leaders" hits hard at these "leading" Republicans:

Washington is full of Republicans with big egos and bigger ambitions. Remember them, Rubio, Cruz, Hawley, Cotton, Lee, Haley. Soon, they'll all be running for president. They're planning for it, even now. They'll tell you they're brave, strong, principled, conservative, but the reality is right in front of you. They're weak, spineless, cowardly, corrupt, shaking in fear of a mean tweet. Traitors to the ideas and ideals of the country. When America needed them to stand tall for a peaceful transition of power, they sided with the loser. When called to end abuses, they shrugged. When called to lead, they cowered. When called to speak the truth, they lied. Call them whatever you like, but don't call them leaders.[35]

The strong words used to describe the six prominent Republicans included in this ad hit hard at the idea that these Republicans chose politics over country and Trump over democracy all because they feared a mean tweet or some other attack from Trump. The ad portrays the current Republican leaders as traitors who have placed their own interests ahead of the interests of the country.

The Lincoln Project also attacked Trumpism. "Never Happens Here" is an ad that focuses on Trump's "autocratic evil" and antidemocratic attempts to bypass the voting results. "Never Happens Here" shows graphic images of the Capitol insurrection and a clip from the presidential debate where Trump tells the White supremacist group Proud Boys to "stand back and stand by." The narrator asks, "We always asked ourselves, it couldn't happen here, could it? It can, and it will. We're now only one presidential election from the end of America as we've known it. For the first time in our history a majority of a major political party refused to accept the result of the presidential election. Violent thugs roam the Capitol streets." Then, the clip from the presidential debate is shown and Trump's voice replaces the narrator as Trump states, "Proud Boys, stand back and stand by." The audio returns to the narrator voiceover, "Tens of millions will now teach their children they live in a country with an illegitimate president. This is how democracy dies. Today, the dividing line in American politics is not between conservative and liberal. It is between those who believe in democracy and those who are killing it by their actions . . . by their silence. Trumpism is an autocratic evil unleashed in America. It must be crushed. The danger is real. The threat is now. If you believe America is worth fighting for join us."[36] "Never Happens Here" combines graphic images of the Capitol under assault with explicit appeals to viewers to join The Lincoln Project and the side of democracy in the fight against autocrats and their self-interests.

Many of The Lincoln Project's postelection ads aired after January 6 used graphic footage from the insurrection, and several ads addressed the insurrection explicitly by pointing the finger at those it deemed responsible. For example, "The Vote" shows clips of several Republican members of Congress who vocally challenged state results—Georgia's Jody Hice, Alabama's Mo Brooks, Texas's Louis Gohmert, California's Scott Perry, Wyoming's Paul Gosar, and Georgia's Marjorie Taylor Greene—objecting to the vote certification for Georgia, Nevada, Wisconsin, Pennsylvania, Michigan, and Arizona, respectively. At the conclusion of the ad, text on-screen shows, "147 Republicans Voted to Overturn the Election Results in 6 states," followed by "Never Forget #TheBigLie" on the final screen.[37] Similarly, in the ad "January 6th, 2021 by the numbers," The Lincoln Project focused on the numbers involved in the outcome of the insurrection: the 414 rioters arrested so far, the 147 Republican members of Congress who objected to electoral votes in six states, the $30 million in property damage, the 140 officers injured, the 2,300 National Guard troops deployed to the Capitol, and the death of three Capitol police officers. It concludes with the number 244, to represent the number of peaceful years of power transition. The backdrop for these ads depicts graphic video from inside the Capitol during the insurrection. It is clear from the advertisements focused on January 6 that The Lincoln Project does not want people to forget about the insurrection. The "by the numbers" approach is effective at drawing attention to how devastating the insurrection was for the nation by focusing on deaths, injuries, and financial damages. But, the power of the ad is in the final figure, which suggests that we have been a nation marked by peaceful transitions of power for 244 years, which was ruined by Donald Trump and his enabling Republican colleagues who were unwilling to accept defeat.

In addition to Trump and his Republican enablers, The Lincoln Project also took aim at American corporations. A unique ad, "Michigan," employs the logos of prominent Georgia and Michigan companies in a "call to action" approach. The ad asserts that the Republican Party is led by people who do not believe in democracy. The ad appears fueled by the public outcry for major companies with headquarters or major operations in Georgia (e.g., Coca-Cola, Delta Airlines, Home Depot) to stand up for the voting rights of people they employ in the state. The ad alleges that corporations sat on the sidelines while Georgia passed the most restrictive voting access laws in the country. The ad turns to Michigan and quickly shows logos for Whirlpool, Little Caesars Pizza, AT&T, Consumers Energy, DOW, Domino's Pizza, Blue Cross Blue Shield, DTE Energy, General Motors, Ford, Kellogg's, Lear, Meijer, and Rocket Mortgage. Each of these companies has major operations in Michigan, so the ad asserts that The Lincoln Project, and by proxy voters in Michigan, will be watching to see whether corporations step up to support the voting rights for their employees in Michigan. The ad uses the phrase "We stand with voters" to suggest that corporate silence or failure to stand up for voter rights suggests that the corporations do not support or believe in American democracy. It is a strategic effort to command engagement from corporations and to place more pressure on legislators.

Even after Biden was inaugurated, The Lincoln Project advertisements continued. The ads took aim at Florida congressman Matt Gaetz after it was alleged that he was engaged in sex trafficking of an underage girl. Josh Hawley and Congressman Kevin McCarthy also received additional attacks in ads from this group. In fact, in an ad called "Kevin McCarthy, you did this," images from the Capitol insurrection are shown while the narrator asserts, "You did this, Kevin McCarthy." As the video continues to show more destruction and violence from the January 6 insurrection, the narrator continues, "You did this" for a total of nine times. The only words in the ad are "You did this" and "Kevin McCarthy." It is unmistakable that The Lincoln Project assigns blame to McCarthy for his failure to stand up to Trump and his willingness to support Trump's lies that the election was fraudulent.

The Lincoln Project remained active in the postelection period. When Trump announced that he would be hosting rallies again during the spring of 2021, The Lincoln Project kept releasing ads and swinging at Trump and Republicans. In the ad "Truthless," Senate Leader McConnell and one of his chiefs of staff, Josh Holmes, are used to suggest that McConnell is using Trump's name only because he knows it can raise money. The ad suggests that McConnell really runs that party and that Republicans are laughing behind Trump's back as they exploit Trump and his followers. An additional attack at Trump focuses on the idea that Trump floated to suggest that he would be back as president in the White House in August 2021. In "How Trump Gets Back to the White House," instructions are shown on-screen for how to reserve tickets from your congressional representative for a White House visit, which implies that the only way Trump gets back to the White House is by way of White House visitor passes secured from his representative.

DISCUSSION

Former president Donald Trump is a very polarizing character. When he entered the political arena and then one by one started knocking off his Republican primary challengers, he made enemies with his rhetorical attacks. He directed personal attacks not only toward his opponents, but also toward established Republicans who did not support him. For example, Trump criticized former Arizona senator John McCain by asserting that he was not a war hero because he was captured and held as a prisoner of war. It is surprising that Republican voters tolerated such a disrespectful and low-down attack of a decorated war hero—especially from someone who received five draft deferments. It is not surprising that two of the founders of The Lincoln Project are former campaign managers for McCain from his 2000 and 2008 presidential campaigns. It is clear that Trump burned some bridges and created some enemies by going after McCain.

The Lincoln Project founders, an admitted group of Never Trumpers, became disenfranchised with Trump in part because he was not promoting conservative values, but also because of fears that a second Trump presidential term would be uncontrolled and dangerous. Not only did The Lincoln Project produce ads quickly, but they did so in very direct and hard-hitting ways. In fact, it appears as though the organization attempted to hold a mirror up to Trump by using the Trump brand of personal, ad hominem attacks. In the general election, The Lincoln Project was "aimed at persuading . . . disaffected conservatives, Republicans and Republican-leaning independents in swing states and districts."[38] In the postelection 2020 environment, The Lincoln Project—despite accomplishing its goal to defeat Trump—demonstrated it will continue to fight until Trump supporters and Trump ideals are defeated.

It is clear from The Lincoln Project's postelection advertising that the battle within the Republican Party is about much more than Trump. While Trump has become the symbolic leader for the Republican Party, it is clear from The Lincoln Project ads that the divide among Republicans reaches beyond Trump to include attacks directed at a range of unprincipled "leaders" in the Republican Party who appear willing to sacrifice truth, honesty, and conservative values so long as they can retain power and continue to raise money while supporting Trump's lies.

The Lincoln Project is certainly novel in American politics. Yes, the nation has had Democratic and Republican groups align against their own party's candidate in the past, but not to the level achieved by The Lincoln Project. Because a vocal, well-funded, and oppositional faction within one of our two political parties is rare, novelty increased the news value for The Lincoln Project. As academic research shows, political advertising has the power to influence the political agenda.[39] The Lincoln Project ads certainly provide a specific example of this, as their ads were featured not only in the mainstream media discussion but also went viral through social media. On YouTube alone, views for The Lincoln Project ads typically approach between five hundred thousand and a million hits, with many exceeding multiple millions of views. In an ever-evolving and -expanding tapestry of campaign communication outlets and niches, The Lincoln Project was a savvy operator able to earn media and public attention.

It is hard to determine whether The Lincoln Project ads converted voters during the election. However, Rick Wilson, the organization's "ad guy," asserted that the ads were particularly effective in Arizona, Georgia, Pennsylvania, Michigan, and Wisconsin. In an interview with *AdAge*, Wilson argued, "We moved former Republicans, independents and current Republicans over what we call the Bannon Line. Steve Bannon, who is no fan of us, said, early in the process, if these guys move 2% or 3% of the Republican vote, Trump is gonna lose. Well, from the metrics we're showing, in the swing states, where we spent I would say 80% to 85% of our resources, we moved the Bannon Line, and crossover Republican votes, between 9% and 13%."[40] According to research from Priorities USA, a powerful left-wing PAC, The Lincoln Project ads "were ineffective in persuading voters in battleground states."[41] The studies appeared to focus on Republican, independent, and former Republican voters. While a definitive answer may not be possible on the effectiveness of The Lincoln Project ads during the campaign, or their efforts to hold Trump and his supporters accountable afterward, analysis from the *Washington Post* shows that "Biden exceeded his national performance among pure independents . . . and also managed to convert more former Trump voters than Trump did ex-Clinton voters" in what it terms the decisive states of Arizona, Georgia, Michigan, Pennsylvania, and Wisconsin.[42] Although the *Washington Post*'s analysis did not attribute The Lincoln Project ads as responsible for shifts in independent voters away from Trump in these five decisive states, its analysis confirms the very movement Wilson credits to the their ads. However, since political attitudes appear deeply entrenched in our current political environment, we question whether a continued strategy that attempts to hold legislators accountable for enabling Trump and failing to support our democratic principles will shift any more voters or simply reinforce attitudes among viewers.

But, it is not hard to show that The Lincoln Project had larger goals than stopping the reelection of Donald Trump. With Donald Trump out of office, The Lincoln Project ads focused on ensuring that Trump is not given power again by challenging the vocal legislators that continue to support him and the lies he perpetuates. In fact, The Lincoln Project focused on the Republican leadership for its ongoing failure to call out Trump's lies, for failing to uphold conservative principles, for supporting lies over truth, and for failing to level honestly with the American people. One could argue that The Lincoln Project's postelection strategy was a prodemocracy strategy. In the postelection period, The Lincoln Project went after Josh Hawley for his leadership in the objection to election certification and Kevin McCarthy for his vocal support for Trump and his effort to overturn the election. But, the ads attacked a host of Republicans who are expected to be running for the 2024 Republican presidential nomination, such as Florida senator Marco Rubio, Texas senator Ted Cruz, Arkansas senator Tom Cotton, Utah senator Mike Lee, Missouri senator Josh Hawley, and former U.S. ambassador to the United Nations Nikki Haley. The ads also attacked supporters of #thebiglie—that the election was fraudulent—by criticizing Georgia's Jody Hice, Alabama's Mo Brooks, Texas's Louis Gohmert, California's Scott Perry, Wyoming's Paul Gosar, and Georgia's Marjorie Taylor Greene for leading the 147 Republicans who objected to certification in six states. The ads raised concerns that the legislators were not supporting democracy, dismissing the votes of millions of Americans, and acting in support of autocratic ideals and individuals. The postelection ads raised larger concerns about the ideals held by the many Republicans who were explicitly vocal of their support of Trump or implicitly supportive through their silence.

What remains less certain is The Lincoln Project's long-term influence. Has The Lincoln Project created a new model for politically savvy individuals to put their resources together to help shape the political environment to suit their specific interests? *AdAge*, a prominent advertising industry publication, bestowed The Lincoln Project with "Marketer of the Year" honors in 2020 based on ads they found so expertly produced and compelling that they immediately would go viral. Given the viral success of The Lincoln Project ads, it will be interesting to observe whether future candidates or PACs will adopt similar strategies in hopes to replicate The Lincoln Project's marketing success. "Democrats for Nixon" disappeared after the group accomplished its goal of reelecting President Richard Nixon in 1972. The ongoing production and distribution of ads from The Lincoln Project in the 2020 postelection environment and deep into 2021 suggest that beyond preventing Trump's reelection, The Lincoln Project has exposed a critical divide, perhaps a crisis of values, within the Republican Party.

NOTES

1. Alexandra Hutzler, "Donald Trump Is First President in Modern History to Never Reach 50% Approval in Gallup Poll," *Newsweek*, January 19, 2021. Retrieved from https://newsweek.com/donald-trump-first-president-modern-history-never -reach-50-approval-gallup-poll-1562653

2. Ibid.

3. Harry Enten, "Latest House Results Confirm 2018 Wasn't a Blue Wave. It Was a Blue Tsunami," CNN, December 6, 2018. Retrieved from https://cnn.com/2018/12/06 /politics/latest-house-vote-blue-wave/index.html/

4. E. Kiely and R. Rieder, "Trump's Repeated False Attacks on Mail-in Ballots," FactCheck.org, September 25, 2020. Retrieved from https://factcheck.org/2020/09 /trumps-repeated-false-attacks-on-mail-in-ballots/

5. E. Kiely, L. Robertson, R. Rieder, and D. Gore, "The President's Trumped-up Claims of Voter Fraud," FactCheck.org, July 30, 2020. Retrieved from https://fact-check.org/2020/07/the-presidents-trumped-up-claims-of-voter-fraud/

6. S. Levine, "Trump says Republicans Would 'Never' Be Elected Again If It Was Easier to Vote," *The Guardian*, March 30, 2020. Retrieved from https://theguardian .com/us-news/2020/mar/30/trump-republican-party-voting-reform-coronavirus/

7. Kim Wyman, "Opinion: I'm the Republican Secretary of State in Washington— and I Believe Voting by Mail Works," MarketWatch, September 30, 2020. Retrieved from https://marketwatch.com/story/im-the-republican-secretary-of-state-in-Wash ington-and-i-believe-voting-by-mail-works-2020-09-22/

8. Ibid.

9. Nathaniel Rakich and Jasmine Mithani, "What Absentee Voting Looked Like in All 50 States," FiveThirtyEight, February 9, 2021. Retrieved from https://fivethirty eight.com/features/what-absentee-voting-looked-like-in-all-50-states/

10. David Turman, "Trump Creates Alternate Reality, Ignores Rule of Law," *Hickory Record*, December 4, 2020. Retrieved from https://hickoryrecord.com/opinion /letters/leter-trump-creates-alternate-reality-ignores-rule-of-law/article_d65d8210 -341d-11eb-bbae-eb6b9ed247fd.html/

11. Donald J. Trump, Election night address, November 4, 2020. Transcript retrieved from http://rev.com/blog/transcripts/donald-trump-2020-election-night -speech-transcript/

12. Ibid.

13. Ibid.

14. Donald J Trump, advertisement, 0:30, December 11, 2020. https://archive. org/details/FOXNEWSW_20201229_140000_Americas_Newsroom/start/9960 /end/10020

15. Angelo Fichera, "Video Doesn't Show 'Suitcases' of Illegal Ballots in Georgia," FactCheck.org, December 4, 2020. Retrieved from https://www.factcheck.org/2020/12/video-doesnt-show-suitcases-of-illegal-ballots-in-georgia/

16. Saranac Hale Spencer, "Nine Election Fraud Claims, None Credible," Fact Check.org, December 11, 2020. Retrieved from https://www.factcheck.org/2020/12/nine-election-fraud-claims-none-credible/

17. Tara Subramaniam, "Fact-Checking Trump Campaign Ad Implying Fraud in Georgia," CNN, December 31, 2020. Retrieved from https://www.msn.com/en-us/news/politics/fact-checking-trump-campaign-ad-implying-fraud-in-georgia/ar-BB1co6C7

18. Paul Steinhauser, "Political Ad Spending Continues Despite End of Election Season," FOX-6 WITI 9 (online), January 23, 2021. Retrieved from https://infoweb-newsbank-com.ezproxy.lib.vt.edu/apps/news/document-view?p=WORLDNEWS&docref=news/1803A7E59F81C008/

19. Center for Responsive Politics, "The Lincoln Project PAC Profile." Retrieved from https://www.opensecrets.org/political-action-committees-pacs/the-lincoln-project/C00725820/summary/2020

20. Lynda Lee Kaid, Juliana Fernandes, and David Painter, "Effects of Political Advertising in the 2008 Presidential Campaign," *American Behavioral Scientist* 55 (2011): 437–56.

21. William L. Benoit, Glenn Leshner, and Sumana Chattopadhyay, *Human Communication* 10, 4(2007).

22. Martin P. Wattenberg and Craig Brians, "Negative Campaign Advertising: Demobilizer or Mobilizer?" *The American Political Science Review*, 93, 4(1999): 891–99.

23. Richard Lau, David J. Anderson, Tessa M. Ditonto, Mona S. Kleinberg, and David P. Redlawsk, "Effect of Media Environment Diversity and Advertising Tone on Information Search, Selective Exposure, and Affective Polarization," *Political Behavior*, 39 (2016): 231–55.

24. Danny Hakim, Maggie Astor, and Jo Becker, "Inside the Lincoln Project's Secrets, Side Deals and Scandals," *New York Times*, March 8, 2021. Retrieved from https://www.nytimes.com/2021/03/08/us/politics/lincoln-project-weaver.html

25. Eileen Shanahan, "Connally to Work to Re-Elect Nixon," *New York Times,* July 15, 1972. Retrieved from https://www.nytimes.com/1972/07/15/archives/connally-to-work-to-reelect-nixon-will-try-to-persuade-other.html

26. Kansaspolitics, "1972 Nixon TV Ad—Democrats for Nixon Criticize McGovern Defense Plan," June 20, 2019. Retrieved from https://www.youtube.com/watch?v=eKfKJL7LLOE

27. Scott Santens, "Democrats for Nixon 1972 Attack Ad against George McGovern," August 1, 2019. Retrieved from https://www.youtube.com/watch?v=PSCIQqnyfCM

28. "Connally Sees More Democrats Supporting Nixon," *New York Times*, September 21, 1972. Retrieved from https://www.nytimes.com/1972/09/21/archives/connally-sees-more-democrats-supporting-nixon.html

29. Dannagal G. Young, "The Lincoln Project and the Conservative Aesthetic," *Society* 57 (2020): 562–68.

30. The Lincoln Project, "Dawn," The Lincoln Project video, 1:00, November 7, 2020. https://lincolnproject.us/dawn/

31. The Lincoln Project, "Democracy," The Lincoln Project, YouTube video, 1:08, November 13, 2020. https://www.youtube.com/watch?v=w0ErQXEzFWA

32. The Lincoln Project, "Oath," The Lincoln Project, 1:00, February 16, 2021. https://lincolnproject.us/oath/

33. The Lincoln Project, "Why We Fight," The Lincoln Project, 1:08. March 29, 2021. https://lincolnproject.us/why-we-fight-2/

34. The Lincoln Project, "Leaders," The Lincoln Project, 1:00, November 19, 2020. https://lincolnproject.us/leaders-missing-video/

35. Ibid.

36. The Lincoln Project, "Never Happens Here," The Lincoln Project video, 1:59, December 16, 2020. https://lincolnproject.us/never-happens-here/

37. The Lincoln Project, "The Vote," The Lincoln Project video, 1:12, April 16, 2021. https://lincolnproject.us/the-vote/

38. Andrew Ferguson, "Leave Lincoln out of It," *The Atlantic*, June 30, 2020. Retrieved from https://theatlantic.com/ideas/archive/2020/06/tactics-lincoln-project /613636/

39. Guy J. Golan, Spiro K. Kiousis, and Misti L. McDaniel, "Second-Level Agenda Setting and Political Advertising," *Journalism Studies* 8, 3(2007): 432–43.

40. Simon Dumenco, "Rick Wilson Ads Actually Worked," *AdAge*, December 9, 2020. Retrieved from https://www.adage.com/article/campaign-trail/lincoln-projects -rick-wilson-ads-actually-worked/2300051/

41. Zachary Evans, "Viral Lincoln Project Ads Did Little to Sway Voters, Study Shows," *National Review*, December 9, 2020. Retrieved from https://www.national review.com/news/viral-lincoln-project-ads-did-little-to-sway-voters-study-shows/

42. David Brady and Brett Parker, "This Is How Biden Eked Out His 2020 Victory," *Washington Post*, February 12, 2021. Retrieved from https://www.washingtonpost .com/politics/2021/02/12/this-is-how-biden-eked-out-his-2020-victory/

Chapter 7

Political Cartoons during the 2020 Postelection Phase

Natalia Mielczarek

Three weeks after the 2020 presidential elections, President Donald Trump wore the pink Energizer Bunny costume from the famous television commercial that advertises durability of the Energizer batteries (figure 7.1). To complete the look, he also put on a set of pink bunny ears and hopped around beating the Energizer Bunny's drum. The logo across the drum advertised a different product, however, than the popular television ad: an "Election Delegitimizer" powered by lies. The compartment where the batteries normally go to fuel the bunny to keep going and going—as the commercial goes—was empty. Underneath it, a new set of instructions was printed for the Election Delegitimizer: "Insert proof." The caption that summarized the scene read: "Still going (somehow) . . ."

With a few strokes of a pen, this single panel in color by Adam Zyglis that was published on December 23, 2020, told one of a number of stories that unfolded across scores of political cartoons during President Trump's "lame duck" period between November 4, 2020, and January 21, 2021. Some zeroed in on the president's conspiracy theories of a rigged election, missing votes, and unruly electors. Others seemed to express a collective sigh of relief at the outcome of the vote on behalf of Uncle Sam and Lady Liberty. A handful conveyed a sense of hope and trust in president-elect Joe Biden and his cabinet to fix the perceived ills that plague the country, from a raging pandemic to an economic crisis. Still some addressed the January 6, 2021, siege on the U.S. Capitol, attempting to deconstruct the participants' motives and pinpoint the source of inspiration that ignited their fervor.

This chapter aims to identify and interpret the dominant themes and recurring visual signifiers that emerged across more than nine hundred political cartoons[1] published during the seventy-two days of the transition period and untangle some of their potential meanings and functions as they—in an

Figure 7.1. "The Delegitimizer." Adam Zyglis, Courtesy of Cagle Cartoons.

overwhelming majority—delivered rhetorical blows to the Republican Party, President Trump, and his supporters. The chapter starts with a brief look at the role that editorial cartoons have played in the American press and at their significant power as visual rhetoric. It then lays out the methodology behind assembling the cartoon corpus and the methods used to decipher their rhetorical work. It concludes with reflections about the possible functions that the political cartoons were likely to serve as ongoing visual commentary during what some historians have called an unprecedented presidential election in U.S. history.[2]

EDITORIAL CARTOONS AND THE AMERICAN PRESS

As "speaking pictures,"[3] editorial political cartoons have been talking to their U.S. readers at least since 1754, with the publication of what has been considered the first editorial cartoon in an American (then Colonial) newspaper. The woodcut drawing entitled "Join, or Die" in the Pennsylvania *Gazette* accompanied Ben Franklin's piece about relations between the colonies and the Iroquois and the growing hostilities between the French and the British. It displayed a snake cut up into eight pieces, each symbolizing a colonial government and labeled with the future state's call letters.[4]

Since then, editorial cartoons have continued to function as contributing voices to public and political discourses, traditionally targeting a canon of favorite topics, from presidents, politicians, and wars to conflicts, the economy, personal flaws, and scandals.[5] As cartoon scholar Peter Duus puts it, editorial cartoons

> provide access to "everyday" reactions to politics that even public opinion polls cannot capture. [They] constitute a vast archive that reveals not only fundamental shifts in political consciousness but also the ebb and flow of political sentiments among the thousands and millions who read them—sentiments left unvoiced by the silence of other texts and other archives.[6]

The genius of editorial cartoons lies in their ability to convey often complex meanings through a combination of just a few lines, colors, and words. Put together, they unfold into more elaborate stories, visual arguments, and mores, frequently by weaponizing satire to criticize, confront, accuse, and often offend those targeted. "It is the ability of cartoons to undermine the legitimacy of rulers, leaving an indelible stain on their public image, that remains one of their most potent and feared attributes."[7] They leave such rhetorical bruises on their targets' egos by tapping into commonly shared and recognized cultural repertoires of symbols, ideas, and stories that are easily accessible and understandable by their readers.[8]

In that sense, editorial cartoons are also visually rhetorical as they produce meanings in the symbolic realm, moving interpretation from the literal to the figurative with the help of multimodal clues of text and image.[9] They are indeed "stark symbolic weapons"[10] because they contain rather than condense or collapse the larger stories they intend to tell; they often point to what is not directly seen by engaging analogy, allusion, hyperbole, metaphor, and other rhetorical devices.[11] They also involve human intervention through their production and anticipate the presence of an audience, two factors that, in addition to the symbolic action, transfigure them from mere drawings into communicative tools of visual rhetoric.[12]

Rooted in the cultural significance of editorial cartoons as visual opinion and guided by the theoretical framework of visual rhetoric, the chapter's analysis set out to answer two overarching questions: What dominant themes and textual hooks emerged in the editorial cartoons of interest during the transition period, and what potential meanings and functions did some selected cartoons produce for the viewer?

CARTOON CORPUS, TEXTUAL HOOKS, AND VISUAL RHETORICAL ANALYSIS

The editorial cartoons considered in this chapter were harvested from www. politicalcartoons.com, one of the most comprehensive databases of political cartoons online, published and maintained by editorial cartoonist Daryl Cagle. The site publishes cartoons daily through syndication of more than eight hundred artists from around the world. The site's search was limited to the time frame between November 4, 2020 (the day after the presidential election), and January 20, 2021 (the day of president-elect Biden's inauguration), and yielded about twelve hundred cartoons that were published on the site during that time window. Of interest were only those that addressed the topic of the presidential election broadly conceived, from the reactions to the election results and allegations of voter fraud to reflections on the Trump presidency and the future under Biden's leadership. Ultimately, 336 cartoons were thrown out as they were deemed topically irrelevant; they covered a range of ideas including football, the mechanism and rollout of the COVID-19 vaccine, and Christmas, motifs that did not directly or indirectly connect with the presidential election. The corpus of 578 political cartoons was then analyzed through a triangulation of three methods: inductive category formation[13] in tandem with thematic analysis,[14] both of which helped to identify the dominant themes among the cartoons, and visual rhetorical analysis,[15] which uncovered suggested meanings and functions of selected cartoons.

Inductive category formation and thematic analysis offer a systematic way of identifying, organizing, and interpreting patterns of meaning across a data set. They summarize the content through reduction procedures that allow a researcher to arrive at a higher level of categories that reflect general themes among the texts. In other words, the approaches are "a way of identifying what is common to the way a topic is talked or written about and of making sense of these commonalities"[16] by looking at the manifest and latent levels of content. In this case, all the cartoons were initially organized into broad categories of topics they addressed, yielding five broad themes. Another round of analysis collapsed two of those themes into one category, ultimately producing four dominant themes that could be identified across the cartoon corpus.

The cartoons of interest recycled a handful of textual hooks[17] that functioned as visual signifiers and contributed to the rhetorical construction of each theme and meanings of the cartoons. Those textual hooks are elements that are reused in texts to become "available for plugging into other forms, texts and intertexts—they become part of the available cultural repertoire."[18] Textual hooks range in content, from characters, gestures, and expressed emotions to poses, sayings, symbols, and scenarios that get recycled for rhetorical purposes of meaning creation.

Visual rhetorical analysis of more than five hundred cartoons in the corpus was certainly beyond the scope of this chapter, particularly in light of a thematic analysis that organized the cartoons into groups of suggested meanings. Four drawings were chosen as representative examples of each theme to demonstrate how they engaged with each topic rhetorically and what functions they potentially served for their viewers as known artifacts of political commentary and provocation. The analysis proceeded in two phases. First, it addressed the nature of each cartoon by looking at its presented and suggested elements. The former consist of the latent components of each drawing—its contents (shapes and forms), colors, media, and materials. The latter are ideas, allusions, and themes that a viewer is likely to conjure when looking at the visual artifact's presented elements.[19]

The second phase featured an analysis of the functions that the cartoons were likely to serve for their viewers; the analysis was rooted in the nature of each image and the theorized functions of cartoons mentioned earlier. It is important to note that a function of an image is different from its purpose; the latter is associated with the author's intended meanings, which were not the focus here. The analysis proceeded from the perspective of the viewer.[20]

PRESIDENT TRUMP TAKES A HIT: THEMES IN EDITORIAL CARTOONS

As noted, the inductive category formation and thematic analysis yielded four dominant themes that emerged in the analyzed cartoons: presidential election 2020, Trump's legacy, the Capitol siege, and transition of power. Each theme included a handful of subtopics that addressed various angles of the four threads. For example, within the Trump's legacy theme, some cartoons focused on the perceived physical and emotional devastation left behind by the president in the form of smoldering rubble and depressed and worried Americans awaiting change. Others highlighted the president's perceived disregard for economic problems and the rising number of COVID-19 deaths in favor of playing golf. Still some judged the Trump presidency as a sinking ship.

The tone and assumed points of view throughout the four dominant themes varied, but an overwhelming majority of the analyzed cartoons expressed vehemently anti-Trump sentiments, often ridiculing and chastising the president for perceived misconduct, fearmongering, and the spread of lies about election results. Some drawings portrayed the presidential election outcome and its fallout from Trump's perspective, channeling his disappointment,

rage, and a sense of wrongdoing. Others, created from an anti-Trump observer's vantage point, relied on satire to comment, lampoon, expose, and
sometimes confront Trump's actions, including claims of a stolen election,
often depicted in the drawings as false and fantastical ravings of a madman
who would stop at nothing to cling to power.[21]

THE PRESIDENTIAL ELECTION THEME AT A GLANCE

The presidential election theme was the most prominent one among the four
in terms of the number of cartoons that addressed it and its staying power
across the seventy-two days of interest. The theme appeared from the day of
the election until the end of November, with some revival after the January
6, 2020, Capitol riot. The subtopic that the cartoons tackled with the highest
frequency within the theme was President Trump's claim of voter fraud, often
fueled by portrayed allegations of missing or miscounted ballots, actions that
the cartoons framed as shrouded in conspiracy theories marred with delusion
and lies. A companion subcategory that often went hand in hand with the
voter fraud idea highlighted strong Republican support for the president's
claims. It paraded various Trump loyalists such as the GOP elephant symbol,
Senator Lindsay Graham, and attorney Rudy Giuliani, all of whom were portrayed as pledging blind allegiance to their leader and his cause.

A handful of drawings also shamed and even admonished the president
and the Republican Party as a whole for their election fraud claims and
perceived fear to contradict such a narrative, always depicted as delusional,
unfounded, and untrue. To that end, some of the drawings presented the
GOP elephant as literally spineless (lying deflated on the ground or holding
its spine in one hand) or looking for a spine. A couple drew the elephant's
head buried in the sand, oblivious to conspiracy theories and unrest among
Trump followers.

Another subgroup of cartoons within this theme focused on the president's
reactions to the election loss, overwhelmingly portraying him as a sore loser
who refused to accept reality. Trump was drawn as outraged, angry, and
restless, often plotting to regain power. Still some, taking the point of view
of the president and his supporters, facetiously depicted the vote counting
process as a clandestine operation riddled with intentional fraud and cheat-
ing, as if attempting to poke fun at the claims of a stolen presidency through
hyperbole. Deploying sarcasm, a few drawings in this category framed the
president's reactions to his loss as a potential lesson for children—that losing is for losers.

TRUMP'S LEGACY THEME AT A GLANCE

Cartoons that addressed this theme were published throughout the time frame of interest, with a particular intensity from mid-December through the inauguration. Their proliferation during this time period was likely prompted by reflections on a fast-approaching end of a political era that came on the heels of the Capitol siege and Trump's second impeachment. The cartoons that illustrated the outgoing president's legacy had nothing positive to say about his character or his accomplishments during his term in office. A drawing by Taylor Jones was a case in point. Published on January 6, 2021, the cartoon shows presidents Buchanan, Johnson, Nixon, and Harding sitting at a table and presiding over an induction ceremony of President Trump to the Society of Worst Presidents in American History. Another cartoon, by Pat Byrnes, shows the White House at sundown with a caption above the building, "End of an Error."

The most prominent subtheme in this category depicted Trump's legacy as one of devastation and dismantling of democracy. Identified as the main culprit behind the ruin, the president emerged as a dangerous, irresponsible, and harmful individual who leaves a path of destruction in his wake. Several cartoons depicted him amid a burning city of rubble, flames, and the occasional bullet flying around. Others captured symbols of democracy and power, including the White House and the U.S. Capitol, in shambles, as if a tornado plowed through them—with fallen walls, devastated furniture, and trash on the floor.

A companion subcategory of the editorial cartoons in the legacy theme also explored devastation of an emotional kind. In one drawing, a weary couple sits on a couch with a daunting question mark hovering above them and a caption that advises them to hold on until the inauguration. Some cartoons seem to have connected the perceived emotional toll of the public to a divided country and a nearly dismantled, in their eyes, Republican Party. More than one cartoon showed the GOP elephant and the Democratic donkey walking in opposite directions or undermining one another. For example, in the cartoon by Dave Whamond published on December 17, 2020, the GOP elephant eats itself by chomping on its leg in a gesture of self-destruction. In another, multiple Republican elephants get into a fight, screaming at and hitting one another in what looks like infighting. In yet another drawing, the elephant and the donkey take two different forks in the same road, walking away from each other without looking back.

The perceived divisions and weariness, some cartoons seemed to suggest, left the country vulnerable to myriad attacks from the outside, including the late 2020 cyberattack perpetrated by Russia on the U.S. government and its institutions. Several cartoons presented Russian president Vladimir Putin tapping into secret government files and daily national security briefings through hacking; one drawing had him make his way to U.S. classified information on a Trojan horse. A handful showed President Trump playing golf while the U.S. institutions were being hacked and compromised, presenting a careless leader who vacated his post in favor of fun.

Another side of Trump's legacy that a number of the cartoons within this theme explored was the president's use of pardons, depicted as frivolous, immoral, for sale, or reserved for the president's cronies. For example, one cartoon converted the White House into a "Pardons" warehouse with a big advertising sign atop. A long line of cars snaked around to the back of the building to a drive-through window to buy pardons on demand. Another had the president working a pardons booth as a salesman—much like an ice cream stand with Trump clad in a white uniform—where each pardon cost $5 million. A handful of the pardon cartoons that coincided with Thanksgiving incorporated turkeys into their composition as another group of pardon recipients. In one such drawing, Michael Flynn, President Trump's former national security advisor convicted for making false statements to federal investigators, occupied the body of a turkey, looking smugly at the viewer while holding a full pardon card from Santa.

THE CAPITOL SIEGE THEME AT A GLANCE

Cartoons that addressed the Capitol riot began to appear on the day of the event and continued during a handful of days following it, with some resurgence during President Trump's second impeachment trial that started in mid-January. The sentiments and activities captured by this theme ran a gamut, from exposés of perceived unconstitutional breaches that damaged democracy (and the Capitol) to admonition and ridicule of those involved. The majority of the drawings, however, did not display the actual act of scaling of the Capitol building. For most, the focus remained on the interpretation of the character, motivations, and ideologies of the participants, including the president himself and members of groups such as QAnon and Proud Boys, reported to have taken part in the riot.[22] They were often portrayed as uneducated, stupid, and even delusional coauthors of conspiracy theories and their perpetrators. For example, in Pat Bagley's cartoon from January 7, 2021, a woman and seven men stand in a group facing the viewer. They are wearing the now-famous red MAGA hats with different slogans meant to illustrate the rioting crowd's mentality: "proudly uninformed," "Trump über alles," "make hate great again," "my lies = your facts," and more. In another, cartoonist Bob

Englehart drew a Trump voter after the Capitol siege, sitting on the ground with a broken arm in a cast, several cuts on his face, a black eye, and a confused, defeated look on his face. A hunting knife, a baseball bat, and a broken wine bottle—presumably the man's weapons—lie at his feet; the title of the drawing sums up the moment: "Sore Loser."

Another topic that some cartoons addressed within the Capitol siege theme was President Trump's perceived involvement in the event as someone who either orchestrated or inflamed the riot by pushing the stolen election narrative and encouraging the participants to act on it. In one such drawing by Dave Whamond, Trump wears his red hat with a new MAGA slogan, "Manipulation and Gaslighting Americans." In another, the president, dressed in a tuxedo and holding a conducting baton, stands on a stage amid flames and rubble to conduct—quite literally—the Capitol siege. With unfolding mayhem behind him, Trump conducts *American Carnage*, the title of the main performance.

THE TRANSITION THEME AT A GLANCE

Similar to the Trump legacy and presidential election themes, the transition theme appeared and lingered following the election and later resurfaced in some cartoons around the New Year, leading up to the January 20, 2021, inauguration. A popular strand of the cartoons addressed the sheer joy and a sense of relief about Biden's victory, framing it as a source of hope for a better future. In one such example by Bob Englehart, Biden and Vice President Kamala Harris are pictured smiling and holding hands as they celebrate their win. A "Welcome Home" sign above their heads hints at the idea of life returning to a pre-Trump "normal" under their leadership. In another drawing, this one by Dave Granlund, the joy around Biden's win is so palpable that the Statue of Liberty and Uncle Sam lock arms in a celebratory jig a few days before the inauguration.

This subtheme also captures a sense of anticipated hope for the future under Biden's reign, reflected literally in the new president's famous aviator sunglasses through the word "unity" in Joe Heller's cartoon. In a drawing by Jeff Koterba, a bald eagle labeled "democracy" and a dove holding a presumed olive branch labeled "unity" look ahead as if into the future, crying. Another drawing in this genre, by J. D. Crowe, depicts Biden's hand placed on a thick book—possibly the Bible—during the inauguration ceremony with a caption that summarizes the postelection hopes: "Let the Healing Begin."

The other prominent subcategory of the transition theme featured cartoons that illustrated an overwhelming amount of work and pending crises that the

Biden–Harris administration would likely face. In a cartoon by John Darkow, as Biden is being sworn into office, anthropomorphized climate change, debt, COVID-19, White nationalism, and the economy hover around the new president demanding his immediate attention, all at the same time. In another, by Jimmy Margulies, the welcome mat at the White House front door resembles a trampled U.S. Constitution, with muddy boot prints staining the "We the people" preamble. The work ahead, as this subgroup of cartoons seems to suggest, is difficult and all-encompassing, and the enormity of the challenge is likely to put much pressure on the new president and his cabinet, as Dave Fitzsimmons's cartoon anticipates. In the drawing, presidents Franklin Delano Roosevelt and Abraham Lincoln come back from the dead to remind a worried-looking Biden as all three glance at planet Earth on fire: "History has its eyes on you." And yet, President Lincoln, in another cartoon, by J. D. Crowe, suggests that the work ahead is manageable, giving the Biden–Harris team a postelection thumbs-up.

The actual ceremony of the inauguration appeared only in a handful of cartoons within the transition theme. When shown, it tended to focus on Biden's win and not Trump's loss, with a few exceptions. When he did make an appearance at the ceremony, President Trump was typically framed as a sore loser—at least twice as actual sour grapes—who continues to cling to the narrative of a stolen election even during Biden's big day. For instance, in a cartoon by Dave Granlund, the president sits in his "Mar-a-Lago bunker" and watches the ceremony, declaring: "My inauguration crowd was way bigger." In another, by Jeff Koterba, Trump swoops in, ready to take the presidential oath himself—his right hand raised and his left hand midair as if resting on a book—despite the fact that Biden is already in the process of reciting it. Other inauguration cartoons featured the new president speaking, smiling, or looking at the crowds (and the readers), sometimes addressing the public.

TEXTUAL HOOKS ACROSS THE FOUR THEMES

The four dominant textual hooks that appeared most frequently and consistently in the political cartoons of interest were four characters: two real-life politicians—Trump and Biden—and two visual symbols embedded in the American political and cultural milieu—the Statue of Liberty and Uncle Sam.

President Trump

The likeness of President Trump appeared in the overwhelming majority of the analyzed cartoons, often as the central character of each scenario. Depending on the theme of the cartoon, Trump's body was engaged in myriad activities, from playing golf and inciting violence among his supporters at the Capitol to looking for lost votes under rocks or working a booth to sell pardons. In the presidential election and the Capitol siege cartoons, however, the president's portrayal was limited to three specific characterizations. In the election theme, Trump was mostly trapped in a visual dichotomy: he was represented either as an impetuous and inconsolable child who throws tantrums after losing an election, or as a delusional tyrant who refuses to accept the results and plots a takeover through a campaign of disinformation and lies. In the Capitol siege theme, the president emerged as the enabler and inciter in chief, leading his supporters to the Capitol.

Trump's portrayal across all themes often involved anger and rage, channeled through facial expressions and activities. For example, the president was frequently shown as yelling, grimacing, pouting, frowning, and turning red while throwing a fit. In a few instances he was seen hitting iconic visual symbols of the United States such as Uncle Sam and the bald eagle or burning furniture in the White House. The Capitol siege theme typically captured the president as the cause of what unfolded that day in Washington, D.C. Cartoonist Ed Wexler, for example, drew the president hooked up to a QAnon brain, suggesting the he and the group are, quite literally, of the same mind.

Regardless of the scenario, the president's likeness almost always appeared in the same ensemble: a dark suit, a white shirt, and a long red tie. The outfit was sometimes completed by Trump's signature red MAGA hat.

Trump Voter/Supporter

Alongside President Trump, the character of a Trump supporter was among the most frequently featured textual hooks when addressing the president's claims of election fraud and the Capitol siege. His portrayal—it was almost always a white male—was mostly consistent across the cartoons and time: a large, middle-aged man, often with a beard, frequently clad in military-style clothing such as fatigues, almost always wearing a red MAGA cap. In many scenarios, the Trump voter also displayed the Confederate flag in a variety of formats, as an emblem on a T-shirt, a belt buckle, or a flag in his hand. His demeanor typically fell into two categories: an angry or grumpy warrior who feels outraged by the perceived election fraud or a dunce who does what he is told without much thought.

The portrayal was even less flattering in those cartoons that ascribed the Trump voter improper and basic English grammar, zealous commitment to the stolen election theory, delusional thoughts, and tenuous contact with reality. For example, in a drawing by Monte Wolverton, which ran on January 17, 2021, a bearded, MAGA-hat-wearing burly man in camouflage fatigues and combat boots stands in front of the Capitol, brandishing a number of weapons, from automatic rifles and a hunting knife to a rocket-propelled grenade, rockets in his backpack, and a fully loaded ammunition belt draped over his chest. With a handful of missiles at his feet, he tells the audience, "Just carryin' these fer my own pertecshun!" This particular cartoon was not the sole example of the militarization of a Trump supporter. The textual hook was almost always equipped with some type of a weapon, suggesting his readiness to fight in the name of his leader, whose name was frequently plastered on his apparel or flags.

The other, more docile portrayal of a Trump supporter pegged him as a naive and not very bright or discerning person who simply followed orders without much thought. One such example by Peter Kuper from January 17, 2021, captures two participants of the Capitol riot sitting and chatting in a basement adorned with the Confederate flag, with one of them working on a laptop. The other reflects over a cigarette pull as he addresses his comrade, "These days they call you a terrorist just for trying to overthrow the government."

The GOP and Republicans

The Republican Party and its members were also among the most popular and visible textual hooks deployed throughout the four themes. They were mostly represented through the party's elephant symbol, though several known Republicans also made an appearance, including Senators Mitch McConnell, Ted Cruz, and Lindsay Graham and Trump's friend and attorney Rudy Giuliani. None fared well in the majority of the cartoons, often emerging as Trump's collaborators, enablers, and servants who were bullied, scared, and submissive to their owner and ruler. In a Bill Day drawing from January 4, 2021, for example, a mesmerized-looking elephant is being instructed to "find me some votes" by Trump's voice coming out of a gramophone. The caption of the cartoon reads, "His Master's Voice," suggesting that the president has direct ownership of the Republican Party.

President-elect Biden

Although Biden's likeness appeared in the postelection cartoons on occasion, it dominated the cartoons within the transition theme leading up to the inauguration. The new president appeared looking almost identical throughout the four themes: clad in a dark suit, a white shirt, a non-red tie, and very often, his signature aviator sunglasses. He emerged in the drawings as the antithesis of his predecessor. He was often drawn as a smiling, happy winner of the presidential race, who—according to the drawings—was long-awaited. A couple of the drawings replaced Biden's grin with the shape of the United States, as if to suggest that the whole country was also celebrating.

A few cartoons poked fun of Biden's age and supposed fragility by reporting on his broken leg and enveloping him in bubble wrap for protection. The overwhelming majority, however, showed him as a leader who is capable, qualified, and ready to tackle an array of crises. For example, in Adam Zyglis's cartoon from December 7, 2020, entitled "Biden's Cabinet Picks," the incoming president is seen putting—or returning—three books labeled "science," "public health," and "history" to a cabinet, hinting at the new president's priorities and values.

Statue of Liberty and Uncle Sam

The two iconic figures that have come to symbolize the United States appeared frequently throughout the four themes, almost always in opposition to President Trump and his supporters. Several cartoons, in fact, depicted Lady Liberty and Uncle Sam either kicking the president out or uttering his signature line from his former reality show *The Apprentice,* "You're fired," as if to carry out the wishes of the voters in a clear gesture of antipathy and disapproval. Uncle Sam and the Statue of Liberty were also seen as endorsing and celebrating Biden's win by dancing, smiling, or, in the case of Uncle Sam, taking a nap four years in the making.

Gifted to the United States by France and dedicated in 1886,[23] Lady Liberty has lingered in the American collective memory since then primarily as a metonym for the United States and its core values of democracy, freedom, and openness.[24] That is also how the character was deployed in the drawings across the four themes. The Statue of Liberty predates the now famous version of Uncle Sam from James Montgomery Flagg's World War I army recruitment poster by thirty-eight years, though the character dates back at least to the War of 1812. Similar to the Statue of Liberty, Uncle Sam has become a visual signifier of the United States, officially adopted as such in 1961 by the U.S. Congress.[25]

EDITORIAL CARTOONS AND VISUAL RHETORIC IN ACTION

Although the political cartoons of interest recycled the same four dominant textual hooks across all themes, they paired them with a variety of other visual and textual elements to build the narrative arc of each drawing. What follows is a series of visual rhetorical analyses of four editorial cartoons that were chosen as representative examples of each of the four themes.

Election Theme: "Trump Declares Victory"

The single panel drawing in color by Jeff Koterba was published on Daryl Cagle's cartoon website the day after the 2020 presidential election (figure 7.2). It features three characters in a horizontal arrangement: a bust of an elderly white man on the left, nearly an entire body of a woman in green in the center-left, and an entire body of a short white man on the right. The man on the left has white hair and is wearing a navy suit, a white shirt, and a blue tie. His arms are raised up with a thought bubble above his head that spells out "C'mon man . . ." The woman in between the two men looks tall and slender and is draped in a green toga. She is sporting a headdress that resembles a crown with spikes coming outward around it. Her right arm is raised up with an open, empty hand; there are two visible dots below it. Her left hand clutches what looks like a tablet with "Too Close to Call" written on it.

Figure 7.2.   "Trump Declares Victory." Jeff Koterba, Courtesy of Cagle Cartoons.

Both the woman and the elderly man to the left look in the direction of the third man positioned in the right corner of the drawing. The man is about a third of the woman's size and roughly equal in dimensions with the other man's bust. He has thick blond hair with bangs that extend beyond his head; his lips are arranged into a circle that resembles a fish's mouth. The man is wearing a dark suit, a white shirt, and a red tie that looks disproportionately long to his short stature. The tie flaps in the air, suggesting that the man is in motion. His legs look airborne; the three dots that look like pebbles behind one of his feet indicate movement. He is holding a flaming torch with "democracy" written on it. The man exclaims five times through a thought bubble as he runs, "I won."

The viewer instantly recognizes that the scene playing out in the drawing is constructed with the help of three of the five dominant visual signifiers: president-elect Biden on the left, the Statue of Liberty in the middle, and President Trump on the right. It is a scene of theft that unfolds on a couple of levels. On the literal level, President Trump is in the process of stealing the torch from the Statue of Liberty, robbing her of her iconic look, thus partially stripping her of her meaning. He rips the torch out of Lady Liberty's prostrated arm by force as indicated by the two falling rocks that are still midair below her hand. The steal just happened as the culprit is still close by, still in the frame. On the figurative level, the torch—here a symbol of a power transfer, presidential continuity, and, more broadly, democracy—gets stolen from its rightful owner, the voters, represented by Lady Liberty. This is a scene of a power grab, as it were, by President Trump, who declares himself a winner while the votes are still being counted. He interrupts the democratic process of elections to preemptively usurp the presidency, a move that is not his to make in the first place. The president is not willing to wait, setting a process in motion to illegally consolidate power.

Trump's actions clearly do not sit well with either of the two other characters, if their facial expressions are any indication. The Statue of Liberty looks stunned, with her enlarged eyes drawn as circles, bulging out in surprise. Her lips are parted, suggesting speechless astonishment. Her emptied hand and arm are still midair, as if frozen in shock after what just happened. Biden's reaction comes in the form of raised hands in a gesture of disbelief and the same catch phrase that he kept uttering during the last presidential debate in October 2020 as an expression of exasperation and annoyance.

Following the election, President Trump would insist that the presidency was, in fact, stolen *from* him and not by him as the cartoon suggests, because of alleged voter fraud.[26] The drawing catches Trump in a lie as he perpetrates the theft himself. As votes were still being tallied on November 4, 2020, the president told his supporters at the White House that day that "Frankly, we did win,"[27] verbally snatching victory from his opponent when there was none to be had then or later. The president emerges in the scenario as a sneaky cheater and a hypocrite who does exactly what he accuses his opponent of doing—stealing the election. Perhaps his physical size in relation to Biden and Lady Liberty alludes to his character; he is half the man that Biden appears to be.

Trump's Legacy Theme: "Trump Destroys GOP"

Drawn by Rick McKee and published on January 20, 2020, this single panel in color shows a scene of a disaster (figure 7.3). Almost the entire frame is filled by what looks like a crater or a hole in the ground with smoke and pieces of debris still floating in the air. The dominant hues in the drawing are brown and gray, with specks of color represented by pieces of clothing, skin, and hair of the two characters caught in the scene, an elephant and a man. The moment is captured from the perspective of someone positioned at the edge of the pit looking down.

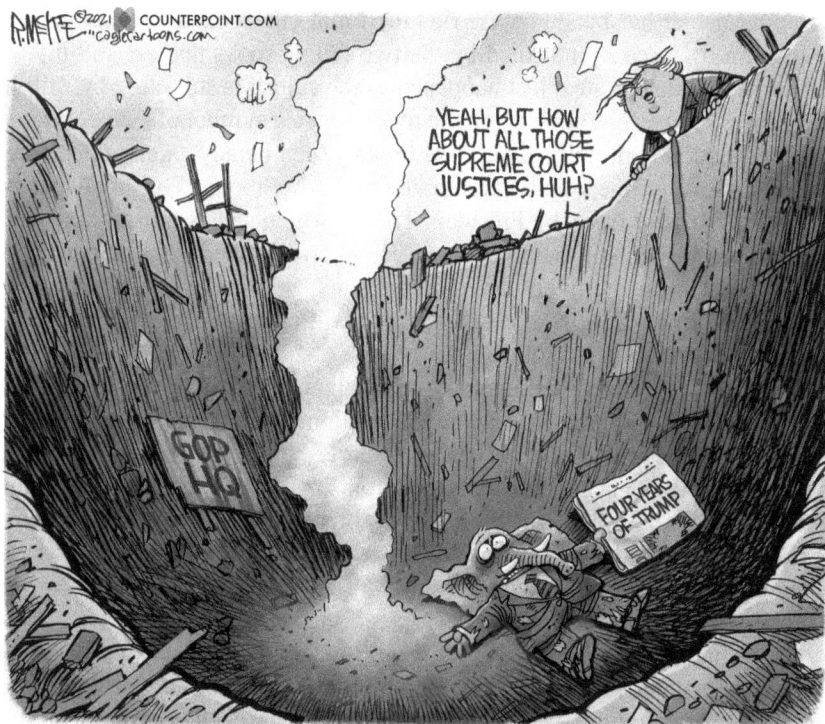

Figure 7.3. "Trump Destroys GOP." Rick McKee, Courtesy of Cagle Cartoons.

The hole looks deep and rounded at the edges, with steep walls that are perpendicular to the ground above and to the base. One wall inside the crater displays a tattered sign with the words "GOP HQ" still visible despite the destruction. The elephant lies on his back at the bottom of the hole, nearly splatted. His eyes are drawn as overly large circles, each with a small dot inside to signify a pupil. The dots are placed close together, making the elephant look cross-eyed and dizzy. Dark semicircles underneath his eyes and several lines meant to look like bunched-up skin create an expression of worry and fear.

The elephant's arms are stretched out; his legs protrude down and are parted as if he were thrown by a blast and landed on his back. The suit he is wearing is ragged, with holes and tears in the jacket and pants. His white shirt is sullied but the tie intact. In his left hand, the elephant holds a newspaper with a banner headline in all capital letters: "FOUR YEARS OF TRUMP." A column of brownish smoke to the elephant's right bellows straight up from the pit.

A white man's bust hanging over the edge of the crater is visible in the upper right corner of the cartoon. He appears unscathed, dressed in a dark suit, a white shirt, and a long red tie that hangs down into the crater. The man looks down at the elephant and says through a thought bubble, "Yeah, but how about all those Supreme Court justices, huh?" He dons strikingly pointy yellow hair, a chubby face, and rosy cheeks. The air around him and over the crater looks thick as indicated by the brownish-gray plumes.

The viewer witnesses the aftermath of a massive explosion that must have happened moments ago, judging by the sheer destruction of the area, the depth of the crater, and the lingering smoke, wood pieces, bricks, and paper still suspended midair. The proverbial dust has not settled yet, but the consequences of the blast are already visible and obvious, in part through the interaction between two dominant visual signifiers in the form of the GOP elephant and President Trump. This is what, the cartoon suggests, the Grand Old Party looks like after four years of Trump's presidency: ruined, scared, and traumatized, with no infrastructure and no help to rebuild. The party, the cartoon suggests, has imploded from within.

The only other person present at the scene is the one who, according to the headline and the cartoon's title, caused the explosion by his implied reckless-ness. Both textual elements accuse the president of destroying his own party, leaving nothing behind but a battered symbol of what it once used to be. But they also seem to absolve the party from any role it might have played in helping to cause the explosion, thus framing Republicans as a collective vic-tim at the bottom of the pit. Trump gets the designation of the villain in this dichotomy, though he justifies his actions by reminding the elephant that his near-death was worth the sacrifice in light of what it has accomplished: the Supreme Court staffed with a majority of conservative judges. Nevertheless, the president seems to be aware of the damage he caused as indicated by his "Yeah, but" at the beginning of his comment.

The elephant and the president are separated physically in the drawing, with the latter in a position to help the former, who finds himself in the hole because of the latter. And yet, the one who can and should help fails to do so, preoccupied by serving excuses for a disaster of his own making, without even so much as a word of sympathy or regret. The elephant, still too shocked to even utter a word, continues to stay down passively, left to his own devices to get himself out of what looks like an existential crisis.

Even though the two are supposed to be allies bound by the same political and ideological membership, their bond transforms into a power play between a perpetrator and a victim. The elephant is clearly not holding the upper hand here as he is battered, bruised, and framed as collateral damage of Trump's political games. The cartoon, in fact, suggests an erosion, if not a complete undoing, of partisan loyalty when the leader sacrifices his own colleagues for the ability to brag and absolve himself of any misconduct. But such a dynamic reflects poorly not only on the president; it also exposes the elephant's allegiance to a dangerous leader, with tragic consequences.

The contrasts that emerge between the elephant and Trump in this panel illustrate the type of relationship the two have come to establish after four years of working together—one of distrust, disloyalty if not betrayal, and unpredictable and reckless behavior that destroys one (the party) but not the other (Trump).

Capitol Siege Theme: "Feeding the Fringe"

The centerpiece of this single panel in color by Adam Zyglis, published on January 15, 2021, is a large sow that is lying on its left side (figure 7.4). It has a human head full of blond hair, pig's ears, a snout, and parted human lips with exposed teeth. The pig looks overweight, having (presumably) farrowed a litter of piglets visible in the drawing—or at least having become their caretaker. Four are seen lined up in front of the pig's belly, suckling. The four piglets also display some human characteristics in that they are wearing hats. One hat is red with "MAGA" written on it; another hat looks like it is made of fur, with a long hook coming out of each side; the third hat seems to be a black helmet with a red logo of a circle and a cross inside it; a sliver of the fourth hat is also visible in the image, displaying a patch of red with a logo of tilted letters *L* on a white background. The piglet quartet is also equipped with a few flags: one yellowish-brown with "Hang Mike Pence" written across it in two rows; another, blue with a white border and an inscription "Trump 2C"; and a third, which is red, with a blue border and a blue *X* stretched across it, with white stars running inside the *X*. A noose made out of rope and three signs with "Stop the steal" lie nearby.

As the visual clues and the title of the cartoon suggest, the drawing captures a literal and symbolic feeding scene between two dominant textual hooks that reveals the type of relationship they have: President Trump plays the role of a nurturing caretaker, and some of his supporters are his ideological offspring

Figure 7.4. "Feeding the Fringe." Adam Zyglis, Courtesy of Cagle Cartoons.

who take on his wisdom with the proverbial mother's milk. Trump does not even have to say anything to deliver his message to his proteges. The cartoon's title distinguishes the piglets as the fringe among Trump supporters, acknowledging that not every Trump follower fits the characterization.

The piglets are easily identified as members or sympathizers of some of the groups that reportedly converged on the Capitol on January 6, 2021, during the "stop the steal" riot. The piglet with the fur hat and horns alludes to the so-called QAnon Shaman, an Arizona man who is a self-proclaimed leader in the pro-Trump QAnon conspiracy theory movement.[28] The piglet with the cross-and-circle logo on his helmet is likely a supporter of White supremacy causes as he dons an iteration of the Celtic Cross interlocked within a circle, a known White supremacy sign classified as a hate symbol by the Anti-Defamation League. The least visible portion of the fourth piglet's hat resembles the Nazi flag with a black swastika in the center of a white circle against a red background, a symbol deployed by a host of White supremacy and neo-Nazi groups in the United States.

In addition to the hats, flags also help to identify the piglets' ideological allegiances. The red flag with the blue *X* is, of course, the Confederate battle flag, another visual sign classified by the Anti-Defamation League as a hate symbol. It has been used by White supremacists, including some Trump supporters, as a symbol of White pride. The noose, a visual signifier of lynching, together with the death threat to Vice President Mike Pence plastered on one of the flags, help to complete the viewer's understanding of the piglets' political and ideological leanings. Put together, the Capitol rioters emerge here as a group of vile characters: racist, violent, and marred in conspiracy theories fed to them by their lifeline pig caretaker.

The feeding presumably takes place before the piglets' participation in the Capitol riot, perhaps as the last stop to get reinforcements, directives, and strength before storming the building. The relationship between the two is one of interdependence. The piglets rely on Trump for food (i.e., life), and Trump relies on the piglets to execute his will, in this case a rebellion against perceived voter fraud. The cartoon, thus, implicates the president as directly responsible for the violence that broke out at the Capitol by feeding his supporters inflammatory rhetoric.

Transition Theme: "Passing the Torch"

Drawn by Dave Whamond, the single-panel cartoon in color was published on Daryl Cagle's site on December 28, 2020 (figure 7.5). Although the cartoon's title inside the drawing is "Passing the Torch," the title on the cartoon website is "Passing the Dumpster Fire." The frame shows busts of two elderly white men as the main characters in the scene. Both are dressed in dark blue suits and white shirts. The one on the left sports a red tie, yellow hair, and a frown indicated by an inverted letter U that stands in for his lips. The man squints as he looks in the direction of his extended left arm and the other man nearby. He is holding a lit torch in the outstretched arm, though the torch looks like a green dumpster with flames and dark bellowing smoke coming from inside it.

The dumpster torch seems to be the focal point of the scene as it is located almost in the center of the composition, hovering above both men. The bright yellow and orange flames shooting upward catch the viewer's attention. The other man, to the right of the torch, looks older than his companion on the left, as indicated by partial baldness, pronounced wrinkles on his forehead, and white hair. He is slender, about half the size of the man with the torch. His eyes seem to be looking away from his counterpart, the extended arm, and the torch, as if refusing to acknowledge their presence. Neither of his hands reach for the torch. His face seems to communicate no emotion other than calmness.

Figure 7.5. "Passing the Torch." Dave Whamond, Courtesy of Cagle Cartoons.

The scene captures the moment of a symbolic power transition between two dominant visual signifiers who make frequent appearances in the transition theme, President Trump and his successor. Neither man, given his facial expressions and body language, seems eager to participate in the exchange. President Trump's face betrays anger, resentment, and maybe even a hint of childishness as he extends his arm to give Biden the torch without so much as a glance at his former opponent. The coldness and bitterness presumably stem from Trump's claims of a rigged election that robbed him of a second term of presidency. Biden, on the other hand, comes across as composed and even detached, as if trying to dismiss Trump and his ill will. He is not clamoring to take over the torch because it is a dumpster on fire—or dumpster fire—a visual signifier in pop culture that stands in for a complete disaster. The cartoon implies that it is the Trump presidency and its legacy that are, quite literally, a hot, burning mess, which Biden is not eager to inherit. Biden appears smaller in stature compared to Trump as he seems to be placed in some geographic (and ideological) distance from the outgoing president and his legacy, which, judging by the robust dark smoke and the shooting flames, is a catastrophe in need of immediate attention.

CARTOON FUNCTIONS AND VISUAL COMMENTARY

The analyzed political cartoons that appeared during the seventy-two days between the presidential elections of November 2020 and the Biden inauguration functioned as a running, mostly one-sided commentary on the perceived (and imagined) tribulations of the Trump presidency, one that culminated in a new era, in which experience, wisdom, and compassion—at least according to some of the drawings—were to return to the White House. The running commentary overwhelmingly detracted from the outgoing president either by infantilizing him as a man-child who could not cope with the electoral loss to Biden or by demonizing him as a delusional "baddie" who destroyed the country and sowed unfounded conspiracy theories among some of his supporters to cling to power.

With such a lopsided and mostly negative visual take on President Trump and his legacy, the cartoons in effect played the role of ideological and moral polarizers that created a striking dichotomy across the four thematic categories by pitting the five dominant textual hooks against each other in a recurring configuration. The juxtaposition, which was visually constructed primarily through hyperbole, often served as the focal point of the drawings' narrative arc. On the one side of the confrontation was the supervillain Trump, who used his powers for selfish, "bad" reasons, and who surrounded himself with rabid supporters and GOP members to carry out his underhanded agenda. On the other side of the moral divide was the idealized, almost savior-like Biden, who was already "good" by the sheer fact that he was not Trump. His supporters included the Statue of Liberty and Uncle Sam, the iconic proxies for all Americans.

As a result, the editorial cartoons of interest created visual shortcuts that summarized the political turmoil of the lame duck period and developed visual archetypes—even caricatures—of President Trump and president-elect Biden to transform complex social issues into rather simplified, easily digestible, and graspable single-panel visual snapshots. In doing so, the cartoons "present society with visually palpable and hyper-ritualized depictions (selectively exaggerated portions of 'reality') that attempt to reveal the essence and meaning of social events."[29]

The running visual-textual commentary of the political cartoons might be likened to the chorus in ancient Greek tragedies. Composed of multiple voices singing and dancing in unison—much like the cartoons of interest in this chapter—the chorus, some have theorized, deployed the alienation effect, an enduring tactic used in dramas for centuries to pause the action.[30] Such interludes in the plot grant the audience opportunities to breathe, register the action, and think through it. In this analogy, the seventy-two days of the "lame duck" period played out as an antient Greek tragedy, with character development and plot twists that saw it all—impassioned rhetoric, failure, triumph, rage, joy, violence, and even death. The editorial cartoons that witnessed these story lines interrupted them to slow down the action so that the audiences—the readers—would have a moment to ponder what they had seen. To do so, the rhetorical work of a chorus and that of an editorial cartoon blended the intellectual with the emotional, the literal with the symbolic, the contemplative with the musical as "perhaps the most effective and direct method for arousing the emotion and passions of the audience while forcing it to think at the same time"[31]—the work that editorial cartoons have been performing in the U.S. media for more than three centuries.

NOTES

1. There were, of course, many more cartoons published during the time period of interest, but this chapter relied on the cartoon site www.politicalcartoons.com for the corpus of analyzed drawings. The site is published by the editorial cartoon artist Daryl Cagle.

2. "Historians' Statement on Congressional Certification of the 2020 Presidential Election" (January 4, 2021). Available on *Politico*'s website at https://www.politico .com/f/?id=00000176-d218-d162-a7ff-f31c5b8c0000.

3. Lester C. Olson, "Benjamin Franklin's Pictorial Representation of the British Colonies in America: A Study in Rhetorical Iconology," *Quarterly Journal of Speech* 73 (1987): 18–42.

4. Donald Dewey, *The Art of Ill Will: The Story of American Political Cartoons* (New York: New York University Press, 2007).

5. Lucy Shelton Caswell, "Drawing Swords: War in American Editorial Cartoons," *American Journalism* 21 (2004): 13–45; Michael A. DeSousa and Martin J. Medhurst, "Political Cartoons and American Culture: Significant Symbols of Campaign 1980," *Studies in Visual Communication* 8 (1982): 84–97; Dewey, *The Art of Ill Will*; Klaus Dodds, "Popular Geopolitics and Cartoons: Representing Power Relations, Repetition and Resistance," *Critical African Studies* 2 (2010): 113–131; Janice Edwards, *Political Cartoons in the 1988 Presidential Campaign: Image, Metaphor, and Narrative* (New York: Garland Publishing, Inc., 1997); Chris Lamb, "Drawing Power," *Journalism Studies* 8 (2007): 715–729.

6. Peter Duus, "Presidential Address: Weapons of the Weak, Weapons of the Strong—the Development of the Japanese Political Cartoon," *The Journal of Asian Studies* 60 (2001): 965–997.

7. Ilan Danjoux, "Reconsidering the Decline of the Editorial Cartoon," *PS: Political Science and Politics* 40 (2007): 245–248; Victor S. Navasky, *The Art of Controversy. Political Cartoons and Their Enduring Power* (New York: Alfred A. Knopf, 2014).

8. Linus Abraham, "Effectiveness of Cartoons as a Uniquely Visual Medium for Orienting Social Issues," *Journalism & Communication Monographs* 11 (2009): 117–165; Ellen Giarelli, "Images of Cloning and Stem Cell Research in Editorial Cartoons in the United States," *Qualitative Health Research* 16 (2006): 61–78; Edwards, *Political Cartoons in the 1988 Presidential Campaign.*

9. DeSousa and Medhurst, "Political Cartoons and American Culture"; Edwards, *Political Cartoons in the 1988 Presidential Campaign*; Sonja Foss, "Theory of Visual Rhetoric," in *Handbook of Visual Communication: Theory, Methods, and Media*, eds. Ken Smith, Sandra Moriarty, Gretchen Barbatis, and Keith Kenney (Mahwah, NJ: Routledge, 2005), 141–152.

10. DeSousa and Medhurst, "Political Cartoons and American Culture," 91.

11. Edwards, *Political Cartoons in the 1988 Presidential Campaign*; Walt Werner, "On Political Cartoons and Social Studies Textbooks: Visual Analogies, Intertextuality, and Cultural Memory," *Canadian Social Studies* 38 (2004): 1–11.

12. Foss, "Theory of Visual Rhetoric."

13. Philipp Mayring, *Qualitative Content Analysis: Theoretical Foundation, Basic Procedures and Software Solution* (Klagenfurt, Austria: GESIS, 2014), 63–107; Axel Philipps, "Visual Protest Material as Empirical Data," *Visual Communication* 11 (2011): 3–21.

14. Virginia Brown and Victoria Clarke, "Thematic Analysis," in *APA Handbook of Research Methods in Psychology* (Washington, DC: American Psychological Association, 2012), vol 2, 57–71.

15. Foss, "Theory of Visual Rhetoric."

16. Brown and Clarke, "Thematic Analysis," 57.

17. Jean Burgess, "'All Your Chocolate Rain Are Belong to Us?' Viral Video, YouTube and the Dynamic of Participatory Culture," in *Video Vortex: Responses to YouTube*, eds. Geert Lovink and Sabine Niederer (Amsterdam, Netherlands: Institute of Network Culture, 2008): 101–109.

18. Ibid., 105.

19. Foss, "Theory of Visual Rhetoric."

20. Ibid.

21. There were nine editorial cartoons in the cartoon corpus that expressed pro-Trump sentiments, some supporting the president's allegations of voter fraud. They were drawn by Gacy McCoy (seven drawings) and Rick McKee (two drawings). They were considered thematic outliers given their small number as compared to the rest of the corpus that overwhelmingly expressed anti-Trump sentiments.

22. Luke Mogelson, "The Storm," *The New Yorker* (2021, January 25): 32–53.

23. National Park Service, "Statue of Liberty: Liberty Enlightening the World" (October 7, 2020).

24. Leo R. Chavez, *Covering Immigration: Popular Images and the Politics of the Nation* (Los Angeles: University of California Press, 2001), 53–81.

25. Encyclopedia Britannica, "Uncle Sam: United States Symbol," retrieved from https://www.britannica.com/topic/Uncle-Sam. Library of Congress, multiple entries about Uncle Sam and propaganda posters during World War I.

26. Jemima McEvoy, "These Are the Voter Fraud Claims Trump Tried (and Failed) to Overturn the Election With," *Forbes* (December 17, 2020).

27. Reuters, "With Results from Key States Unclear, Trump Declares Victory" (November 4, 2020).

28. Erin Donaghue, "Capitol Rioter Known as 'QAnon Shaman' Will Be Jailed until Trial," *CBS News* (January 16, 2021).

29. Abraham, "Effectiveness of Cartoons as a Uniquely Visual Medium," 119.

30. Albert Weiner, "The Function of the Tragic Greek Chorus," *Theatre Journal* 32 (1980): 205–212.

31. Ibid, 211.

Chapter 8

Litigating Victory

An Analysis of 2020 Postelection Lawsuits

Cayce Myers

The storming of the U.S. Capitol on January 6, 2021, was the culmination of months-long conflict over the results of the 2020 presidential election. The riot followed the pro-Trump "Save America" rally where thousands of Trump supporters came to show their support for the president and protest what they believed was a stolen election. This flashpoint in the 2020 presidential election will likely be remembered as the boiling point where Trump supporters took extralegal means to delegitimize the democratically held presidential election. However, the fight over the legitimacy of the 2020 election has a much deeper history, which goes back even before the November election: Lawsuits by both parties and presidential candidates echoed the issues of election legitimacy, voting rights, and the myriad of new voting accommodations made because of the COVID-19 pandemic. Understanding the roots of the storming of the U.S. Capitol requires an understanding of the underlying legal controversy that surrounded the 2020 presidential election.

The litigation surrounding the 2020 election was something both candidates discussed during the campaign, and both used it as a fundraising talking point. President Trump's Save America PAC and the Republican National Committee raised money for election challenges, and by December 2020 the *Washington Post* reported that President Trump raised approximately $170 million from his claims of election fraud (although only some of the money raised was going to actual legal challenges).[1] Trump fundraised focusing on election fraud with one fundraising text stating, "The Left will try to STEAL this election!"[2]

The certification of the election results even became a political issue. Nowhere was this more evident than in the Georgia special election for U.S. senator. In the runoff, Trump made an endorsement of Senator Kelly Loeffler (R-GA), who committed to object to the election results of 2020 in the U.S.

Senate (she ended up not objecting after the storming of the Capitol).[3] Trump also made a campaign issue out of the electoral result in Georgia, vowing to campaign against Republican governor Brian Kemp and Republican Georgia secretary of state Brad Raffensberger, who had resisted Trump's request to overturn the Georgia election results in the presidential election. Trump said that he believed Kemp and Raffensberger were not even Republicans, and that he was "treated badly" by both officials.[4] Kemp would go on to receive great criticism from his own party after this, creating doubt about his political future in his reelection. He and the Georgia General Assembly would go on to pass a voter law that made changes for absentee ballots, curtailed mobile voting centers, and made substantive changes to the State Election Board, including removing the secretary of state from it.[5]

Democrats and Joe Biden also fundraised based on election challenges. Biden's campaign began fundraising for potential postelection litigation, although in a low-key way. The Biden's Lawyers Committee fundraised by calling donors and explaining that unless the election results showed Biden handily winning, there would likely be postelection litigation that would go on into December 2020.[6] After the election, Biden's team went on to ask for $30 million to combat the lawsuits that Trump and his supporters were bringing in individual states. The fund called The Biden Fight Fund, a joint campaign committee by Biden's campaign and the Democratic National Committee (DNC), ended up with slightly over $19 million from October through December 2020.[7] Biden would continue to engage in postelection fundraising, sending one email to donors stating, "We can't allow Trump to win any of these lawsuits just because we can't afford to fight back. We need to be able to show up in court to defend Joe and Kamala's victory . . . and to do that we are counting on a surge of donations today into the Biden Fight Fund."[8]

The money, campaign rallies, speeches, and politics of the postelection are significant. They led up to the event of the storming of the U.S. Capitol, an event previously unthinkable in modern American politics. However, the roots of the postelection turmoil lie in the allegations of voter fraud, voting laws, and the new statewide measures taken in light of the COVID-19 pandemic. This chapter examines the litigation surrounding the 2020 presidential election by examining multiple federal and state lawsuits filed both before and after the election.[9] Examining these lawsuits shows that claims of election fraud and disenfranchisement by Trump did not meet the legal threshold for overturning the 2020 election. However, the claims made in many of these lawsuits set up political talking points for the 2022 midterm election and eventual 2024 presidential election. The chapter concludes with an analysis of the legal and political impact of election lawsuits in 2020 and provides predictions of what role these types of suits may play in the future of American politics.

AMERICAN VOTING LAWS: A BRIEF OVERVIEW OF CONSTITUTIONAL ISSUES AND ENFRANCHISEMENT

Federal law over the past 240 years has dealt with the issue of who can vote, and how that right can be ensured. James Madison in Federalist 57 directly addressed the importance of voting in federal elections, and how the federal and state governments should stay out of the laws governing it. To Madison, it was important that voting rights be enshrined in the Constitution, writing:

> Who are to be the electors of the Federal Representatives? Not the rich more than the poor; not the learned more than the ignorant; not the haughty heirs of distinguished names, more than the humble sons of obscure and unpropitious fortune. The electors are to be the great body of the people of the United States.[10]

Nearly two hundred years later the sentiment of the importance of voting as essential to democracy was reiterated by U.S. Supreme Court Justice Hugo Black. Writing in 1964 Justice Black summed up the importance of voting rights in *Wesberry v. Sanders,* stating:

> No right is more precious in a free country than that of having a voice in the election of those who make the laws under which, as good citizens, we must live. Other rights, even the most basic, are illusory if the right to vote is undermined.[11]

However, the nature of voting laws in the United States has not been as straightforward as Madison and Black may have hoped. Litigation as an election strategy has a long history in American politics. Dating back to the nineteenth century, the American legal system has played a role in elections, sometimes even determining their outcomes. Part of the reason for this is the way American elections work. They are certified by states, and states under Article I, section 4 determine many of the intricacies of the logistics of actually holding an election.[12] In fact, in the history of U.S. election laws, it has been the states, not the federal government, that have caused many of the issues that courts have to grapple with. To understand the implications of the pre- and post-2020 presidential election litigation, it is important to provide an overview of U.S. election law, and the history of litigating election outcomes.

The arc of voting rights in the United States has been a gradual inclusivity of voters, with barriers gradually being removed based on property ownership, race, gender, and age. However, the fight for this expansion of the electorate has been glacial, and, at times, hard fought. American voting rights in the eighteenth century were based on property ownership, and it would not be until the mid-nineteenth century when that barrier was removed for White male citizens (North Carolina was the last state to remove the requirement in

1856).[13] However, the property qualifications for voting slowly eroded, with most White men being able to vote in the United States as early as 1789 (estimates range from 50 to 75 percent of the population).[14] Even women could vote in New Jersey until 1807, and landowning free African Americans could vote in a handful of states prior to the Civil War.[15] Federal law dating back to Article I of the U.S. Constitution established voting rights in the United States, but it was not until the post–Civil War era that there was a concerted federal effort to regulate voting rights within states.[16] Until 1870, the U.S. Constitution was silent on managing voting, and, as a result states regulated voting rights. However, a series of constitutional amendments changed the nature of voting in the United States starting with the Fourteenth Amendment, ratified in 1868, which gave citizenship to all freed slaves, and the Fifteenth Amendment, ratified in 1870, which gave African American men the right to vote.[17]

Federal law tried to put some enforcement of the new rights given to former slaves, especially voting rights. The Enforcement Act of 1870, also known as the Civil Rights Act of 1870, protected voting rights of African American men who were intimidated from voting because of groups such as the Ku Klux Klan.[18] Signed into law by President Ulysses S. Grant, the law gave the president the power to use the military to suppress any attempts to block the enforcement of these voting rights, and it declared disallowing voters from exercising their right to vote based on race or prior servitude to be illegal.[19] However, U.S. Supreme Court holdings in *United States v. Reese* and *United States v. Cruikshank*, both decided in 1876, undercut much of the law and the Fifteenth Amendment protections given to African Americans.[20] The more significant of the cases, *United States v. Cruikshank*, held that the Bill of Rights, the first ten amendments of the U.S. Constitution, did not apply to states or private parties.[21] Writing for the majority, Chief Justice Morrison Waite held that the Equal Protection Clause and Due Process Clause of the Fourteenth Amendment did not apply to individuals, but did apply to states. The result was that violations of the Enforcement Act of 1870 did not apply to a series of defendants who killed several men, both African American and White, during an armed confrontation in the Louisiana governor's election in 1872.[22] The result of this decision was a continuation of disenfranchisement of African American voters in the South and a rise of poll taxes and literacy tests given as prerequisites to voting.[23]

The disenfranchisement of African American voters would continue during the late nineteenth and first half of the twentieth centuries. However, by the late nineteenth century the women's suffrage movement gained momentum, and some states recognized women's right to vote as early as 1870 (Wyoming).[24] However, universal women's suffrage in the United States did not occur until 1920 with the ratification of the Nineteenth Amendment.[25] Still, Native Americans did not have voting rights in some states until the twentieth century with the passage of the Indian Citizenship Act of 1924.[26] Some states did not recognize Native American voting rights until much later, with Maine and Utah still having some form of disenfranchisement of Native Americans until the 1960s.[27]

It was the 1960s, however, that would be a watershed moment for the development of voting rights laws in the United States. The U.S. Supreme Court under Chief Justice Earl Warren handed down several definitive cases on voting, establishing the principle of one man, one vote, which was the concept that votes could not be diluted through unique representation laws. The first decision, *Baker v. Carr*, decided in 1962, held that redistricting was a justiciable question, as opposed to a political one, which meant that federal courts could hear redistricting cases. The impact of the case was significant. Writing for the majority, Justice William Brennan reformulated the political question doctrine (the doctrine of when a legal question is political as opposed to legal) stating that under the Equal Protection Clause of the Fourteenth Amendment questions about malapportionment were not exempt from judicial review.[28] This led the court to strike down several laws that related to disproportionate election processes that diluted certain groups. These systems the court reviewed typically were structured to give rural communities a greater power within the election system and diluted the voice of voters in urban areas. One such example was Georgia's county unit system. In 1963 the court struck down Georgia's county unit system, in which counties voted in units that gave a disproportionate number of votes to less populated rural counties, finding it was unconstitutional holding that it undermined the concept of one man, one vote.[29] Writing for the majority Justice William Douglas noted, "The conception of political equality from the Declaration of Independence, to Lincoln's Gettysburg Address, to the Fifteenth, Seventeenth, and Nineteenth Amendments can mean only one thing—one person, one vote."[30]

By 1964, the U.S. Supreme Court had gone further in its establishment of case law that upheld the concept of one man, one vote. In 1964 the court ruled in *Wesberry v. Sanders* that the allocation of U.S. House of Representatives had to be proportional to the population and that congressional districts had to be equal in population.[31] That same year, in *Reynolds v. Sims*, the Court applied the same population issues of representation on state legislatures holding that those districts also had to have equal amounts of population represented in each district.[32]

Other barriers to voting also were eliminated in the mid-1960s. The Twenty-Fourth Amendment of the U.S. Constitution, ratified in 1964, banned poll taxes in federal elections, a practice that had been in place since the late nineteenth century.[33] The U.S. Supreme Court subsequently held that poll taxes violated the equal protection clause of the Fourteenth Amendment in *Harper v. Virginia Board of Elections,* which ended poll taxes in state elections.[34] Voting age also was lowered in 1971. As a result of the Vietnam War and the criticism that soldiers could be drafted to go to war but could not vote, the voting age in the United States was lowered to eighteen in the Twenty-Sixth Amendment.[35]

Perhaps the most significant voting law in the 1960s came from federal statute, not U.S. Supreme Court rulings. In 1965, President Lyndon Johnson signed the Voting Rights Act of 1965, which banned racial discrimination in voting.[36] This outlawed literacy tests, laws that explicitly provided racial discrimination in voting, and a preclearance requirement for some voting districts. It is the preclearance requirement that sought to combat disenfranchisement in certain states and local governments that require review of any changes to laws or voting practices by the U.S. attorney general and the U.S. District Court for the D.C. Circuit. That provision of the act, known as section 5, identified districts for review under a coverage formula that was ultimately struck down by the U.S. Supreme Court in 2013.[37] With the coverage formula removed, the section 5 review process of the Voting Rights Act of 1965 is, in effect, unenforceable.[38] The ending of the preclearance requirement was predicated on the historical changes in elections since 1965. Many of the original areas covered by preclearance had minority officials, and voting participation had radically changed from 1965 to 2013. For example, of the six states originally covered by the Voting Rights Act of 1965, the number of African American elected officials had increased by 1,000 percent.[39] The result of elimination of the preclearance formula is that federal review of voting laws has changed. Critics have argued this has led to an increase in restrictive voting laws that facilitate voter disenfranchisement.

VOTING IN THE TWENTY-FIRST CENTURY: THE ISSUE OF STATE-BY-STATE STANDARDS

Vote counting and the processes of collecting ballots have produced election challenges going back to the 1876 presidential election between Rutherford B. Hayes, the Republican, and Samuel Tilden, the Democrat. Interestingly, that election hinged on vote counting procedures in Florida and the Reconstruction Republicans' attempt to use vote counting procedures to ensure a Republican victory (they succeeded).[40] The presidential election of 1876 was prescient of the well-known 2000 presidential election between George W. Bush and Al Gore, which ended only thirty-nine days before Inauguration

Day (Tilden and Hayes ended only two days before the inauguration).[41] These types of disputes illustrate the complexities and the idiosyncratic nature of state election laws. In U.S. history the law of how elections actually work is set by the states, not the federal government. While the 1960s was an era when federal law strengthening the protection of voter enfranchisement, states, such as Minnesota, were perfecting state recount measures and establishing the structure for election challenges.[42] By the 1970s the U.S. Supreme Court precedent in *Reynolds v. Sims*, the 1964 case over congressional district apportionment, had been used to develop a series of lower court decisions that increased the federal government's role in invalidating elections based on the Fourteenth Amendment.[43] It is this tension between federal intervention and state-specific election law that would be the hallmark of election issues in the twenty-first century.

No issue has been so divisive in modern election law as voter ID legislation. Framed by Democrats as a Republican attempt to suppress low-income and minority voters who tend to vote Democratic, the issue of voter ID laws has become a touchstone of an increasingly partisan political environment. Republicans charge that voter ID helps reduce fraud in elections and preserves the integrity of the election process. Indiana established a voter ID law by its Republican-controlled legislature. That law was challenged, and the U.S. Supreme Court upheld the voter ID laws, 6–3, in a plurality opinion in 2008.[44] The court upheld the law based on the ground that Indiana had an interest in addressing voter fraud. Following this ruling, other states followed suit in passing voter ID laws, with a greater number of voter ID laws being passed after the U.S. Supreme Court's decision in *Shelby County v. Holder*, which struck down the preclearance formula of the Voting Rights Act of 1965.[45]

The issues of voter ID, voter fraud, and voter disenfranchisement, have been entrenched upon a Republican–Democratic basis. However, in 2008, former Democratic president Jimmy Carter and former Republican secretary of state James Baker III found that both sides' concerns regarding voter ID had merit.[46] Voter ID laws continued to face criticism with Texas's voter ID law being challenged in a series of lawsuits starting in 2011 and ultimately ending in 2018.[47] However, voter ID law is nuanced and varies state by state. In some states voter ID requires a government-issued ID with a photo. However, in some states when a voter cannot produce that ID the voter may vote without the ID and have their vote counted, and some stricter states mandate that the voter take additional steps to prove their ID before the vote is counted.[48] As of 2020, thirty-five states have some type of law that requests or requires voters to provide ID before voting.[49]

Other voting regulations by states impact voter participation and would become particularly large issues in the 2020 election. None is so impactful on voter turnout than early voting. Currently there are forty-three states, plus the District of Columbia, that allow early voting in an election (Connecticut, Kentucky, Mississippi, Missouri, New Hampshire, and South Carolina do not).[50] Some of the early voting varies even within the state itself with county clerks making the decision on whether to start early voting on Saturdays or Sundays in certain states.[51]

Related to early voting is absentee voting, which began as a mechanism for military personnel to vote during the Civil War and later in World War II. The federal government created two laws that directly deal with military absentee voting: the Uniformed and Overseas Citizens Absentee Voting Act (UOCAVA) enacted in 1986 and the Military and Overseas Voter Empowerment Act (MOVE Act) enacted in 2009.[52] However, it was not until the 1980s that absentee ballots came into widespread use on Election Day starting with California, which allowed absentee requests for any reason.

By 2020, there were twenty-nine states with no-excuse absentee ballot request processes. All states offer mail-in absentee voting, and that option has increased in popularity compared with in-person day-of voting from 1998 to 2018 (day-of voting is still the dominant method, however).[53] By 2020 the MIT Data and Science lab reported that more votes were mailed in than cast in-person in the presidential election.[54] Some states have even gone so far as to make all of their voting by mail (Oregon, Utah, Colorado, Washington, and Hawaii). Mail-in ballots can also be returned to a drop box and returned by another person in some states, and voters can also hand deliver their ballots to a voting location.[55] In 2020, mail-in balloting became a big issue politically with several states automatically sending out ballots to all registered voters (California, District of Columbia, Nevada, New Jersey, and Vermont).[56] The criticism of vote by mail is the issue of fraud, and some studies show that fraud is actually a rare occurrence. According to a study by Project Vote, a voter turnout nonprofit that advocates for voter mobilization of low-income and minority voters, voter fraud sometimes is conflated with voter error.[57]

In addition to early voting and mail-in ballots, there are other mechanisms to increase voting. One controversial measure is ballot collection, or, pejoratively called ballot harvesting, which is the process by which third parties are allowed to pick up and deliver ballots to voters. As a practice it varies state by state and is a process that was at the root of a 2018 voter fraud case in the North Carolina congressional election for the Ninth District. That case involved election irregularities that included allegations that voters received absentee ballots they never requested, the collection of unsealed ballots by third parties, and the illegal ballot collection by a Republican operative.[58] That case eventually led to a revote in the election because of the level of election fraud, especially illegal ballot harvesting.[59] According to the National Conference of State Legislatures, twenty-six states allow someone other than the voter to return a ballot, but twelve of those states place a limit on the amount of ballots a third party can return to prevent undue influence on the voter.[60] Some states also place restrictions on who the person returning the ballot can be, but some states have a more permissive view, allowing the voter to designate anyone to return the ballot.

The closeness of elections also presents a unique situation for recounting ballots. In some states a close election automatically warrants a recount regardless of whether a candidate requests it. The vast majority—forty-one—of states and the District of Columbia allow a requested recount from a candidate, party, or group.[61] However, nine states (Arizona, Connecticut, Florida, Hawaii, Illinois, Mississippi, New York, South Carolina, and Tennessee) do not have a requested recount process, and only six of those states have recounts that are triggered by close votes within a percentage (e.g., Arizona requires there to be a .01 percent margin).[62] Recount requests are very nuanced among the forty-one states that do allow them. For example, in Massachusetts and Pennsylvania recounts can occur with voter petitions.[63] Thirty-nine states allow candidates to ask for recounts, but among those states, twelve require the margin of victory to be within a specific percentage.[64] Still other states have recount provisions that allow political parties to request a recount (Colorado, Indiana, Michigan, Oregon, South Dakota, and Washington).[65]

It was the idiosyncratic nature of state election laws, specifically recount protocols, that set the stage for the largest and most publicized election law challenge—Florida's presidential recount in 2000. That recount made its way up to the U.S. Supreme Court in an unprecedented move by a body that thought of itself as apolitical. In the Court's decision in *Bush v. Gore,* the decision addressed first whether the recount in Florida should be stopped, and whether a recount should resume using a statewide standard.[66] The recount Florida had been using involved a county-by-county recount system that the U.S. Supreme Court in *Bush v. Gore* voted 7–2 violated the Equal Protection Clause of the Fourteenth Amendment. The impactful decision, however, was the 5–4 decision, along ideological lines with conservative justices in the majority, that Florida could not institute a statewide standard for recounts before the safe harbor deadline of December 12, 2000. Because of that, George W. Bush won the electoral votes in Florida.

Interestingly, *Bush v. Gore* as precedent is limited, and it presented some question on the precedential value of the case in contemporary law. Writing in the equal protection analysis, the majority wrote, "Our consideration is limited to the present circumstances, for the problem of equal protection in election processes generally presents many complexities."[67] However, the impact of *Bush v. Gore* was significant, not only for the law but for the public consciousness of elections. In 2002 the Help America Vote Act (HAVA), which banned the punch card ballot used by Florida in 2000, passed Congress and was signed into law by President Bush. The National Commission on Federal Election Reform, headed by Democratic president Jimmy Carter and Republican Gerald Ford, was also created to address election issues, particularly the safe harbor guidelines that made the election decision so fast. However, the largest impact of 2000 was the recognition that close elections have very uncertain outcomes. The U.S Supreme Court in *Bush v. Gore* took that case at its own discretion. There was no law or constitutional provision that mandated it decide the case and, as a result, the outcome of the election. In effect, the law today could allow for a *Tilden vs. Hayes* 1876–style outcome; one that resulted in a purely political solution.[68]

LITIGATION IN THE 2020 ELECTION

Preelection Lawsuits

Numerous lawsuits were filed prior to the 2020 election, with most of the lawsuits focused on state-level changes that were made related to the COVID-19 pandemic. These lawsuits were from several states that were mainly in highly contested places such as Pennsylvania, Arizona, and Georgia. *USA Today*'s analysis of lawsuits filed between January 1 and October 23, 2020, showed that there were over 230 preelection lawsuits in federal courts.[69] That number was higher than during the presidential elections of 2016, 2012, and 2008.[70] The issues in the suits revolved around COVID-19 procedures on mail-in ballots, extended vote tabulation, and accommodations for disabled voters.

Major cases involving the 2020 presidential election were filed in highly contested or populous states, and the decisions were made very quickly given the timeliness issues of the lawsuits. This was clearly present in a series of cases that focused on election deadlines and when mail-in votes would be counted. In Arizona, a toss-up state in 2020, the state Democratic Party sued the Arizona secretary of state regarding failure to have proper signatures on absentee ballots corrected by Election Day.[71] The Arizona Democratic Party sought a permanent injunction against the state mandating signatures being corrected by 7 p.m. Election Day, and instead wanted to have voters have up to five days after voting ended to correct the error. The U.S. District Court for the District of Arizona granted the permanent injunction, but the U.S. Court of Appeals for the Ninth Circuit granted a stay of the injunction holding that the time allotted under Arizona law did not place an undue burden on voters.[72]

Similarly, *Mi Familia Vota v. Hobbs* was another Arizona case that involved the Arizona law involving the deadline for voters to register for 2020.[73] In that case plaintiffs Mi Familia Vota, a Latino voting organization that supports Latinos and Latino immigrants, and Arizona Coalition for Change, a group dedicated to register voters, sued Arizona over the October 5 deadline to register as an absentee voter because of COVID-19. Prior to the pandemic, the groups were registering on average 1,523 voters a week, but that number dropped to 282 a week. They sued arguing the registration deadline of October 5 violated the First and Fourteenth Amendments under due process. The U.S. District Court for the District of Arizona granted an injunction on Arizona from enforcing the October 5 deadline and extended the deadline to October 23. The Republican National Committee appealed the decision to the U.S. Court of Appeals for the Ninth Circuit, which held that the injunction could remain in place until October 15, essentially providing ten more days for registration than the Arizona statute allowed.[74]

Arizona was not the only state where voter registration rules were at issue. In Michigan the Michigan Alliance for Retired Americans sued the secretary of state over Michigan laws regarding absentee ballots, specifically the requirement that absentee ballots be received by 8 p.m. on Election Day, law that limits who may handle and deliver a voter's ballot, and the required postage for mail-in ballots.[75] The Michigan Court of Claims issued a partial preliminary injunction on the enforcement of these election laws, specifically allowing ballots received up to fourteen days after the election be counted and removing the law regarding who could possess ballots. However, the Michigan legislature appealed and the Court of Appeals of Michigan held that the 8 p.m. restraint on the ballot drop-off was constitutional, and that Court of Claims exceeded its jurisdiction by issuing a permanent injunction.[76] A similar case occurred in Georgia where The New Georgia Project, a voting rights group that registers voters, sued Georgia over the state law that required absentee ballots be turned in by 7 p.m. on Election Day.[77] The U.S. District Court for the Northern District of Georgia issued a preliminary injunction, which was later stayed by the U.S. Court of Appeals for the 11th Circuit. Writing for the majority, Judge Britt Grant said that the long-standing Georgia statute was "reasonable and nondiscriminatory" and stayed the District Court's preliminary injunction, which had posed its own new deadline (counting all ballots received after the election).[78]

The deadlines for accepting ballots were a major legal issue in several states. In North Carolina, the General Assembly made certain changes to election laws including reducing the witness requirement to one person for absentee ballots, allowing for ballot tracking, and creating an online system for absentee ballot requests. However, the North Carolina State Board of

Electors provided additional COVID-19 measures allowing absentee ballots to be counted up to six days beyond the original deadline. This change was appealed eventually to the U.S. Supreme Court, which denied an injunction of this change and left the extended deadline in place.[79]

The changes to election laws because of COVID-19 also involved constitutional questions of executive power of governors and state legislatures. For example, in Minnesota there was a case that challenged the power of the secretary of state to allow extending the time for vote counting absentee ballots.[80] The setting of election laws is normally the purview of the state legislatures, and the U.S. Court of Appeals for the 8th Circuit held:

> The [Minnesota] Secretary's attempt to re-write the laws governing the deadlines for mail-in ballots in the 2020 Minnesota presidential election is invalid. However well-intentioned and appropriate from a policy perspective in the context of a pandemic during a presidential election, it is not the province of a state executive official to re-write the state's election code, at least as it pertains to selection of presidential electors.[81]

The end result was the deadline extension was suspended.

Other cases also involved whether executive orders could be used to change state election laws. A New Jersey case, *Trump v. Way*, challenged the governor's executive order mandating all voters receive mail-in ballots.[82] The executive order mandated that all voters in New Jersey receive ballots by mail and that all votes mailed in would be counted up to two days after Election Day. Donald Trump's campaign sued the New Jersey secretary of state predicated on the argument that an executive order violated the state legislature's right to determine electors.[83] However, the New Jersey state legislature then passed a law that reiterated the New Jersey governor's executive order. The U.S. District Court for New Jersey denied Trump's request to block the changes made that allowed counting of ballots prior to Election Day and accepting mailed-in ballots after polls close. The District Court denied the injunction request.[84] Similar to New Jersey, California's Governor Gavin Newsom issued an executive order under the California Emergency Services Act (CESA) to send all registered voters ballots by mail.[85] A California judge ruled that this executive order overstepped the governor's power, but, like New Jersey, the California legislature passed legislation that mirrored the order making the constitutionality of the executive order a moot issue.[86]

Voter turnout would be important to making Texas a potential swing state, and many of the lawsuits in Texas involved ballot access and voting. Traditionally a Republican presidential stronghold, Texas, which last voted Democratic in 1976, has been thought to potentially be a state where Democrats could make inroads, especially after the strong showing of Congressman

Robert Francis "Beto" O'Rourke in the 2018 senatorial election. In 2020, there were a series of cases about drive thru voting within Harris County, Texas, the state's most populous county. Drive thru voting is a process by which voters cast ballots at a Drive Thru Voting (DTV) station, show their ID, and vote using a portable handheld voting machine.[87] One case, *Hotze v. Hollins,* challenged the drive thru voting system in Harris County.[88] The plaintiffs, a group of Republican voters and office holders, made a general claim that the drive thru system violated the Equal Protection Clause of the Fourteenth Amendment along with violating Article I, section 4, clause 1 of the U.S. Constitution, which details that the time, place, and manner of elections for the U.S. House and Senate is determined by state legislatures.[89] The U.S. District Court for the Southern District of Texas held that the plaintiffs lacked standing and lacked a particularized grievance under the Equal Protection clause. The case was dismissed by the District Court, and the U.S. Court of Appeals for the Fifth Circuit also denied the plaintiff's motion for an injunction banning drive thru voting.[90] This same issue was also raised at the state level with the plaintiffs seeking a writ of mandamus to halt the Harris County drive thru voting precinct and to throw out 127,000 votes cast using that system.[91] Similar to the federal court, the Texas Supreme Court denied the injunction request on the drive thru voting system. Later, the Texas Supreme Court also denied a writ of mandamus request to throw out 127,000 votes cast in Harris County in the drive thru voting precinct.[92]

Other lawsuits also continued in Texas regarding the way votes were tabulated and mail-in ballots worked. One case was the *Texas Democratic Party v. Abbot*, the governor of Texas's absentee voting rule that allowed those only over sixty-five years of age or with a disability to vote by mail without an excuse.[93] The Democratic Party of Texas, along with other plaintiffs, sued stating that the vote-by-mail exception rationale violated the Twenty-Sixth Amendment of the U.S. Constitution, which bars laws that prohibit voters over eighteen years of age from voting on account of age. The U.S. District Court for the Western District of Texas granted a preliminary injunction stating that laws that differentiated vote-by-mail qualifications based on age violated the Twenty-Sixth Amendment, because the plaintiffs met the requirements of a preliminary injunction, which included a likelihood of success on the merits of the claim and a public interest.[94] The preliminary injunction was appealed to the U.S. Court of Appeals for the Fifth Circuit who set aside the injunction, and later issued a decision stating that the age requirement on absentee voting did not violate the Twenty-Sixth Amendment; the decision was appealed to the U.S. Supreme Court, which denied certiorari in 2021.[95]

The decisions by Governor Abbot also included his drop-off voting stations, which were limited to one per county in Texas, which has 254 counties. This was challenged in *Texas League of United Latin American Citizens v. Abbott*, in which the U.S. District Court for the Western District of Texas under a variety of constitutional and federal statutes including the First Amendment, Fourteenth Amendment, the Voting Rights Act of 1964, and the Enforcement Act of 1871,[96] agreed with the plaintiffs and granted an injunction on limiting the amount of drop-off sites for the election. However, the U.S. Court of Appeals for the Fifth Circuit reversed the District Court's ruling holding that the drop-off site limitation was likely constitutional and that one drop-off site per county could proceed for the 2020 election.[97]

There was also a lawsuit with multistate plaintiffs against President Trump. In *Washington v. Trump* fourteen states—including Colorado, Connecticut, Illinois, Maryland, Michigan, Minnesota, Nevada, New Mexico, Oregon, Rhode Island, Vermont, Virginia, and Wisconsin—sued President Donald Trump regarding his changes to the U.S. Postal Service (USPS) and its relationship to the 2020 election.[98] Specifically the plaintiffs claimed that the Trump administration's changes to the USPS, including not treating election mail as first-class mail, and other changes that result in delays in delivery have an adverse effect on elections. The suit asked for a preliminary injunction on the Trump administration's changes to the USPS. The U.S District Court for the Eastern District of Washington granted the injunction and later clarified it regarding extra postal trips and the efforts made to treat election mail as first-class mail.[99]

While these cases represent just a cross section of the lawsuits filed prior to the 2020 presidential election, they show that rules of the election were a major political and legal issue. States sought to facilitate greater voter participation in light of COVID-19 and also had to contend with whether those measures would provide a benefit to one candidate or party. The postelection litigation would amplify this issue, with Trump and his supporters claiming that some of the new mechanisms put in place during COVID-19 actually were designed to help Democrats and Joe Biden.

Postelection Lawsuits

Donald Trump made a political issue out of the voting laws and even voting machines in 2020, calling Dominion Voting Systems, a company that manufactures voting systems and software, "horrible, inaccurate and anything but secure."[100] Trump made many claims after the election involving lost votes due to Dominion Voting Systems (no evidence was found of this), the switching of Trump votes to Biden because of Dominion Voting Systems (it was in fact human error), and that the FBI and Department of Justice were not looking into voting fraud (Attorney William Barr said the DOJ had found no level of fraud that would have changed the outcome of the election).[101] On January 6, 2021, *USA Today* reported that Democratic election lawyer Marc Elias found that Trump or Trump allies had filed sixty-two election lawsuits in state and federal courts.[102] However, Trump's lawsuits had supporters in the Republican Party, with Senator Lindsey Graham (R-SC), who donated $500,000 to Trump's postelection legal defense fund, saying, "Democracy depends upon fair elections. President Trump's team is going to have the chance to make a case, regarding voting irregularities. They deserve a chance to make that case. I'm going to stand with President Trump."[103] However, Graham warned that claims made about election fraud could not be based on suspicion alone, saying, "General statements are not enough. We've got to be specific."[104] It would be that lack of specificity and evidence that proved problematic for the postelection litigation strategy.

Postelection lawsuits filed by Trump and his supporters were largely unsuccessful, and many were dismissed or withdrawn. At one point, Trump lost six lawsuits in a single day.[105] However, there were prolonged legal battles that continued into the first part of 2021. Litigation by President Trump and his supporters focused on a few key states including Pennsylvania, Georgia, Arizona, Nevada, and Wisconsin. These states were all won by Joe Biden but, with the exception of Nevada, had been won by Donald Trump in 2016.

One of the biggest lawsuits involving the 2020 election was *Texas v. Pennsylvania et al.*, which was filed by Texas attorney general Ken Paxton and alleged that Pennsylvania, Georgia, Michigan, and Wisconsin unconstitutionally changed state election laws by not using state legislatures.[106] The case was unique in that the U.S. Supreme Court had original jurisdiction in the case, because the court has original jurisdiction involving disputes between states. The lawsuit was viewed as a Republican attempt to claim that the election changes in 2020 by executive branch officials violated Article II of the U.S. Constitution.[107] The lawsuit was filed on December 8, 2020, before the safe harbor time that Congress was to certify the results of the Electoral College. On December 9, President Donald Trump filed a motion to intervene in the case to join as a plaintiff.[108] The states of Missouri, Alabama, Arkansas, Florida, Indiana, Kansas, Louisiana, Mississippi, Montana, Nebraska, North Dakota, Oklahoma, South Carolina, South Dakota, Tennessee, Utah, and West Virginia (all states Trump won in 2020) also filed amici briefs supporting the Texas attorney general's lawsuit. However, the case was not without its Republican critics. In Georgia, the spokesperson for the attorney general, Chris Carr, criticized that the lawsuit was "constitutionally, legally and factually wrong about Georgia."[109] Ultimately the U.S. Supreme Court refused to hear the case, with Justices Samuel Alito and Clarence Thomas stating that they believed the U.S. Supreme Court could not deny a case in original jurisdiction.[110]

Pennsylvania was narrowly won by Donald Trump in 2016, and it was the site of many accusations of voter fraud by the Trump campaign. Lawyer Rudy Giuliani argued that Trump observers were disallowed from witnessing vote counts in largely Democratic areas and Philadelphia. Because of this, Giuliani asked for the invalidation of seven hundred thousand ballots, which was denied 5–2 by the Pennsylvania Supreme Court.[111] One of the biggest cases from Pennsylvania involved an appeal from the Supreme Court of Pennsylvania, which involved election law changes that permitted hand-delivered ballots at locations other than the Election Board and a thirteen-day extension of absentee and mail-in ballots, among other changes.[112] That decision was appealed under the question of whether the court's decision in amending election law, as opposed to the Pennsylvania state legislature, violated the U.S. Constitution Articles I and II.[113] In February 2021 the U.S. Supreme Court denied certiorari in a case involving the COVID-19 election measures taken in Pennsylvania, which included that extended deadlines for mail-in ballots could only be made by the state legislature.[114] That denial ended the litigation of the 2020 election and what was most likely the strongest argument Donald Trump had in litigating the 2020 presidential election.

Perhaps one of the most widely publicized Pennsylvania cases was *Donald J. Trump for President v. Boockvar*, which was a federal lawsuit in the U.S. District Court for the Middle District of Pennsylvania.[115] In that case Trump's campaign requested the invalidation of millions of votes based on the argument that the Pennsylvania secretary of state's notice and cure procedure for defective mail-in ballots was a violation of equal protection laws. The case gained national media attention not only for the request, but also because Trump's lawyers changed three times during the lawsuit.[116] District Court Judge Matthew Brann issued a decision that was highly critical of the lawsuit, saying:

> This Court has been presented with strained legal arguments without merit and speculative accusations, unpled in the operative complaint and unsupported by evidence. In the United States of America, this cannot justify the disenfranchisement of a single voter, let alone all the voters of its sixth most populated state. Our people, laws, and institutions demand more.[117]

On appeal the U.S. Court of Appeal for the Third Circuit agreed, with Judge Stephanos Bibas, who was appointed by Trump, writing, "Free, fair elections are the lifeblood of our democracy. Charges of unfairness are serious. But calling an election unfair does not make it so. Charges require specific allegations and then proof. We have neither here."[118]

In Georgia, Trump lost to Joe Biden by just over eleven thousand votes after two statewide recounts. Georgia had a contentious governor's election in 2018, and the Democratic challenger, Stacey Abrams, went on to register an estimated eight hundred thousand new Georgia voters since her defeat.[119] This narrow loss for Trump prompted several lawsuits and harsh criticism for Georgia's Republican governor, Brian Kemp, and Secretary of State Brad Raffensberger. In one unique Georgia challenge, Trump supporter and celebrity attorney Lin Wood sued the Georgia secretary of state challenging the certification of the election and requesting new election rules for the upcoming Georgia Senate runoff. The U.S. District Court for the Northern District of Georgia dismissed the suit because of Wood's lack of standing as a Georgia voter, and the U.S. Court of Appeals for the 11th Circuit affirmed.[120] Trump also sued the governor of Georgia and the secretary of state, requesting that the results of the presidential election in Georgia be decertified. A judge for the U.S. District of the Northern District of Georgia denied the request.[121] Trump's campaign also sued in the Superior Court in Chatham County, in the Eastern Judicial Circuit, over the issue of late ballots counted. The judge dismissed the suit.[122]

Similar cases occurred in Arizona, Nevada, Wisconsin, and Michigan. In Arizona there were several lawsuits that proceeded called the "Sharpie lawsuit," because they alleged that Maricopa County ballots were invalidated because of the use of Sharpie pens on the ballots. The lawsuits were filed in Maricopa County Superior Court, a state trial court, and eventually dropped.[123] However, the bigger case in Arizona was brought by Sidney Powell, in U.S. District Court for the District of Arizona, claiming that election fraud in Arizona warranted setting aside the ballots in Arizona.[124] The U.S. District judge dismissed the suit for both standing and lack of evidence to support the claim. Another challenge came from the state Republican Party chair, who sued challenging the signature verification process in Maricopa County. The lower court dismissed the suit, and the Arizona Supreme Court affirmed the decision.[125] Nevada's litigation was similar, with the Nevada Supreme Court affirming a dismissal of an election challenge of mail-in voting and voting machines. The original suit asked for Nevada to replace the electors for Joe Biden with those for Donald Trump or annul the election. The trial judge in the First Judicial Circuit of Carson City allowed for the presentation of evidence, but the plaintiffs could not produce evidence that would warrant the election being overturned, and the case was dismissed. The Supreme Court of Nevada affirmed the dismissal.[126] In Wisconsin, Trump filed a suit alleging that election procedures "tainted" fifty thousand ballots.[127] The U.S. District Court for the Eastern District of Wisconsin dismissed the complaint, and the U.S. Court of Appeals for the 7th Circuit affirmed.[128] Other cases in Wisconsin filed by Trump supporters failed to achieve the result of overturning the election, including In re William Feehan filed by Sidney Powell, Trump's lawyer who famously referred to her legal fight as "the Kraken," seeking a writ of mandamus from the U.S. Supreme Court, and *Mark Jefferson v. Dane County, Wisconsin*, which challenged the mail-in ballot system in Wisconsin.[129] In Michigan Trump's challenges to election procedures were rejected by the Federal Court of Claims.[130] Other pro-Trump plaintiffs had a similar outcome in Michigan, with the courts dismissing the suits.[131]

One of the most unusual postelection challenges came from a lawsuit filed by Texas representative Louie Gohmert, a Republican, and Republican Party members against Vice President Mike Pence in the U.S. District Court for the Eastern District of Texas. In that case the plaintiffs sought to have the vice president empowered to select alternative electors from the Electoral College under the claim that the Electoral Count Act of 1877 was unconstitutional.[132] The Electoral Count Act of 1877 is a law that was the outgrowth of the disputed election of 1876 between Tilden and Hayes. It essentially takes away the authority of Congress to decide how electoral votes are counted, and instead gives that power to the states. The purpose is to remove Congress from creating a uniform voting system by which counting can occur to favor a political candidate. This act also works in tandem with the Twelfth Amendment of the U.S. Constitution, which states that the vice president opens the electoral votes. However, the vice president's role in that count is limited. The judge in the U.S. District Court dismissed the suit on standing.[133] The plaintiffs appealed to the U.S. Court of Appeals for the 5th Circuit, which affirmed the lower court's dismissal.[134]

It is also important to note that many of Trump's and his supporters' lawsuits were withdrawn before a decision could even be made. Lawsuits in Michigan, Pennsylvania, Arizona, New Mexico, and Wisconsin were dropped for a variety of reasons, with one law firm withdrawing from a suit in Pennsylvania.[135] In total none of Trump's lawsuits created a change in the election outcomes, and his postelection litigation failed as a strategy. However, doubts persist, and even at the time of this writing the issues in the 2020 election vote counting continue. In Arizona, Maricopa County is conducting a hand recount of the votes, which many believe foreshadows a new election norm of challenging the administrative processes of all elections, despite the outcome.[136]

IMPACT OF LITIGATION ON 2024 AND BEYOND

In elections it is thought that the most important thing to win is to get the most votes. However, as the litigation around the 2020 presidential election shows, part of the process of getting the most votes involves the laws regulating voting itself. Voting locations, early voting, ballot drop-offs, mail-in ballots, absentee ballots, drive thru voting, post–Election Day counting, signature verification, absentee requests, and even who makes the rules about voting (legislature or court) makes a difference in elections. If anything, the biggest takeaway from the litigation of the 2020 presidential election is that lawsuits, both by Republicans and Democrats, are part of the election process. They are, in many ways, as important as the campaigning itself, because as we have seen historically in the United States sometimes elections come down to what votes count.

Looking at the 2020 presidential election, it is clear from a voting stand-point that the preelection litigation was significant, especially because the logistics of the 2020 presidential election changed because of COVID-19. Mail-in ballots, early voting, and post-Election Day vote counting became major issues that had the potential the determine outcomes in a variety of races. It is also evident that the issue of the election litigation was impor-tant for both sides and that Republicans, Democrats, and their supporters were part of the litigation process to create a certain outcome politically. If anything, the legal process became an extension of the political campaigns of 2020 in a way that was unlike previous elections. Even at the time of this chapter's writing, Florida Republicans are reassessing their legal stance on mail-in voting, because it is thought to actually help Republicans in that state's elections.[137]

Of course, the biggest issue in the post-2020 presidential election was the storming of the U.S. Capitol on January 6, 2021. That event was preceded by the Save America rally, in which both President Trump and his lawyer Rudy Giuliani spoke. Trump claimed that there was widespread voter fraud in Wisconsin, Pennsylvania, and Georgia, saying:

> All of us here today do not want to see our election victory stolen by a bold and radical left Democrats which is what they are doing and stolen by the fake news media. That is what they have done and what they are doing. We will never give up. We will never concede. It doesn't happen. You don't concede when there's theft involved.[138]

Giuliani made reference to having a "trial by combat" in relation to the elec-tion outcome, later claiming it was taken out of context and was a "Game of Thrones" reference.[139] The purpose behind the rally and criticism of the process was to encourage objection to the counting of the electoral votes making Joe Biden president of the United States. After the storming on the U.S. Capitol, debate over vote counting was suspended, but when the debate resumed, 147 Republican lawmakers (8 senators and 139 U.S. representatives) supported at least one objection to the count.[140] Later, Trump would be impeached for a second time in the House of Representatives and acquitted in the U.S. Senate for incitement of an insurrection.

Setting aside the Trump impeachment issue, the criticism of the election and its outcome has some likely roots in the litigation pre- and postelection. The lawsuits demonstrate that the change of the election processes in light of COVID-19 presented a legal issue that also emerged as a political talking point and eventual rallying cry. These pre- and postelection lawsuits also demonstrate that in a political context, litigation, even its anticipation, can be used as a campaign issue and, somewhat more importantly, a fundraising issue. This can be seen in Trump's postelection speech at the Conservative Political Action Conference (CPAC) in 2021, in which he continued the narrative of the fraud in the presidential election, blaming the court system. He said, "We have a very sick and corrupt electoral process that must be fixed immediately. This election was rigged and the supreme court and other courts didn't want to do anything about it."[141] Even Dominion Voting Systems would go on to bring a lawsuit against former Trump attorney Sidney Powell and Rudy Giuliani for defamation.[142]

So, what do these lawsuits mean for American politics? It's hard to imagine that society, let alone the U.S. election system, will return exactly to where it was prior to COVID-19. There are no doubt going to be some permanent changes. Voting in the United States has evolved legally since the nineteenth century, typically in the form of increasing enfranchisement. This first occurred with demographic groups, and in the twenty-first century it is now focused on the mechanisms of voting itself. The pre- and postlitigation of the presidential election of 2020 showed that rules matter—quite a lot. The changes to voting logistics will continue, and it is already apparent that the issue of voting is at the forefront of 2022 midterms and is already at issue for the presidential election of 2024. The impact of Trump's postelection lawsuits was minimal in a legal sense because they were unsuccessful in changing the election outcome. As a political issue they had resonance with his supporters, and the allegations made in the suits will continue. Of course, there is political pushback on this narrative. However, the end result is that elections in the United States are highly polarized and sometimes come down to razor-thin margins. That means politicians now have to go after every vote and hire lawyers to make sure those votes are counted.

NOTES

1. Josh Dawsey and Michelle Ye He Lee, "Trump Raises More than $170 Million Appealing on False Election Claims," *Washington Post*, December 1, 2020, https://

www.washingtonpost.com/politics/trump-raises-more-than-150-million-appealing
-to-false-election-claims/2020/11/30/82e922e6-3347-11eb-afe6-e4dbee9689f8
_story.html; Jarrett Renshaw and Joseph Tanfani, "Donations under $8K to Trump
'election defense' Instead Go to President, RNC," *Reuters*, November 11, 2020,
https://www.reuters.com/article/uk-usa-election-trump-fundraising-insigh-idINK
BN27R30B. Some of the money raised for election challenges had to go over a certain
threshold amount of $8,000 before it went to recount efforts. Donations under $8,000
were used for other political purposes.

2. Ibid.

3. Caroline Kenny, "Kelly Loeffler Says She Will Object to the Certification of
Biden's Electoral College Win," *CNN* online, January 4, 2021, https://www.cnn
.com/2021/01/04/politics/kelly-loeffler-david-perdue-electoral-college-certification
/index.html; Tia Mitchell, "U.S. Sen. Kelly Loeffler Says She Will No Longer Object to
Biden's Win in Georgia," *Atlanta Journal-Constitution*, January 6, 2021, https://www
.ajc.com/politics/politics-blog/us-sen-kelly-loeffler-says-she-will-no-longer-object
-to-bidens-win-in-georgia/ITBOOXVKHJGA3GAIHQZDUPMHVY/.

4. Emily Czachor, "Trump Lashes Out at Ga. 'Republican' Governor Kemp
ahead of Rally to Support GOP Senators," *Newsweek*, December 20, 2020, https://
www.newsweek.com/trump-lashes-out-ga-republican-governor-kemp-ahead-rally
-support-gop-senators-1556216; Tamar Hallerman and Tia Mitcheell, "Trump
Campaigns for Loeffler and Perdue in High Stakes Election Eve Rally," *Atlanta
Journal-Constitution*, January 4, 2021, https://www.ajc.com/politics/live-trump
-campaigns-for-loeffler-and-perdue-in-high-stakes-election-eve-rally/R7E5SMX2R
JALPNS7JFZ65W6WTY/.

5. Georgia General Assembly, Election Integrity Act of 2021, Georgia SB
202, signed into law March 25, 2021, https://assets.documentcloud.org/documents
/20527915/sb-202-as-passed.pdf.

6. Elena Schneider and Natasha Korecki, "Biden Camp Quietly Raises Money for
Post-Election Court Brawl," *Politico*, November 2, 2020, https://www.politico.com
/news/2020/11/02/biden-camp-fundraising-post-election-433803.

7. "Biden Fight Fund Financial Summary," Federal Election Commission, accessed
April 23, 2021, https://www.fec.gov/data/committee/C00762229/?cycle=2020.

8. Nicole Goodkind, "Why Joe Biden Is Still Fundraising after Winning the Election," *Fortune,* November 25, 2020, https://fortune.com/2020/11/25/why-joe-biden
-is-still-fundraising-money-2020-election-results-winner/.

9. This chapter does not examine all the election lawsuits in 2020 because they are
too many to analyze for a single book chapter. According to one estimate there were
230 preelection lawsuits and 62 postelection lawsuits for a total of 292 lawsuits filed
in federal and state courts during the 2020 election. The outcomes of these suits varied
from being withdrawn or dismissed to adjudicated at the appellate level. This chapter
focuses on major lawsuits that were adjudicated at the trial or appellate court level. For
a longer list of postelection lawsuits, see Jacob Shamsian and Sonam Seth, "Trump
and His Allies Filed More than 40 Lawsuits Challenging the 2020 Election Results.
All of Them Failed," *Business Insider*, February 22, 2021, https://www.business
insider.com/trump-campaign-lawsuits-election-results-2020-11.

10. James Madison, Federalist No. 57, *The Federalist Papers*, Library of Congress, https://guides.loc.gov/federalist-papers/text-51-60.

11. *Wesberry v. Sanders*, 376 U.S. 1, 17 (1964).

12. U.S. Const., art. I, §4.

13. Stanley Engerman and Kenneth Sokoloff, "The Evolution of Suffrage Institutions in the New World," *The Journal of Economic History* 65 (2005): 891–921, 907. Engerman and Sokoloff note that even though property requirements ended by 1856, tax requirements endured into the twentieth century in Rhode Island and Pennsylvania. The idea of paying taxes as a substitute for property qualifications began during the colonial era, and had a longer duration in the United States as a voting prerequisite than property ownership.

14. Stephen Scott, "George Washington: The American Franchisee," The Miller Center, University of Virginia, https://millercenter.org/president/washington/the-american-franchise.

15. Engerman and Sokoloff, "The Evolution of Suffrage," 904. Only six states (all in New England) gave African Americans the right to vote.

16. U.S. Const., art. I.

17. The Fourteenth Amendment in effect nullified the *Dredd Scott v. Sanford*, 60 U.S. 383 (1857) decision, which held that African Americans essentially were not guaranteed any rights under the U.S. Constitution whether they were free or enslaved. The Fourteenth Amendment also ended any question of the constitutionality of the Civil Rights Act of 1866, 14 Stat. 27-30 (1866), which was passed through a veto override of President Andrew Johnson. That act provided equal protection under the law, and African Americans enjoy the legal rights and protections afforded to White citizens of the United States.

18. Enforcement Act of 1870, Pub. L. No. 41-114, 16 Stat. 140 (1870).

19. Ibid.

20. *United States v. Reese*, 92 U.S. 214 (1876); *United States v. Cruikshank*, 92 U.S. 542 (1876).

21. *United States v. Cruikshank*, 92 U.S. 542 (1876).

22. Ibid. This case arose from a riot involving the 1872 Louisiana governor's race in which former Confederate soldiers and Ku Klux Klan members killed state militia members at the Grant County Courthouse in Colfax, Louisiana.

23. Ibid. This holding would later be overturned by a series of cases that incorporated specific amendments from the Bill of Rights to the states, with the incorporation of the First Amendment right to assemble being incorporated in 1937 in *De Jonge v. Oregon*, 299 U.S. 353 (1937). The holding in *Cruikshank* also held that the Second Amendment did not apply to states. It would be 2010 when that right was incorporated in the holding of *McDonald v. City of Chicago*, 561 U.S. 742 (2010).

24. See Jennifer Billock, "Women Have Been Voting in Wyoming for 150 Years, and Here Is How the State Is Celebrating," *Smithsonian Magazine*, June 7, 2019, https://www.smithsonianmag.com/travel/women-voting-wyoming-150-years-here-how-state-celebrating-180971263/.

25. U.S. Const. amend. XIX.

26. Indian Citizenship Act of 1924, Pub. L. No. 68-175, 43 Stat. 253 (1924).

27. "Securing Indian Voting Rights," *Harvard Law Review* 129 (2016): 1731–1754, 1735.

28. *Baker v. Carr*, 369 U.S. 186 (1962). This case arose out of a redistricting issue in Tennessee, which had not redistricted its congressional map since 1901. The issue of judicial review involved examining the Equal Protection Clause in the Fourteenth Amendment with the Guarantee Clause found in U.S. Const., art. IV, § 4. This contrasted with a U.S. Supreme Court opinion in *Colegrove v. Green*, 328 U.S. 549 (1946), where Justice Felix Frankfurter wrote that the Guarantee Clause gave the state legislatures the power to set the time, place, and manner of elections. In that 1946 decision the court held that only the U.S. Congress, not the U.S. Supreme Court, could evaluate malapportionment.

29. *Gray v. Sanders*, 372 U.S. 368 (1963). In the county unit system, there were 410 county unit votes, which disproportionately diluted the influence of residents in Fulton County, where the City of Atlanta is located. The court specifically said that the Georgia county unit system was not analogous to the federal Electoral College because the Electoral College was enshrined in the U.S. Constitution, art. II, § 1.

30. Ibid., 381.

31. *Wesberry v. Sanders*, 376 U.S. 1 (1964). This case came from Georgia, where congressional districts were not equal in population in the Fifth Congressional district that included urban areas of Fulton, DeKalb, and Rockdale Counties that had a population two to three times larger than other Georgia congressional districts.

32. *Reynolds v. Sims*, 377 U.S. 533 (1964).

33. U.S. Const. amend. XXIV.

34. *Harper v. Virginia Board of Elections*, 383 U.S. 663 (1966).

35. U.S. Const. amend. XXVI.

36. Voting Rights Act of 1965, Pub. L. No. 89-110, 79 Stat. 437 (1965).

37. *Shelby County v. Holder*, 570 U.S. 529 (2013).

38. Ibid. The court noted the coverage formula, which was written in 1965 and revised in 1970 and 1975. The formula looked at the history of voting discrimination, and whether there was low voter turnout at the time the formula was created. It was originally set to expire within five years of its creation. The Voting Rights Act of 1965 preclearance formula had not changed since the 1970s, but the act was reauthorized by Congress in 2006.

39. Ibid., 547.

40. Edward Foley, *Ballot Battles: The History of Disputed Elections in the United States* (New York: Oxford University Press, 2016), 119–125.

41. Ibid., 117. Foley notes that the issue in 1876 is an example of an election challenge that did not end up being decided in the courts, whereas the 2000 election was decided by the U.S. Supreme Court. He argues that the 1876 election challenge was a much messier challenge because of the lack of court intervention, whereas the 2000 election challenge was more structured because of the court involvement. The result in 1876 was eventually decided by Congress in what has become known as the Compromise of 1877, which effectively ended Reconstruction in the South in exchange for Republican Rutherford B. Hayes to win the election.

42. Ibid., pp. 237–246. Minnesota led the way on state recount measures in its 1962 governor's election where the margin of victory was only ninety-one votes, or .0073 percent.

43. Ken Starr, "Federal Judicial Invalidation as a Remedy for Irregularities in State Elections," *New York University Law Review* 49 (1974): 1092–1125; *Bush v. Gore*, 531 U.S. 98 (2000). In 1974 Ken Starr, who would go on to be a judge of the U.S. Court of Appeals for the D.C. Circuit, solicitor general, and Whitewater independent counsel, wrote a law review article stating that *Reynolds v. Sims* would eventually lead to federal court involvement in overturning many close elections, almost fore-shadowing the *Bush v. Gore* decision in 2000.

44. *Crawford v. Marion County Election Board*, 553 U.S. 181 (2008).

45. *Shelby County v. Holder*, 570 U.S. 529 (2013).

46. Jimmy Carter and James Baker III, "A Clearer Picture on Voter ID," *New York Times*, February 3, 2008, https://www.nytimes.com/2008/02/03/opinion/03carter .html. Carter and Baker had served on a 2005 Commission on Federal Election Re-form, which suggested the creation of a federal real ID for voting purposes. However, both Republicans and Democrats rejected that idea.

47. Alexa Ura, "Plaintiffs Say Texas Voter ID Fight Is Over," *Texas Tribune*, August 8, 2018, https://www.texastribune.org/2018/08/08/plaintiffs-say-texas-voter -id-fight-over/.

48. "Voter Identification Requirements: Voter ID Laws," National Conference of State Legislatures, https://www.ncsl.org/research/elections-and-campaigns/voter-id .aspx.

49. Ibid.

50. "State Laws Governing Early Voting," National Conference on State Legis-latures, https://www.ncsl.org/research/elections-and-campaigns/early-voting-in-state -elections.aspx. Delaware has a law allowing early voting, but it does not go into ef-fect until 2022.

51. Ibid.

52. Uniformed and Overseas Citizens Absentee Voting Act, Pub. L. No. 99-410, 100 Stat. 924 (1986); Military and Overseas Voter Empowerment Act, Pub. L. No. 111-84, 123 Stat. 2190 (2009).

53. Sarah Eckman and Karen Shanton, "Early Voting and Mail Voting: Overview & Issues for Congress," Congressional Research Service, March 27, 2020, https:// crsreports.congress.gov/product/pdf/IF/IF11477.

54. "Voting by Mail and Absentee Voting," MIT Election Data + Science Lab, last updated March 16, 2021, https://electionlab.mit.edu/research/voting-mail-and -absentee-voting.

55. Eckman and Shanton, "Early Voting and Mail Voting: Overview & Issues for Congress."

56. MIT Election +Science Lab, "Voting by Mail and Absentee Voting."

57. Lorraine Minnite, "The Politics of Voter Fraud," Project Vote, http://www .projectvote.org/wp-content/uploads/2007/03/Politics_of_Voter_Fraud_Final.pdf. This is not to say voter fraud does not ever exist. In 1997 the *New York Times* covered a rural Georgia county that had systemic issues of alleged voter fraud that included

being paid for votes in elections. See Kevin Sack, "Georgia Gets Tough on a County Tradition: Vote Buying," *New York Times*, March 23, 1997, https://www.nytimes.com/1997/03/23/us/georgia-gets-tough-on-a-county-tradition-vote-buying.html.

58. Molly Reynolds, "Understanding the Election Scandal in North Carolina's 9th District," *Brookings*, December 7, 2018, https://www.brookings.edu/blog/fixgov/2018/12/07/understanding-the-election-scandal-in-north-carolinas-9th-district/.

59. National Conference of State Legislatures, "VOPP: Table 10: Who Can Collect and Return an Absentee Ballot Other Than the Voter," February 15, 2021, https://www.ncsl.org/research/elections-and-campaigns/vopp-table-10-who-can-collect-and-return-an-absentee-ballot-other-than-the-voter.aspx.

60. Ibid.

61. National Conference of State Legislatures, "Election Recounts," November 24, 2020, https://www.ncsl.org/research/elections-and-campaigns/automatic-recount-thresholds.aspx.

62. Ariz. Rev. Stat. § 16-661.

63. Mass. Ann. Laws ch. 54, § 135; 25 Pa. Stat. § 3261.

64. The twelve states that require the margin of victory to be within a certain percentage are: Delaware, Georgia, Missouri, Montana, New Hampshire, North Carolina, North Dakota, South Dakota, Texas, Utah, Vermont, and Virginia. Further complicating that process is that the margin of victory varies among those twelve states.

65. National Conference of State Legislatures, "Election Recounts."

66. *Bush v. Gore,* 531 U.S. 98 (2000). The issue of the state recounts involved an issue of whether undervotes, those votes not tabulated by the voting machines, should be included.

67. Ibid., 109.

68. Foley, *Ballot Battles*, 139–148.

69. Alan Gomez and Kevin McCoy, "Federal Election Lawsuits Have Already Set a Recent Record. A Look at 2020 in the Courts," *USA Today*, October 30, 2020, https://www.usatoday.com/story/news/nation/2020/10/30/courts-reject-voting-rights-extensions-in-covid-shadowed-elections/5998149002/.

70. Ibid.

71. *Arizona Democratic Party v. Hobbs*, 976 F.3d 1081 (9th Cir. 2020). Arizona's electoral votes went to Biden, but only narrowly, with just over ten thousand votes.

72. Ibid.

73. *Mi Familia Vota v. Hobbs*, 977 F.3d 948 (9th Cir. 2020).

74. Ibid.

75. *Michigan Alliance for Retired Americans v. Secretary of State*, ___N.W.2d___, 2020 WL 6122745 (Mich. Ct. App. 2020).

76. Ibid.

77. *The New Georgia Project v. Raffensberger*, 976 F.3d 1278 (11th Cir. 2020).

78. Ibid.

79. *Circosta v. Moore*, 141 S.Ct. 46 (2020).

80. *Carson v. Simon*, 978 F.3d 1051 (8th Cir. 2020).

81. Ibid., 1060.

82. See *Donald J. Trump for President v. Way*, SCOTUSblog, accessed May 4, 2021, https://www.scotusblog.com/election-litigation/donald-j-trump-for-president-v-murphy.

83. *Trump v. Way*, No. 20-10753 (D.N.J. 2020).

84. Ibid.

85. Ca. Exec. Order No. N-64-20 (May 8, 2020), https://www.gov.ca.gov/wp-content/uploads/2020/05/05.08.2020-EO-N-64-20-text.pdf

86. *Gallagher v. Newsom*, Court Order, Superior Court of Sutter County, https://htv-prod-media.s3.amazonaws.com/files/final-ruling-1605331770.pdf.

87. Drive Thru Voting, Harris County Elections, https://harrisvotes.com/drivethruvoting.

88. *Hotze v. Hollins*, No. 20-20574, 2020 WL 6440440 (5th Cir. Nov. 2, 2020).

89. Complaint, *Hotze v. Hollins*, No. 4:20-cv-03709, 2020 WL 6373661 (S.D.Tex. October 28, 2020); U.S. Const., art. 1§ 4, cl. 1; U.S. Const. XIV amend.

90. *Hotze v. Hollins*, No. 20-20574, 2020 WL 6440440 (5th Cir. Nov. 2, 2020).

91. At issue in the mandamus was Texas governor Greg Abbot's executive order that suspended two provisions of the Texas Election Code, specifically that the early voting in Texas begins on the seventeenth day before Election Day and that early voting ballots must be delivered in person to the voting clerk's office.

92. In re Steven Hotze, M.D., Harris County Republican Party, Hon. Keith Nielsen, and Sharon Hemphill, 610 S.W.3d 909 (Tex. 2020); In re Steven Hotze, M.D., Wendell Champion, Hon. Steven Toth, and Sharon Hemphill, No. 20-0751, 2020 WL 5939131 (Tex. Oct. 7, 2020); see Jake Bleiberg, "Texas High Court Denies GOP Effort to Reject Houston Votes," *AP* Online, November 1, 2020, https://apnews.com/article/election-2020-donald-trump-virus-outbreak-houston-elections-57796e23983587f358127dfe050070a3.

93. *Texas Democratic Party v. Abbot*, 461 F.Supp.3d 406 (W.D.Tex. 2020). The statute in question is Tex. Elec. Code §§ 81.004-.004. An underlying issue in this case was COVID-19 risk and a Travis County state court judge who does not have immunity to COVID-19 to qualify as disabled under the Texas statute.

94. *Byrum v. Landreth*, 566 F.3d 442 (5th Cir. 2009). This case law establishes the four-part test to determine whether a preliminary injunction is granted. However, a preliminary injunction is not a final disposition of the case. It is only a temporary relief requested by a plaintiff in a lawsuit.

95. *Texas Democratic Party v. Abbot*, 978 F.3d 168 (5th Cir. 2020), cert. denied 121 S.Ct. 1124 (2021).

96. *United Latin American Citizens v. Abbott*, 493 F.Supp.3d 548 (W.D. Tex. 2020), 978 F.3d 136 (5th Cir. 2020).

97. *United Latin American Citizens v. Abbott*, No. 20-50867, 2021 WL 1446828 (5th Cir. Feb. 22, 2021); *Texas League of United Latin American Citizens v. Hughes*, 978 F.3d 136 (5th Cir. 2020).

98. *Washington v. Trump*, 487 F.Supp.3d 976 (E.D. Wash. 2020).

99. Ibid., *Washington v. Trump*, No. 1:20-CV-03127-SAB, 2020 WL 6588502 (E.D. Wash. Oct. 2, 2020).

100. Ann Gerhart, "Election Results under Attack: Here Are the Facts," *Washington Post*, March 11, 2021, https://www.washingtonpost.com/elections/interactive/2020/election-integrity/.

101. Ibid.

102. William Cummings, Joey Garrison, and Jim Sergent, "By the Numbers: President Donald Trump's Failed Efforts to Overturn the Election," *USA Today*, January 6, 2021, https://www.usatoday.com/in-depth/news/politics/elections/2021/01/06/trumps-failed-efforts-overturn-election-numbers/4130307001/.

103. Joseph Bustos, "Trump Needs to Show Specific Evidence of Election Fraud in Court, SC's Graham says," *The State*, updated November 8, 2020, https://www.thestate.com/news/politics-government/election/article247013687.html.

104. Ibid.

105. Kyle Cheney and Josh Gerstein, "Donald Trump's Brutal Day in Court," *Politico*, December 4, 2020, https://www.politico.com/news/2020/12/04/donald-trump-in-court-443010.

106. *Texas v. Pennsylvania*, 141 S.Ct. 1230 (2020).

107. U.S. Const., art. II.

108. Motion to Intervene, *Texas v. Pennsylvania*, 141 S.Ct. 1230 (2020).

109. Adam Liptak, "Texas Files an Audacious Suit with the Supreme Court Challenging the Election Results," *New York Times*, updated December 11, 2020, https://www.nytimes.com/2020/12/08/us/politics/texas-files-an-audacious-suit-with-the-supreme-court-challenging-the-election-results.html.

110. *Texas v. Pennsylvania*, 141 S.Ct. 1230 (2020). It is worth noting that cases of original jurisdiction are exceedingly rare in the U.S. Supreme Court, with only 123 cases between 1789 and 1959, and only 140 petitions since 1960 in which almost half were denied. See Federal Judicial Center, "Jurisdiction: Original, Supreme Court," https://www.fjc.gov/history/courts/jurisdiction-original-supreme-court.

111. In re Canvassing Observation, 241 A.3d 339 (Pa. 2020).

112. *Pennsylvania Democratic Party v. Boockvar*, 238 A.3d 345 (Pa. 2020).

113. U.S. Const., art I; U.S. Const., art. II.

114. *Republican Party of Pennsylvania v. Degraffenreid*, 141 S.Ct. 732 (2021).

115. *Donald J. Trump for President v. Boockvar*, ___F.Supp.3d__ 2020 WL 6821992 (W.D. Pa. Nov. 21, 2020).

116. Alan Fuer, "Judge Dismisses Trump Lawsuit Seeking to Delay Certification in Pennsylvania," *New York Times*, updated December 8, 2020, https://www.nytimes.com/2020/11/21/us/politics/pennsylvania-trump-court-ballots.html.

117. Ibid., *1.

118. *Donald J. Trump for President v. Secretary of Pennsylvania*, 830 Fed.Appx. 377 (3d Cir. 2020).

119. Danny Hakim, Stephanie Saul, and Glenn Thrush, "As Biden Inches Ahead in Georgia, Stacey Abrams Draws Recognition and Praise," *New York Times*, updated January 8, 2021, https://www.nytimes.com/2020/11/06/us/politics/stacey-abrams-georgia.html.

120. *Wood v. Raffensberger*, 981 F.3d 1307 (11th Cir. 2020), cert. denied, 141 S.Ct. 1379 (2020); *Wood v. Raffensberger*, ___F.Supp.3d___, 2020 WL 6817513 (N.D. Ga. Nov. 20, 2020).

121. *Trump v. Kemp*, ___F.Supp.3d__, 2021 WL 49935 (N.D. Ga. Jan. 5, 2021).

122. In re Enforcement of Election Laws and Securing Ballots Cast or Received After 7 p.m. on November 3, 2020, SPCV20-00982 (Chatham County Superior Court, Nov. 5, 2020), https://www.wsav.com/wp-content/uploads/sites/75/2020/11/Order-On-Petition-To-Command-Enforcement-Of-Election-Laws-2.pdf.

123. Bree Burkitt and Jen Fifield, "Sharpie Lawsuit Officially Dropped by Plaintiffs Hours after Biden Win Announced," *Arizona Central*, November 7, 2020, https://www.azcentral.com/story/news/politics/elections/2020/11/07/sharpie-lawsuit-officially-dropped-plaintiffs-hours-after-biden-win-announced/6209529002/.

124. *Bowyer v. Ducey*, ___F.Supp.3d___, 2020 WL 7238261 (D.Ariz. Dec. 9, 2020).

125. *Ward v. Jackson*, No. CV-20-0343-AP/EL, 2020 WL 8617817 (Ariz. Dec. 8, 2020), cert. denied 141 S.Ct. 1381 (2021).

126. *Law v. Whitmer*, 477 P.3d 1124 (Nev. 2020).

127. *Trump v. Wisconsin Election Commission*, ___F.Supp.3d___, 2020 WL 7318940, *1(E.D.Wis. Dec. 12, 2020).

128. *Trump v. Wisconsin Election Commission*, 983 F.3d 919 (7th Cir. 2020), cert. denied, ____ S.Ct. _____, 2021 WL 850635 (2021); *Trump v. Wisconsin Election Commission*, ___F.Supp.3d___, 2020 WL 7318940 (E.D.Wis. Dec. 12, 2020).

129. In re William Feehan, ____ S.Ct.____ , 2021 WL 769780 (March 1, 2021); *Mark Jefferson v. Dane County, Wisconsin*, 951 N.W.2d 556 (Wisc. 2020). Zach Montellaro and Kyle Cheney, "Pro-Trump Legal Crusade Peppered with Bizarre Blunders," *Politico*, December 3, 2020, https://www.politico.com/news/2020/12/03/sidney-powell-trump-election-lawsuit-442472. Powell was removed from the Trump legal team in November 2020 but continued with efforts to challenge the election.

130. *Trump v. Benson*, No. 20-1567C, 2020 WL 6689092 (Fed. Cl. Nov. 12, 2020) (lawsuit requesting stop counting absentee ballots).

131. *King v. Whitmer*,___ F.Supp.3d____, 2020 WL 7134198 (E.D. Mich. Dec. 7, 2020); *Constantino v. Detroit*, 950 N.W.2d 707 (Mich. Superior Ct. 2020); *Stoddard v. City Election Commission of the City of Detroit*, 20-014604-CZ (Third Judicial Circuit Court of Mich., Nov. 6, 2020). See Emily Bazelon, "Trump Is Not Doing Well with His Election Lawsuits. Here's a Rundown," *New York Times*, updated November 25, 2020, https://www.nytimes.com/2020/11/13/us/politics/trump-election-lawsuits.html.

132. *Gohmert et al. v. Pence*, ___F.3d. ___, 2021 WL 17141 (E.D.Tex. Jan. 1, 2021).

133. Ibid.

134. *Gohmert et al. v. Pence*, 832 Fed.Appx. 349 (5th Cir. 2021).

135. Bazelon, "Trump Is Not Doing Well with His Election Lawsuits"; "Trump Asks to Drop Voting Allegations in New Mexico, For Now," *Associated Press*, January 12, 2021, https://apnews.com/article/election-2020-donald-trump-state-elections-lawsuits-general-elections-66d53e1e68b331c8b0bd86887dfc252b; Rachel Adams,

David Enrich, and Jessica Silver-Greenberg, "Once Loyal to Trump, Law Firms Pull Back from His Election Fight," *New York Times*, November 13, 2020, https://www.nytimes.com/2020/11/13/business/porter-wright-trump-pennsylvania.html. The law firm Porter, Wright, Morris & Arthur withdrew.

136. Rosalind Helderman and Josh Dawsey, "As Trump Seizes on Arizona Ballot Audit, Election Officials Fear Partisan Vote Counts Could Be the Norm in Future Elections," *Washington Post*, April 29, 2021, https://www.washingtonpost.com/politics/trump-arizona-recount/2021/04/29/bcd8d832-a798-11eb-bca5-048b2759a489_story.html. The recount is said to be focused not on Trump's loss but on the administrative process surrounding vote counting in the county.

137. Amy Gardner, "Florida Republicans Rushed to Curb Mail Voting after Trump's Attacks on the Practice. Now Some Fear It Could Lower GOP Turnout," *Washington Post*, May 3, 2021, https://www.washingtonpost.com/politics/florida-republicans-mail-voting/2021/05/02/4c133920-a9bf-11eb-8c1a-56f0cb4ff3b5_story.html.

138. Julia Jacobo, "This Is What Trump Told Supporters before Many Stormed Capitol Hill," *ABC News* Online, January 7, 2021, https://abcnews.go.com/Politics/trump-told-supporters-stormed-capitol-hill/story?id=75110558.

139. Julie Gerstein, "Rudy Giuliani Says His 'Trial by Combat' Comment during Trump's January 6 Rally Was a 'Game of Thrones' Reference, Not a Call to Violence," *Business Insider*, January 13, 2021, https://www.businessinsider.com/giuliani-claims-trial-by-combat-comment-game-of-thrones-reference-2021-1.

140. Harry Stevens, Daniela Santamariña, Kate Rabinowitz, and John Muyskens, "How Members of Congress Voted on Counting the Electoral College Vote," *Washington Post*, January 7, 2021, https://www.washingtonpost.com/graphics/2021/politics/congress-electoral-college-count-tracker/.

141. Justin Vallejo, "Donald Trump's C-PAC Speech—Read the Full Transcript," *The Independent*, March 1, 2021, https://www.independent.co.uk/news/world/americas/us-politics/donald-trump-cpac-speech-2021-b1809208.html.

142. Nick Coransaniti, "Rudy Giuliani Sued by Dominion Voting Systems over False Election Claims," *New York Times*, updated April 28, 2021, https://www.nytimes.com/2021/01/25/us/politics/rudy-giuliani-dominion-trump.html.

Index

181

Black Lives Matter (BLM), 39, 40, 42, 44, 63, 103
Bloomington, Indiana, 76
blue states, red states *vs.*, 16
Boxer, Barbara, 38
Brandenburg, Clarence, 76
Brandenburg v. Ohio, 75, 76, 77, 79, 82, 83, 85
Brann, Matthew, 166
Breitbart, 62
Brennan, William, 155
Brooks, Garth, 24
Brooks, Mo, 75, 117, 121
Buchanan, James, 131
Burke, Kenneth, 44–45, 91
Burns, Lisa M., xii, 1–27
Bush, George W., 11, 24, 156–57, 159–60
Bush, Jeb, 45
Bush, Laura, 24
Bush v. Gore, 159–60
BuzzFeed News, 11
Byrnes, Pat, 131

Cabinet, 15
Cagle, Daryl, 128, 138, 144
California Emergency Services Act (CESA), 162
Calvert, Clay, 76, 80, 82, 84
cancel culture, 66
candidates (2020 election), 2–6
capitalism, 93
Capitol riots (January 6, 2021), xi–xiv, 1, 2, 5, 17–19, 22, 41, 81, 82, 116–17, 151; as carnivalesque concept, 98–99, 103–6; as cartoon theme, 132–33; contrast of coverage on Summer Riots of 2020 and, 63; immediate aftermath and, 35–38; MAGA at, 20–21; political cartoons of, 135, 142–44; postelection and, 61–62; redux of, 43–44; semantics of debate on, 62–63. *See also* insurrection
Carmichael, Stokely, 39, 42

carnivalesque concept, xiii, 92, 93–97, 101–2; Capitol riots as, 98–99, 103–6; the critic and, 103–6; liberalism and, 100
Carpini, Michael Delli, 52
Carter, Jimmy, 157, 160
cartoons. *See* editorial cartoons; political cartoons
censorship, press and corporate: postelection and, 56–57; social media and, 57
Center for Responsive Politics, 112
CESA. *See* California Emergency Services Act
the challenge period, xii, 2; transition period and, 12–16
Chansley, Jacob, 98
Chauvin, Derek, 39
Cheney, Liz, 73; on insurrection, 74
Cineas, Fabiola, 79
Civil Rights Act of 1870, 154
civil rights movement, 39–40
Civil War, 63, 113, 154; military and voting during, 158
Claiborne County, Mississippi, 76, 77–78
Clinton, Bill, 24
Clinton, Hillary, 3, 7, 45, 73, 120
CNN, 10; on Capitol riots, 62
Colbert, Stephen, 97
Coll, Steve, 66
colonialism, 93
Columbia University, 66
Connally, John, 113
Conservative Political Action Conference (CPAC), 170
conspiracy theories, 7, 14, 17, 21–21, 132, 143
Constitution, xv, 104; American voting laws and, 153–56; defenses of, 13; obedience to, 38. *See also specific topics*
Conway, George, 112–13
Conway, Kellyanne, 113
Cotton, Tom, 116, 121

159–60; rights in Michigan, 118; in
Texas, 163; in twenty-first century,
156–60. *See also* mail-in ballots
Voting Rights Act of 1965, 156

Waite, Morrison, 154
Wall Street Journal, 22
Warnock, Raphael, 15, 112
Warren, Earl, 155
Washington D.C., 39–40; summer
protests in, 41–42
Washington Post, 13, 18, 22, 38, 40,
41, 45, 53, 120; on Capitol riots, 62,
151
Washington v. Trump, 164
Wesberry v. Sanders, 153, 155
Westboro Baptist Church, 79
Wexler, Ed, 135
Whamond, Dave, 144

White House, 25, 39, 40
White supremacists, 105, 116–17
"Why We Fight" advertisement, 115–16
Wilmington, Delaware, 11, 21
Wilson, Richard Ashby, 78
Wilson, Rick, 112–13, 120
Wisconsin, 59, 167–68
Wittes, Benjamin, 4
Wolverton, Monte, 135–36
"Women for America First," 17
Wood, Lin, 167
World War II, 158
writ of mandamus, 163, 168
Wyman, Kim, 108–9

Young, Dannagal, 113–14
YouTube, 20

Zyglis, Adam, 125, 137, *143*

About the Contributors

Lisa M. Burns is professor of Media Studies at Quinnipiac University. She teaches courses including Media, History & Memory; Media & Society; Media Trend Forecasting & Strategy; Political Communication; Media Critics & Influencers; and Celebrity Culture. Her research interests include media history, political communication (particularly media coverage of U.S. first ladies and presidents), public/collective memory, and media criticism. Burns's edited collection *Media Relations and the Modern First Lady: From Jacqueline Kennedy to Melania Trump* was released in 2020 (Lexington Press). Her previous book, *First Ladies and the Fourth Estate: Press Framing of Presidential Wives* (Northern Illinois University Press), was published in August 2008. She has also published several journal articles and book chapters on first ladies.

Robert E. Denton Jr. holds the W. Thomas Rice Chair in the Pamplin College of Business and is professor and director of the School of Communication at Virginia Tech. Denton is the author, coauthor, or editor of thirty-two books, several in multiple editions, on the presidency and political campaigns. His most recent volumes include *The 2020 Presidential Campaign: A Communication Perspective,* Robert E. Denton Jr., ed. (Rowman & Littlefield, 2021), *Studies of Communication in the 2020 Presidential Campaign,* Robert E. Denton Jr., ed. (Lexington Books, 2021), and *Political Campaign Communication: Principles and Practices,* 9th ed., with Judith Trent and Robert Friedenberg (Rowman & Littlefield, 2019).

Scott W. Dunn is an associate professor in the School of Communication at Radford University. He studies political communication, and his current

research interest is young people's engagement with politics. He is the author
of numerous articles, book chapters, and professional research papers.

W. Wat Hopkins is professor in the School of Communication at Virginia
Tech. His primary area of research is communication law and the First
Amendment. In addition to numerous journal articles, Hopkins is the author
of *Communication and the Law, 2021 Edition* (Vision Press, 2021), *Mass
Communication Law in Virginia,* 4th ed. (with Cayce Myers) (New Forums
Press, 2016), and *Mr. Justice Brennan and Freedom of Expression* (Praeger,
1991). He is also editor of the journal *Communication and the Law* (Taylor
& Francis).

Courtney L. Marchese is an associate professor of interactive media and
design at Quinnipiac University. She teaches a wide range of design theory,
research, and technical skills at the undergraduate and graduate level. She is
also a professional designer with over a decade of experience specializing
in data visualization, information graphics, user experience design, and us-
ability studies. Using a human-centered design approach, Marchese has created a number of databased multidisciplinary projects, including a nationally
recognized award-winning voter education initiative based on political data
from the renowned Quinnipiac Polling Institute. Her forthcoming book from
Bloomsbury Press is titled *Information Design for the Common Good.*

Natalia Mielczarek is an assistant professor in the School of Communication
at Virginia Tech. Her research interests include visual communication, iconic
images, and digital participatory culture and virtual content. In addition to
several book chapters, her recent work has appeared in *Journalism and Mass
Communication Quarterly* and *Visual Communication Quarterly.*

Cayce Myers is an associate professor and director of Graduate Studies at
the School of Communication at Virginia Tech. Dr. Myers's research focuses
on laws that affect communication practice and the historical development
of American public relations, social media, and media history. Myers is
the author of *Public Relations History: Theory, Practice, and Profession*
(Routledge) and coauthor of *Mass Communication Law in Virginia* (New
Forums Press). He holds a Ph.D. and M.A. from the University of Georgia
Grady College of Journalism and Mass Communication, a LL.M. from the
University of Georgia School of Law, a J.D. from Mercer University Walter
F. George School of Law, and a B.A. in political science and history from
Emory University.

Theodore F. Sheckels is the Charles Potts Professor of Social Science as well as professor of English and communication studies at Randolph-Macon College. He earned his Ph.D. and M.A. from Pennsylvania State University. Dr. Sheckels has contributed numerous articles and book chapters to publications within his field and has published six books. His research interests include the political dimensions of Margaret Atwood's fiction, presidential debates, political conventions, and lesser-known political communicators from the twentieth century.

John C. Tedesco is a professor in the School of Communication at Virginia Tech. His areas of research interest include political communication, presidential campaign communication, and public relations. He is coauthor of two books, *Civic Dialogue in the 1996 Presidential Campaign: Candidate, Media, and Public Voices* (Hampton Press) and *The Internet Election: Perspectives of the Web in Campaign 2004* (Rowman & Littlefield). He has authored numerous book chapters, articles, and research papers.

Benjamin Voth is an associate professor and director of debate and speech programs in the Dedman College of Humanities and Sciences at Southern Methodist University. He is a leading national scholar on debate and the power of the human voice. He is the author of three books on how individual communication abilities can positively change the world: *James Farmer Jr.: The Great Debater* (Lexington Books, 2017), *Social Fragmentation and the Decline of American Democracy: The End of the Social Contract* (Palgrave Macmillan, 2017, with Robert E. Denton Jr.), and *The Rhetoric of Genocide: Death as a Text* (Lexington Books, 2014 and 2016). *The Rhetoric of Genocide* won the American Forensic Association's 2015 top national book award, the Daniel Rohrer Memorial Outstanding Research Award, for research in the field of speech and debate. His most current book is *Debate as Global Pedagogy: Rwanda Rising* (Lexington Books, 2020). He is currently an advisor to the Bush Institute and the Debate Fellow for the Calvin Coolidge Foundation in Vermont.

www.ingramcontent.com/pod-product-compliance
Lightning Source LLC
Chambersburg PA
CBHW071413290326
41932CB00047B/2847